Anti-Social

Anti-Social

Nick Pettigrew

C

CENTURY

3 5 7 9 10 8 6 4

Century
20 Vauxhall Bridge Road
London SW1V 2SA

Century is part of the Penguin Random House group
of companies whose addresses can be found at
global.penguinrandomhouse.com

Copyright © Baby Rocket Ltd, 2020

First published in the United Kingdom by Century in 2020

This book is substantially a work of non-fiction based on the life,
experiences and recollections of the author. Names of people,
places, dates, sequences and the detail of events have been
changed to protect the privacy of others.

www.penguin.co.uk

A CIP catalogue record for this book is available
from the British Library.

HB ISBN 9781529124774
TPB ISBN 9781529125733

Printed and bound in Great Britain by Clays Ltd, Elcograf S.p.A.

Penguin Random House is committed to a sustainable future
for our business, our readers and our planet. This book is made
from Forest Stewardship Council® certified paper.

To Squibb,

loveyouspringrolls

Author's Note

This book was written back when the word 'Corona' suggested a brand of beer rather than a virus that would reach every corner of the planet. Even as I write this note, quite how the Coronavirus will come to permanently change the world we live in is yet to be seen.

The optimist in me (who, despite everything happening right now, refuses to go away) thinks there will be changes for the better. Maybe we'll come to value social care a bit more or restore our health service to where it's always deserved to be. I hope we'll stop viewing low-paid work as low-value work and realise there is such a thing as society. Even if it's nothing more than people washing their hands after going to the toilet, that will be something.

What won't change is fundamental human nature and, whatever a post-virus world looks like, it's going to contain people whose behaviour is a burden to others. So long as that exists, people doing my job will need to exist. In heaven there's no need for us, in hell it's too late for us, and in between we'll just crack on with it.

All of what follows is true. All of it has either happened directly to me or has been relayed to me by a colleague. My job requires no embellishment. Exaggerating would be like drinking Red Bull to swallow ketamine or putting go-faster stripes on a lightning bolt. There's no point. Identifying details, dates and names have been changed to protect the innocent and guilty, as well as those who swear they're not guilty but obviously are.

Prologue

I am an anti-social behaviour officer. If you're talking to me, something in your life has gone wrong. These are the kinds of things I hear day in, day out:

'I just don't want to hear the word "cunt" shouted repeatedly at 3am every night any more. I don't think that's unreasonable.'

Perhaps your life has become unbearable due to the person living above you and their fondness for crack, the company of strangers and non-specific dance music. People will tell you that drugs have helped produce some of the finest music ever created, and they may be right – but I can also tell you that *heavy* drug use produces the worst taste in music imaginable. I have yet to receive a complaint about a crack den blasting out Nick Drake at unsociable hours.

Walking past a neighbour's door and hearing them chant 'Kill the kids, kill the kids' inside their flat, when you know that they live on their own (unlike the family with four kids downstairs), is not everybody's cup of tea. Or maybe you find being called a 'paki twat' rather bothersome. Evidence tends to suggest it can grate after a while.

'You can't evict me, I've got asthma.'

On the other hand, the reason your life resembles somebody beating a social worker around the head with an *EastEnders* script might be... you. Personal responsibility tends to be unfashionable these days, a bit pull-up-your-bootstraps-and-get-a-haircut-for-goodness'-sake. But sometimes you have to hold your hands up and say, 'You got me.' Like the time one of our more troubling residents was stopped by police as he chased a neighbour down the road while waving an entire car exhaust-pipe mechanism around his head like a steampunk Darth Vader. His first words were, 'Yeah, I know how this looks...'

If your neighbour complains about a leak coming from your flat, and when the plumbers break in they find a fully-operational hydroponic cannabis factory and no signs of habitation, it's hard to blame an over-developed sense of entrepreneurship. If you beat a disabled neighbour so badly they lose sight in one eye, saying it was a tiff that got out of hand will cut very little mustard. And don't piss over your balcony onto the patio below and tell me it's raining.

'We've tried literally everything to make this person go away – is there anything you can do?'

Or maybe you're a social worker, a mental health worker, a police officer, a firefighter, a dog warden or even a vicar, and you've been landed with somebody who is a massive pain in the arse to the general population. You're either incapable of dealing with them or you just can't be bothered – so who are you going to call? Given that the Ghostbusters don't exist, the person you're going to call is me, or at least somebody like me.

Anti-social behaviour is like pornography: hard to define, but you know it when you see it. Several acts of parliament have tried to pin it down with varying degrees of success. The definition of ASB:

(a) conduct that has caused, or is likely to cause, harassment, alarm or distress to any person,

(b) conduct capable of causing nuisance or annoyance to a person in relation to that person's occupation of residential premises, or

(c) conduct capable of causing housing-related nuisance or annoyance to any person.

is the current, less-than-catchy attempt. It can encapsulate everything from hoarding your own piss in milk cartons to smearing faeces across the letterbox of a gay couple's flat because, well, they're gay.

The 1998 Crime and Disorder Act laid the groundwork for what most people understand as ASB – anti-social behaviour. It was an attempt to drag all the scraps of sub-criminal behaviour that annoyed people into one set of laws. It gave birth to the ASBO, a headline-friendly piece of legislation that no longer exists but to which people still refer, much to the irritation of every ASB officer in the country. It's like somebody suggesting dirigible airships continue to be a concern, or that 78rpm records are still purchasable from your local branch of Our Price.

The 1998 act was, frankly, a right old mess. Unwieldy and often unworkable, it proved baffling to the magistrates being asked to enforce it, and it gave too many agencies too many hard-to-define powers, when all they needed was one big legislative stick to wave about with 'STOP THAT' painted on it.

One job it did end up producing was mine. Any local council or social landlord – charities which provide low-cost housing to people in need – had to prove they had a procedure (local authorities love writing a procedure as it's far easier than actually doing anything) for dealing with ASB. The procedures that resulted, festooned as they were with flowcharts, mission statements and key performance indicators, tended to boil down to this: 'We'll give it to the ASB officer to deal with.' And so it was that at the turn of the millennium, bored with answering every type of call imaginable in the call centre of a social landlord (telling people what their rent balance is or booking a repair for a blocked toilet or leaky roof hundreds of times a day can get a bit repetitive), I decided to become an ASB officer.

I've done it ever since, with varying degrees of success, failure, infestations of frogs, sobbing, anger and envy (I am, of course, the envy of my friends who graduated at the same time as I did, and now do something hard to define in the media which seldom involves a heroin addict vomiting on their shoes. Except for the ones who ended up in music journalism, obviously).

What follows is a year in my job: a job I've done for over a decade, and which has stretched the limits of my patience, compassion and sanity. By the end, I hope you will have some insight into how the framework that keeps society functioning is now a spun-sugar latticework of making do, doing without and hoping nothing goes tragically wrong.

Zeno of Elea was born in Greece in 495 BC, and was a philosopher, because everybody in ancient Greece seemed to be a philosopher. He wrote a series of paradoxes, which were questions of the kind usually posed by somebody at 2am after an evening smoking weed. One of them said that an arrow fired at a target travels half the distance between the two. Then half the remaining distance. Then half again, and so on. On this basis, the arrow should never hit the target. We're now living in a Zeno's Paradox of austerity. If you reduce funding by half and a service still operates, then surely you can halve funding again, and then again? But people can't be halved, and when nobody is around to do a job that's needed – looking after the elderly, the addicted and the insane – that job becomes everybody's. And not everybody is equipped to do it.

This book is only one person's opinion. I don't claim to have a magic pill to make everything better because I'm not a newspaper columnist. I'm not going to pretend I don't see things through the prism of my own background and my personal politics. But what I can guarantee is that any opinion I offer has been tempered by a decade and a half dealing with society at its most vulnerable. I'd like to think that gives me a bit more insight than a private education, an Oxbridge degree and being parachuted into a safe parliamentary seat would. I give you a money-back guarantee you will never see me on *Question Time* saying we should bring back hanging for littering.

This book follows a year during which I look more closely at my job than ever before, and thought about the effect it's having on me. Am I naturally a dour, cynical person with a sense of humour as bitter as cheap coffee, or has the job made me that way? Am I actually helping people any more, or am I doing just enough to steer clear of a public inquiry? Do I want to hurtle into middle age doing a job that kicks the psychological shit out of me every day? Do I really want to start a new career from scratch when my joints ache every morning and I've started needing reading glasses?

By the end of this book, even if I have answered none of the other questions above, I will have answered at least one: Do I really want to do this any more?

January

Password: Stressed101
Medication: Sertraline 50mg

2 January

'She's back again. She's throwing water at our house and staring through the windows. Please do something.'

As usual after the Christmas holidays, I have come back to a pile of messages from people with nobody else but me to contact about the ways their neighbours' lives have rubbed up against theirs: parties, arguments, nocturnal hoovering and loud sex. The usual.

But this one stands out because this was meant to have been sorted. Carla was meant to be dying in hospital and Rachel was meant to be relieved about that.

Rachel and her family are a typical family living in a large city: man and wife plus two kids. Her spouse has a loose grasp of English and they both have a firm grasp of their Christian faith. They live their quiet, normal life in a house entirely too small for them, the kind of tenants who'd never contact the council about their home unless it was on fire.

Last year, Rachel contacted me to say her neighbour's behaviour was getting too much. Carla was shouting at Rachel's family, putting threatening notes through the letterbox, telling malicious lies about the family to the other neighbours, banging on the doors and windows. Carla was starting to scare Rachel's kids. One kid had started wetting the bed, and the other was refusing to go to school in case the 'bad woman' was out there.

Carla was the bad woman – but 'bad people' in the realm of ASB are varying shades of Bad. Carla's behaviour was Bad, no question, and her Bad behaviour required action and, eventually, consequences. More than that, though, Carla's case was like playing Jenga with complicated medical and psychiatric factors. When faced with such a difficult case, one's first instinct is to stay clear. However, that's not an option for me, because dealing with cases like Carla's is kind of what I get paid to do and washing my hands of it would, I'm sure, lead to questions being asked of me. Let's see when you would have wanted to leave well alone. . .

Born in South America, Carla had language issues, spoke only very basic English, and preferred to read messages in English rather than having it spoken to her. If you saw her in the street, your first concern would be that a passing breeze might blow her away. Physically very slight, she also seemed on the brink of collapse. She always seemed to be trying to inhabit as small a space as possible.

Still on board?

She had mobility issues, was partially paralysed down one side and needed a walking stick (which she also used to bang on her neighbour's door several times a day). All of this contributed to her depression diagnosis.

Shall I go on?

Her depression could also be explained by the fact that her child had been taken into care at birth (and eventually adopted) due to Carla's inability to cope. Visitors to her flat said she kept the spare room furnished with a made-up cot for the day she regained custody of the child she was never going to see again.

I know. I *know*.

This probably explained her anger towards figures of authority, causing her to lash out at social workers, her GP and anyone else who tried to help. 'Help' had become synonymous with having her kid taken away.

Sitting above all this, like a clenched fist of plutonium in her head, was a progressive, incurable brain tumour that elbowed aside the parts of her mind that dealt with anger management, impulse control, sight, hearing and mobility, and disorientated her completely. She'd been diagnosed just before she became pregnant, and had been told to terminate her child because the same hormones that would make the baby in her womb flourish would also be greedily lapped up by the tumour in her head. She was heading down a road that would ultimately kill her and make her lose control along the way.

Carla chose her baby over treatment and, in doing so, indirectly chose to become lame, dissociative, deaf, rage-filled, in constant pain (did I mention the chronic pain or did I spare you that?) and, ultimately, childless.

And this was who I'd had arrested for breaching her order and taken to court. Because there was the very real risk that the tumour pressing on Carla's brain might cause her to do something irreparably bad. Her neighbour couldn't cope any more. Neither could local support services, due to the usual mix of bureaucracy, missed opportunities, apathy and chronic underfunding.

When there are no other options available, I do the thing that keeps me awake at night, because *there are no other options available*. Court action was the only way to break the cycle and if it meant me upping my self-medicating dose of beer of an evening, so be it.

When Carla was arrested for the fifth time in three weeks for breaching her court order, the custody sergeant took one look at her and said, 'Not in my cells. No chance.'

This is usually done with a mixture of concern for the person arrested and the desire to avoid the number of reports you need to write if somebody snuffs it in your custody cell.

I had my own opinions on her mental health, but these would, understandably, not be medically or legally recognised. All I could do was ask that somebody qualified to diagnose her did so. If you're arrested and police feel you're in need of urgent medical or psychiatric treatment, you're taken to a 'place of safety' to be treated. In this case, it was the nearby psychiatric ward, whose staff immediately sectioned her.[1] Her prognosis looked bad, and it was expected her next home would be a palliative care facility. She was in her forties, seven stone, desperately unhappy and terminally ill.

Now, though, she's back in her house, and back screaming at the shadows in her mind, exorcising them by making Rachel's life a misery. A broken, dying, mentally fractured woman and a terrified, worn-down family; a dysfunctional support network and a legal system not fit to deal with things like this.

---

1 The Mental Health Act 1983 allows medical professionals to keep people in hospital care for the safety of themselves and others, even if the patient would rather remain at large talking to Elvis or the dragon that lives in their wardrobe. The threshold for sectioning is a lot higher than most people realise. Merely being loopy isn't enough to deploy the big butterfly nets. Your loopiness has to manifest itself in a way that might harm you or harm others. It's viewed as an option of last resort for dealing with somebody's mental illness. The patient's liberty and personal dignity is paramount, and sectioning can be a distressing and demeaning process. And it has absolutely nothing to do with the lack of bed spaces or how much paperwork is involved. Definitely not.

And in the middle of it, me, with all eyes pointed my way looking for a solution where there isn't one. It is 9.15am. It is 2 January. Happy New Year.

4 January

I'm told a new person – Simon – will be starting with the team on Monday, as we've been two people short for months. Our ASB Team is part of a larger organisation that, like other local councils, Arms' Length Management Organisations and Registered Social Landlords up and down the country, provides low-cost housing for those in need. As ASB officers, we manage thousands of properties, with each ASB officer covering about 3,000 properties – so when you're two people short, it is noticeable and you want to recruit as soon as you can.

The problem is that anybody who can do the job is doing the job somewhere else. It requires such a specific set of skills that finding somebody with transferable experience and training them up is a massive ballache and usually doesn't work.

I ask my boss about Simon.

'He's not done the job before, but he's good at taking statements so we should be able to get him up to speed.'

Welcome aboard, Simon.

7 January

People have legitimate concerns about their data being misused, especially if that data is sensitive in nature. But one thing that defines the police in terms of data protection is that they hate telling any other organisation anything.

It's a historical bias. Even though the concept of a working partnership between police and landlords is over fifteen years old, officers tend to view anybody not carrying a baton as a potential suspect. To some degree this is understandable. The nuggets of information they do share with us can be really valuable to the wrong people.

I've known weeks in advance that a property was going to be raided for drugs and firearms. A quick phone call to the right people, suggesting they have a clear-out of their attic before 5am next Friday, could save them thousands of pounds in seized items, as well as making sure trusted workers can carry on making them money rather than being tied up in court cases.

It would be dishonest to say that this isn't sometimes an enticing prospect. Who wouldn't want to book a two-week holiday in a place with no concrete or crackheads, acquired via a thirty-second phone call? Drug dealers would pay handsomely for intel like that. But I don't do that for a variety of reasons, paramount amongst them being, it's immoral, and I'd get caught. The fact that any self-respecting drug dealer would kick the information out of a pudgy, middle-aged civilian like me for free is beside the point.

That's not to mention the other ways I could abuse the information police provide me with. I could let the local head-the-ball know the address of a sex offender who lives around the corner. Or tell an abusive partner where their terrified ex and kids are now staying. Someone on the estate would probably love to know which of their neighbours have attempted suicide, beat their kids or are on metha-done. The combination of having gossip at your fingertips and the willingness to divulge it to human garbage is not a mix that makes you suitable for this job.

Tenants are always terrified somebody will know they've spoken to me. Over the years I've perfected the fol-lowing reassurance, which seems to work: 'If you tell me something in confidence and I breach that confidence, I'll get fired. And I'll deserve to. I have a mortgage to pay, so believe me, I won't do that.' Our tenants have no reason to trust me, and I don't blame them, but tell somebody you'll get sacked for not doing your job properly and they tend to believe you.

A case which perfectly illustrates the difficulty in get-ting people to share data came up last year. Operation Poland was set up by police to deal with drug dealers in the area. Drugs aren't an issue in the estates I cover, in the same way that water isn't a talking point in the Atlantic Ocean: they permeate every element of my work. The people who take drugs, the people stepping over their prone bodies on the way to work, the petty crime it attracts, the police hours lost to dealing with it, the vomit and piss that needs cleaning, the dealers tearing around cul-de-sacs in hire cars. Imagining this job with drugs no longer a problem is like trying to imagine the colour red no longer exists.

So Poland was set up to wag a finger at the hurricane of crack and heroin blowing around the tower blocks. The details of the operation might be useful in dispelling some myths about 'the drug problem' – something I hope you live in too nice an area to have experienced.

Op. Poland uncovered the following structure. The system is run from the cars that ferry the drugs to the users. Two people on pushbikes serve each car. These are the bottom of the food chain and typically the youngest. The average starting age is in the lower teens, as they have loads of energy for cycling around and no criminal record, so if they get caught, they're not going to jail. 'Getting caught' is not much of an issue anyway, as they never carry any cash or drugs. They're there to corral the buyers, like itchy, catatonic sheep, to the agreed drop-off point. They might make £50 a day, which when you're thirteen is pretty decent.

Six street dealers are spread across the two cars (almost always hire cars, as this makes the police tracking licence plates pointless and it means they can big it up in a nice new Audi rather than their mum's shitty Corsa). They'll make £150 a day for an eight-hour shift. The driver drives, the front passenger makes the handovers, and the guy in the back keeps hold of the money and the weapons to defend the money.

This eight-man (equal opportunities haven't hit the drug dealing trade yet, it's never women) crew is served by a single mobile phone number. In their wisdom, phone companies have set up 'media hubs' across our estates, sleek monoliths with LCD screens featuring happy, attractive-looking people doing happy, attractive-looking stuff on a video loop. They offer free WiFi, and allow people to charge their phones and browse for local services as well as, most importantly, make thirty-second phone calls free of charge. These hubs very quickly became crackhead standing stones, with groups of six or more addicts, bedding over their shoulders, huddled around the speaker with a phone number scrawled on a piece of paper, waiting to hear where to go.

Once a location off the main road is given, the push-bike riders make sure the addicts do what they are told, herd any stragglers towards the right corner, and make sure they don't get impatient and shuffle off elsewhere in search of a fix. You know when you're waiting to get served at the bar for your first drink on a Friday evening? It's that, multiplied by 4,741, with added leg ulcers.

Finally, the boys (car-based dealers usually run a little older, somewhere between eighteen and mid-twenties, after they've proved trustworthy) turn up in the car and swiftly do the handovers while parked in the middle of the road. There's no point in being furtive. It's everywhere. Who's going to stop them?

As many as a dozen sales take place in one stop, usually a 'one and one' (one wrap of crack, one of heroin, because who doesn't like a chaser with their beer?) for £20. The drugs are wrapped in a scrap of colour-coded plastic, taken from the kind of carrier bag corner shops use: red-and-white plastic for heroin and blue-and-white plastic for crack. The tiny wraps are passed from the mouth of the dealer to the mouth of the addict. Even if a ninja police officer sprang out of the glove compartment to arrest everyone, the evidence can be swallowed before it can be stopped. An addict won't even feel the effect of their one-and-one. The dealer will worry about ingesting the merchandise later.

A dozen transactions can be done in under two minutes, then it's off to the next location to do it again – roughly one set of drop-offs every five to ten minutes, every hour, twenty-four hours a day. Any expert in the service industry will tell you the drug trade is doing it right: give the customer what they want; take the product to them; be on call at all hours. Possibly best they avoid the 'slice up the torso of a customer wasting your time by not having enough money' part, though.

All of this trade comes from one phone number, remember. Over all the estates the dealers covered, Operation Poland found evidence of eight phone numbers being overseen by two dealers operating from a nearby flat. In turn, those two dealers were being supplied by a mid-level dealer with product in bulk. When he was eventually caught, he had 95 kilos of pure cocaine in his house, the same as 190 bags of flour or one adult warthog, if that makes it easier to visualise. Enough to keep eighties Hollywood running for six minutes.

Operation Poland monitored calls to each phone number over a four-month period. Each phone averaged over 200 phone calls every single day from customers eager to make a purchase. Before paying out wages, buying produce, solicitors' bills, car hire costs, baseball bat purchases, etc, etc, they made over £2 million a year. If that sounds a lot, I should point out that that was *per phone*. Eight phones made a gross profit of over £16 million a year for the two people just two rungs up the ladder.

So why do we ask, 'Why do people become drug dealers?' rather than 'Why wouldn't they?'

Back to Operation Poland. The operation was set up, the test purchases were made by undercover police, the properties were raided, arrests were made, the Crown Prosecution Service (CPS) prepared charges, the cases went to court and the sentences were handed down.

On average the dealers in the cars got two-year sentences (sometimes suspended) and the mid-level people they worked for were given about four years each. Current sentencing guidelines suggest offenders serve half their sentence.

All of this happened without any police officer thinking to tell the landlord of over twenty of the dealers involved, despite the fact that drugs and weapons had been found in the addresses that the council had asked me to keep free of, well, drugs and weapons. Despite the fact that I can evict families who knew what was going on and turned a blind eye. Despite the fact that one dealer managed to buy his mum's £315,000 flat (which I manage) in cash a few years ago. In spite of all the ways I can support the work they did, using legal powers that have existed for years, they thought it best not to tell me.

Police *really* don't like sharing information.

9 January

Simon has taken sixteen hours (fourteen if you don't count the two lunch hours I spent as far away from him as possible) to get on every single nerve-end I possess. It's almost impressive, the way he manages it.

He doesn't chew his gum with the open-mouthed ferocity of my former colleague Irene, who sounded like a slug doing press-ups. Nor does he engage me in conversations about conspiracy theories, as does the caretaker called Nigel who works on an estate I manage, and who knows who *really* controls the United Nations (clue: it's 'the Jews').

But Simon does suggest I haven't been doing my job on cases he's 'helping' with, a malevolently beatific Dolores Umbridge smile on his face. He can waste an hour of my time making me explain how CCTV cameras work in conjunction with local authority powers, the legislation that covers CCTV use, and so on. He's new to the job and I wouldn't expect him to know these things. But if a work experience teenager peered over the head of a surgeon and said, 'Is that meant to be bleeding?', you'd expect them to be a bit miffed.

And then there's the stationery.

He approached our stationery cupboard (the one

thing local authorities always seem to find money for is stationery. No idea why) like a nun waiting for Lourdes to open. Most of his time so far has been spent arranging ring-binders, folders, plastic sleeves, Post-it notes, different coloured pens, staplers (yes, plural) and other gewgaws to tackle a workload he hasn't yet been given. I'm scared to give him a print-out of all the team's contact numbers because I know a unicorn-themed, laminated version will soon appear on my desk.

10 January

Raul is only in his early thirties but has packed a lot into his short life: firearm offences, robbery, public order and drug offences. Lots and lots and *lots* of drug offences. Common factors among most arrested drug dealers are stupidity and laziness. They don't get caught after elaborate sting operations using deep cover detectives and state-of-the-art surveillance techniques. They run a red light in an expensive hire car with two of their mates, the stereo blaring, a machete in the boot and forty wraps of crack in the glove compartment. They have eighty visitors to their flat every day and wonder how the neighbours knew what was going on.

Dealers don't seem to realise that weed absolutely reeks, so if you have a pillow case full of the stuff in your living room, any copper walking past your front door might smell it. My wife is a home-cooking gadget nerd and has a sous vide – one of those water baths you cook stuff in for twelve hours in a vacuum-sealed bag. (Her addiction to cookery gadgets has resulted in a one-in, one-out policy. A new piece of gadgetry can only cross the threshold if another piece is heading in the opposite direction.) You can buy the vacuum sealer and a hundred bags for under thirty quid, and this would make a dealer's weed undetectable to the human nose. No drug dealer (who gets caught) bothers to do this because it requires a modicum of effort.

Incidentally, on the smell of drugs: the abilities of sniffer dogs are quite incredible. Speaking to a dog handler on a housing estate sweep, he told me two stories that seem impossible. On one occasion, his dog indicated – that is, showed interest in a way that the handler knew to interpret as the presence of drugs – on the rucksack of a festival-goer. The bag was searched with no drugs apparent. The dog then indicated for a tin of hair wax that was still sealed. When opened, the surface of the hair wax was untouched and smooth. When the team dug to the bottom of the tin, they found a dozen ecstasy pills wrapped in cellophane. The fact the dogs can smell anything over the odour of a festival-goer is an achievement in itself.

On another occasion, the dog singled out somebody in a queue for a nightclub. She was searched and no drugs were found. On a hunch, the handler asked, 'You had drugs on you and you swallowed them, didn't you?' Dumbfounded, the woman said yes. The dog had detected the smell of ecstasy *inside a human body.*

But let's return to Raul. Cinema is obsessed with criminal masterminds, but your average street level drug dealer is generally a criminal gobshite. Raul is no exception. Back in October, his flat was raided and police found a royal flush in drug-dealer poker: multiple mobile phones, a stack of self-seal bags (those little bags, usually decorated with cannabis-leaf logos, that you see discarded on the pavement), and more money than somebody in Raul's situation should have had access to, as well as a smorgasbord of cannabis, crack and spice (the synthetic drug that turns people into the walking dead, rather than star anise).

So in late December, police raided his flat again, because obviously the previous raid hadn't stopped Raul from being a drug dealer. He's in his early thirties, has never had a legitimate job in his life and has a criminal record so long it requires an index – he's hardly going to give it all up to become a primary school teacher, is he?

When they kicked down his door, Raul wasn't at home but his mate was. While police were in the process of arresting the friend and searching the flat, Raul came back home. Despite the police car parked outside, despite the kicked-in door, despite the sound of coppers turning over his flat, Raul walked straight into the living room and was immediately nicked. They found a phone on him with thousands of drug-deal messages on it. He hadn't had the sense to judge the situation and just keep walking past his flat.

He took it in good humour, though, did Raul. He told the arresting officers in the van on the way to the station that when he was bailed, he was going to wait outside the police station and throw acid in the face of the first copper he saw. This is the kind of thing that causes a defence solicitor to pinch the bridge of his or her nose and reach for the coffee.

So, I go to Raul's block of flats to see if he's been causing a nuisance to other residents. Generally speaking, violent drug dealers don't tend to make good neighbours. If we can prove he's caused a nuisance, it gives us more legal options as to how to deal with him.

On the floor above his, I notice there's a mountain of post piled outside the door of one particular flat. As I get closer, there's the unmistakable odour of cat piss, expired meat and pear drops. Once you've smelled Dead Human, it's something you never forget. My first was several years earlier. Tenants reported they'd not seen their elderly neighbour for a while, so I went with an experienced housing officer to see if the tenant was at home. My colleague opened the letter box, sniffed, and said, 'Nope, he's dead.' Seeing my look of confusion, she told me to get a noseful myself. And there it was: a smell like a joint of meat that's been left out at room temperature for several days and the pear-drop smell of the ketones that are part of the decomposition process.

My more experienced colleague called the police, as they can force entry into a property without a warrant in order to do a welfare check, and told them our concerns. A sergeant arrived with a probationer – a newly qualified police officer they pair with a more experienced officer to show them the ropes. It was clear this was his first dead body, too. When they came back out of the flat to confirm our tenant had died, the probationer was the colour of a Granny Smith apple.

Real death is seldom dignified. Our tenant was in his seventies with a history of ill health, and was found by the police wedged between his bed and the wall. They thought he was probably going for a late-night wee, had a heart attack and ended up head-down in his bedroom. They estimated he'd died a couple of weeks before, and it being summer, he'd started to . . . leak somewhat.

This is how a lot of people end their lives: not in a pristine hospital bed, arms crossed over their chests, surrounded by loved ones, but arse-up in a council flat, dripping bodily fluids into the threadbare carpet, with some spotty constable trying their best not to vomit on them.

Back to today's corpse. There's no answer at the door, which isn't a surprise, so I have to return to the office, where the database shows that the tenant is an eighty-year-old man named Albert, who has lived in the flat since the early 1970s, has mental health issues and has steadfastly refused any help from social services.

I call our police team and request a welfare check. When they force entry, they find Albert wrapped in a duvet on his living room floor. The experienced sergeant tells me the flat is one of the worst he's ever seen. Albert has – had – no bed, no running water and no electricity. Every room is piled with clutter and there is cat shit everywhere. Cobwebs drape down like a fairground haunted house. There's also £12,000 in cash – Albert has no next of kin, so unless environmental health finds a will under one of the bags of faeces, it will go to the government (who seemed to do little to help Albert while he was alive).

People from the Celia Hammond Animal Trust attend and take Albert's two cats to be rehoused, but they think there may be more of them in the flat, hiding from the unusual sound of police breaking down a door. They ask if somebody (me) can go back to the flat, leave some food behind and see if it gets eaten.

11 January

The following day, I go to Albert's flat armed with a bottle of water, a bowl and some cat biscuits. It seems such a stupid thing to be concerned about, but it feels like the only thing I can do for Albert now – make sure his cats are looked after.

The flat is every bit as bad as the police suggested – worse than any crack den I've ever visited. Albert loved animals and our troops. Pictures of squaddies and Labradors cut from newspapers adorn the walls. A small Christmas tree in his living room is a punch in the heart. I *pssspssspsss* and rattle the biscuit bag to coax out any remaining cats, but there's no response, so I leave behind a bowl of water and pile of biscuits, which I'll check after the weekend.

The last thing I see before I leave is the empty patch of floor in the living room where Albert ended his days. The police told me one thing which will haunt me forever: 'We think when he died he was writing out Christmas cards to himself from his cats.'

For some light relief, I'm given another case on the same day. This time it's a woman in her thirties who has made multiple rape allegations, is a crack addict, was recently picked up by police after being found punching herself in the face in the street, and is currently being coerced into having her flat used as a 'shooting gallery' (that is, a place where people can take their drug of choice in relative peace and quiet) for heroin addicts. So there's that.

14 January

I go back to check Albert's flat and there are no more cats to catch, thankfully. But I do go home immediately to put my clothes in the wash and have a shower. Some smells don't go away quickly.

17 January

A GP appointment to change my depression medication. The Sertraline isn't working any more. I'll miss the jingle I sing to myself when I take it ('Maybe he's born with it – maybe it's Sertraline') but that's not reason enough to persevere with it. I can feel the numbness descending that usually presages a full-blown depression slump so we agree to try Mirtazapine and see if that does the trick. I'm warned side-effects may include increased appetite and vivid dreams.

21 January

'Have a drink if you've never seen a Nazi paedophile's dick.'

There's a drinking game, more popular in America (where drinking is viewed as something that requires an excuse) than in Britain (where drinking is something you only stop when you're on antibiotics or asleep), in which somebody makes a statement and everyone else has to take a drink depending on whether it's true for them or not.

For example, if you were sitting with a group of rugby players and said 'Have a drink if you've never shoved something up your mate's arse for a bet,' it would be a pretty cheap round. One of the benefits of an ASB job is that it gives you an armoury of potential 'If you've never . . .' to ensure you never have to buy a drink during that game.

In the morning, I receive a call from the boss. I'm to go to a flat because the police are there arresting one of our tenants, and they want to make sure the flat is in a safe condition to be secured once he's taken away. If he's charged with a serious offence and remanded in custody, the flat could sit empty for weeks or even months. You don't want to live adjacent to a flat with leftover food, leaking pipes or a pet that has been left unattended for months.

Ordinarily, this kind of call comes after a police raid, as the drug trade doesn't lend itself to good housekeeping. Cannabis factories are usually death traps of bypassed fuse boxes, overloaded plug points and leaking hydroponic kits installed by people who like cannabis more than they like passing electrical installation certificate checks.

This was different. The tenant was being arrested for sending abusive mail. Not, as I originally thought, to one of his neighbours (people send floridly abusive letters to their neighbours for the smallest of things, from a barking dog to owning a functioning washing machine), but to the police.

And by abusive, I mean 'full of Nazi imagery and anti-semitic threats' abusive. 'Calling specific police officers a paedophile' abusive. 'Mocking a police officer who died defending parliament from a terrorist attack' abusive. A step up from a tiff about dropped fag ends.

This guy had been caught thanks to DNA from the letters. Hate-mail correspondents don't cut untraceable news type with a scalpel, wearing surgical gloves and a sterile jumpsuit like in the films. They're seldom that meticulous. This one had even licked the envelope flap.

'So they ran a DNA test on the letters? That's expensive, isn't it?' I ask my boss.

'It is, but the letters were getting worse and they were worried he meant business.'

'They must have had the DNA on file already to get a match.'

'They did. He's a registered sex offender.'

'A Nazi sex offender? Right.'

When I arrive, there are a dozen coppers in attendance. They confirm that the property is heavily hoarded, hence us being called. The homes of hoarders can cause a raft of issues for surrounding tenants, so I would have to check for rodent droppings, rotting food, piles of flammable rubbish, etc.

However, the main concern for police right now is the Nazi sex offender not dying. When he answered the door and officers told him why they were there, he promptly collapsed. If you're seventy-four years old, and have a heart condition and a permanent place on the sex offenders' register, knowing you're going back to jail can place a strain on your nervous system.

Paramedics continue working on him, trying to save a life like his, showing impartiality in the face of illness as they always do. Meanwhile, the police are bemoaning how much work his inconsiderate cardiac arrest is going to cause them. Injury during arrest attracts the attention of the IOPC (Independent Office for Police Conduct). A death will lead to a full inquiry. Either way, every scrap of paperwork relating to the arrest will be scrutinised to make sure the neo-Nazi sex criminal was treated fairly.

And somebody has left a bit of necessary paperwork back at the station. Something as simple as that could nullify the legality of the arrest, turning a pain-in-the-arse situation into a seventy-two-piece orchestra of piss. A PC is dispatched to see if they might not have left that document in the car. (Translation: 'Do not come back without a copy unless you want to be teaching road safety to schoolkids for the next twelve months.')

A sergeant greets me. 'On the bright side, you've got an empty flat to let out now,' he grins.

'True. I wonder if they'd be happy moving in quicker if we didn't redecorate?'

'Yeah. Just tell them they can have it on Monday if they don't mind all the swastikas on the wall. See what they say.'

A police officer from Ringfence is also present. Ringfence is the unit that oversees violent and sexual offenders, making sure they don't pop over to Thailand for a relaxing break with some local kids or move into a flat above a crèche. It's a job few people could do, myself included.

Their client is still hovering between life and death, lying on the communal balcony outside his front door, paramedics working away. It is obvious that whatever happens, there is no way I am going to be needed any time soon. Police confirm this a short while later, saying that his flat is a crime scene that will need searching for offensive and illegal material. The reason so many officers had turned up in the first place was the risk of dangerous items, home-made devices and so on. With the amount of junk he had stored, it would be tomorrow morning at the earliest before I would be back.

I go to the floor above to report back to the office in private. I didn't realise the block layout is staggered like a ziggurat, so when I step out onto the communal balcony, I am looking down on the pale, naked figure of our tenant. Paramedics have to cut off the clothes of a patient in his condition to administer defibrillation, check for secondary injuries, put in IV lines and so on.

I can, and there's no easy way of saying this, see his dick.

As they give him CPR, his dick jiggles slightly with every chest compression. Thirty dick jiggles, two bagfuls of air into the lungs, thirty more dick jiggles. Jiggle, jiggle, jiggle. Breathe. Jiggle, jiggle, jiggle. And so on.

Later that day, I am informed he died at the scene, two hours after we left. Paramedics had worked to save his life for over four hours, without success.

So, another bullet of horror to add to the 'have a drink if you've never' ammunition. 'Have a drink if you've never seen a Nazi paedophile's dick.' I seldom play that drinking game these days, though. All my friends end up shitfaced by 8pm and I go home stone cold sober.

Here's why I'm with my other half. When I tell her about my day, she says, 'Awww. He's with Hitler now.'

24 January

I have to call a complainant in a colleague's absence. It is, I am assured, urgent. This is a case that has dragged on for over six months, generated reams of paperwork and is no closer to being resolved. I read the email trail to familiarise myself with the salient aspects of the case before calling the victim to discuss our case strategy going forward.

'Is that Ms V—?'

'Yes.'

'It's Nick. I've read the notes in my colleague's absence and have been asked to give you a call. I can see the diary sheets of events covering December and this month. It's just. . .'

'Just what?'

'. . . it's just that generally speaking, we wouldn't consider a child rolling a marble across the floor to be anti-social behaviour.'

ASB is in the eye of the beholder. And for this tenant, a toddler occasionally running across the living room floor or rolling some marbles about was beyond the pale.

'Did you read the other parts? Where he keeps dropping a toy truck on the floor?'

I had.

'It's too much. It makes the walls shake and the light fittings swing.'

Don't ask how fucking big the toy is, don't ask how fucking big the toy is...

'It's ruining our lives.'

It's always ruining their lives. When a victim reports ASB, three things are guaranteed:

1: The doctor has told them they've got depression. (This is almost never backed up by a GP note, proof of medication, a psych report or anything other than them feeling a bit fed up. As a diagnosed and medicated depressive for over two decades, I find it a little offensive – like claiming to be a paraplegic when you stub your toe.)

2: Some, if not all, of the occupants in the victim's home will have asthma. It must sound like a yoga class for overweight nuisance phone-callers in their place. What this has to do with their neighbour watching TV late at night is never adequately explained.

3: IT IS RUINING THEIR LIFE.

After a Herculean effort in not telling Ms V— to shove the marbles up her arse (taking care not to fart them out and disturb the neighbours living below her, obviously), it's agreed that my colleague will pick up the case where she left off.

27 January

Yeah, about the vivid dreams the GP mentioned. A more accurate description on the box might be 'Caution:

Mirtazapine may cause dreams that appear to have been filmed by Christopher Nolan in 4K Ultra-HD and soundtracked by Hans Zimmer kicking the shit out of an orchestra.'

They're also making me irritable, and in a job that could make Gandhi tell Mother Teresa to go fuck a goat, that's less than ideal. Might have to have another word with the GP.

28 January

The Ringfence officer calls to give an update on their deceased former client. The investigation into the threatening letters will run alongside the investigation into his death to make sure the police acted properly during their visit.

I worked with this officer a while back on another case. A new tenant was causing problems with his neighbours and during an argument mentioned he was a sex offender, which is as strange a way to win an argument as you're likely to hear.

I had not been told about his past. Police disclose information on a need-to-know basis, and Ringfence had risk-assessed the tenant and decided we did not need to know. I wasn't told specifics about his past, but his Ringfence officer helped fill in some of the blanks.

After he complained about the condition of the flat we

had provided for him ('It's a dump, I've lived in much nicer places than this,' he moaned), his Ringfence officer said, 'I'm guessing that flat is nicer than the cell he sat in for twenty years.' It was a way of telling me the gravity of what he'd done without actually telling me.

But now he had paid his debt to society and was living in a property I managed, and I was obliged to treat him with courtesy and respect, making sure he was happy in his new home where nobody was trying to put ground glass into his food or beat him to death with a bar of soap in a sock.

The reason for disclosing his past soon became clear. It was how he got himself a new flat when his current one was not to his liking. In the two years he had been free, this was his third. He'd annoy the neighbours, let them know he was a paedophile, let his Ringfence officer know he'd let the neighbours know and let the system do the rest.

I managed to maintain my professionalism by thinking about those around him. A petrol bomb through his window would place the family upstairs at risk. A vigilante beating on the way home from the off-licence would put an otherwise-innocent neighbour in jail for carrying it out. So I wrote the report, agreed his life was at risk and approved his transfer away from the estate. I manage to feel OK about having done that almost 90 per cent of the time.

31 January

A joint visit with somebody from CMHT (the community mental health team) to see Candice. Last year, Candice threw a bike at her neighbour and started punching them. After police issued a caution and we took her to court, things have been somewhat fraught where she lives. This is not helped by Candice calling the victim's dad an 'ugly cunt' whenever she sees him, or spitting on the floor whenever she passes the victim on the street.

Today's visit is with the mental health team because Candice is psychotic. If you've not worked with psychotics as part of your job, you're liable to think of them as people wheeled around on gurneys wearing masks and saying rude things to FBI agents. This is seldom, if ever, the case.

Candice's psychosis is simply a function of her schizophrenia, which she is taking medication to treat (or rather isn't, hence the downturn in her behaviour). Candice's psychosis simply means her grip on reality is looser than that of most people, but it doesn't automatically mean she's going to harm anyone.

This is a difficult sell to the neighbours of schizophrenics, who may have witnessed psychotic episodes. Especially if the neighbour kicked you down some stairs during one of them. But the court was satisfied that, while Candice was

curb-stomping her neighbour, her capability to understand the consequences of her actions was only temporarily
impaired. They were also satisfied that her new drug regime
would minimise the likelihood of it happening again (as
long as you actually take it, Candice, for fuck's sake).

As a result, we could not get a court order granted
against Candice for the assault or take tenancy action
against her: because while she was doing it, she didn't know
what she was doing. Imagine explaining that to somebody's
bruised and grazed face and to their crestfallen mother. If
you think it would make you feel like a useless piece of shit,
you'd be quite right.

I asked the victim to get back in touch if the neighbour
started getting all stair-kicky again, and over the last few
weeks, Candice has been a bit of a handful. I complete the
appointment with the psych visitor and it is decided that,
while Candice is currently functionally psychotic, she doesn't
pose enough of an immediate risk to self or others to be
sectioned. Apparently, her grasp on what she's done to her
neighbour, her perceived persecution by everyone in the
block where she lives and her desire, at the age of forty-five,
to finally pursue her dream career as a jockey isn't enough
to have her carried away.

The psych visitor will see Candice on a weekly basis and
wait for her condition to sufficiently worsen (she clearly isn't

taking her medication, as evidenced by her inability to show us any of her tablets) for her to be sectioned again.

Once in hospital, her psych medicine regime will be settled, possibly via a slow-release anti-psychotic injection (known as a depo injection), until she is well enough to be released (Candice wants to avoid hospital at all costs, as a side-effect of most anti-psychotics is to make the patient's weight balloon like De Niro preparing for a film, which is no good for an aspiring jockey).

This cycle is likely to be repeated until Candice dies.

Not an easy visit, so I'm glad to get back to the office. Simon is there, asking if I know how to order four-hole hole punches, while he carefully arranges the two tenant interviews he's managed to complete since he arrived in colour-coded folders.

My boss is waiting to speak to me, and takes me into a side room.

'They're doing another Operation Poland in a few weeks. There are going to be 200 coppers involved. We're going to get the info as and when it arrives. And I want you to coordinate it as it comes in so we can serve them eviction notices.'

There's never somebody around when you need them, to push you down some stairs so you can have a few weeks of sick leave, is there?

February

Password: HadEnough101
Medication: Mirtazapine 15mg

1 February

Sixty-nine.

I run my monthly report of how many cases I'm supposedly dealing with, and that's the figure that comes back:
sixty-nine. I haven't even the energy to say *'Nice'* to myself.
(There's a juvenile online convention that whenever the
number sixty-nine appears, you say *'Nice'* to mark its sexual
connotation. I am a very juvenile person and wholeheartedly subscribe to this sort of thing.)

There are no industry standards on how many cases are
too many for an ASB officer. Even now, it's too new a job,
relatively speaking, and the role is too nebulous to apply
such standards. An ASB officer working in the home coun-
ties commuter belt will not be doing the same job as their
colleague working in central Birmingham, for instance.

Many years ago, I worked for a small RSL (registered

social landlord, a type of charity that offers low-income housing for those in need) whose housing stock was primarily located in Mayfair. On my first day I was handed a brick-thick file, the most serious current case they were dealing with and one they hoped an experienced ASB officer like me might be able to finally crack.

There will be many tales of deprivation and depravity, heartbreak and misery in this book so I can't warn you every time one appears. All I will say is that you should sit down with a stiff drink to hand, turn your phone off and make peace with your god before proceeding. Ready? Good.

Doris was in her seventies and lived in a ground floor flat in a 1920s-built complex, equidistant from the King's Road and the Thames. In the flat next door lived her neighbour Beryl, who was of a similar age. Both had lived there for decades and were initially friends, but time had soured their relationship. Some now-forgotten slight had lodged a tiny splinter in their happy handshake of a friendship, and over the years this had become inflamed, swollen and infected.

Hard as it is to believe that two rational human beings could act this way, but as I read through the file I learned that Doris had a habit of sweeping the path in her garden, and letting the dead leaves and dirt encroach onto Beryl's front garden. In turn, when Beryl tidied her garden, she'd move Doris's plant pots to one side when sweeping up and not put them back.

I know. The horror. The inhumanity. I lasted six months in that role before resigning due to a fear I would leap into the Thames out of sheer boredom, with Doris and Beryl's case file tied around my feet to anchor me.

Sometimes the contrast between workloads can exist in the same job. Another RSL I worked for had properties spread across London, from the leafy outer suburbs to the inner city of pre-gentrification King's Cross. In the space of one week I dealt with two ends of the scale.

First, I attended a residents' meeting, at which the hot topic was kids riding their skateboards on the pavement rather than the designated cycle path. Brows were furrowed, tea was drunk and voices were very slightly raised trying to resolve this thorny issue. I don't remember whether it was featured on *Newsnight* or not.

Three days later, I had a call from police to say one of our properties – a stone's throw from King's Cross – had been raided and three machete-owning crack dealers had been arrested. Left behind was our tenant, Harry.

Harry was a gentle, broken Irishman in his late forties who wanted little more than to slowly drink himself to death. He frequented the same local pubs as the street sex workers that used to be a common feature of King's Cross before the artisan fishfinger pop-up restaurants and designer water bars took over.

Happy for the company (I never got the sense he wanted anything more from them than that), Harry told the girls he chatted with to pop round if they ever needed to get out of the cold, use the loo or have a cup of tea. One sex worker took him up on his offer, accompanied by three men who said they would very much like to sell crack from his flat.

To emphasise their enthusiasm, they beat Harry up and told him the whole flat, save for his tiny back bedroom, was now theirs to run their business from. When police eventually raided the property, it was clear he had been coerced, so he wasn't arrested. The problem was, as the officer on the phone pointed out, the actual drug dealers could only be held for twenty-four hours as there wasn't enough evidence to remand them in custody. Being the type of people who take a dim view of anyone disturbing their commercial enterprise, and given that Harry had escaped arrest, I knew they would make a beeline back to his flat and seek to remonstrate with him via the medium of machete. His already-unsafe home could very soon become a fatal place to be.

I made my way to Harry's flat and told him to gather whatever stuff he couldn't leave behind. This took a depressingly short amount of time, and involved a few items of clothing, a battery-operated radio and a 2.5-litre bottle of Frosty Jacks cider, the preferred beverage of the alcoholic, being both relatively cheap and ludicrously strong. I tried some once out of curiosity and it tasted like licking the inside of a television. While it was plugged in.

I told Harry we were on our way to the homeless persons' unit (where I would subsequently sit with him for three hours to ensure they found him somewhere else to stay) so he couldn't take the cider with him. Before you could say *sláinte*, he started gulping down as much as his stomach could manage, leaving the rest of the bottle behind. As we reached the hallway to his front door, his stomach decided it actually couldn't manage, and vomited back up two litres of fizzy nightmare onto the lino floor.

I'd like to think that later that evening, the newly released and vengeance-bent crack dealers burst into Harry's flat and crashed to the floor like homicidal Keystone Cops, slipping around on his last goodbye to his home.

Anyway, sixty-nine cases. Not nice. As I say, there's no set rule as to how many 'too many cases' are, but sixty-nine is definitely pushing it. There are different ways to reduce a workload that high. You can eliminate, for example:

- Duplicate cases (when three different tenants have complained about the same issue, why have three cases open when you can lump them into one?);
- Dead cases (they haven't complained for six months so you phone them with crossed fingers, heart in your mouth, and ask if it's still a problem, praying they say it's naturally resolved itself so you can close the case. This is where my previous work in sales comes in handy and I channel that 'Overcoming Objections' training day I yawned through some time in the late nineties);
- 'Moved away' cases (the dream scenario, where one or both of the parties involved in the dispute has moved house so you can close the case without having to speak to either of them).

All you're doing, though, is shuffling deckchairs – none of it really changes the tsunami of crap headed your way. But if it gets the Excel report down to a single page, it feels that little bit less overwhelming.

2 February

One of the main tools I use to deal with problem behaviour is the ASB injunction. In formal terms, ASB injunctions are a civil power granted to local authorities under the 2014 Crime and Policing Act which require a two-stage evidentiary test to be met to the balance of probabilities, whereby the court is satisfied that the respondent has engaged, or has threatened to engage, in anti-social behaviour, and that the granting of the order is just and convenient to prevent the respondent from engaging in further anti-social behaviour. In non-formal terms, it's a court order to try and stop people from being dickheads.

Anyone over the age of ten can be the subject of an injunction and while they typically run for between twelve and twenty-four months, the court can grant them 'until further order', i.e. until the subject convinces the court to cancel them because they're not a dickhead any more or until the subject drops dead, whichever happens first.

They typically list things people must refrain from doing, and these things should be behaviour of which they have been proven guilty. For instance, you can't get an injunction prohibiting somebody from murdering goats while dressed as Spiderman unless they have a penchant for doing that.

Over the years, we have had to finesse the way these prohibitions are worded. A big problem on our estates is cars with young males in them selling drugs and groups of lads on street corners doing the same. Successive challenges to our injunctions have seen the prohibition of dealing on street corners get gradually more pedantic. 'You must not congregate in a group of three or more people' seems easy to understand and lacking ambiguity. But the aforementioned challenges have morphed this into 'You must not congregate in a public place (other than a place of worship, sporting event or activity intended for vocational or training purposes) in a group of three or more people (i.e. two other people with you comprising the third person), except for immediate family members.'

Likewise the car-dealer injunctions have gone from 'You must not be in a vehicle with three or more people' to 'You must not be present in a private vehicle (which excludes trains, buses and other modes of public transport) in a public place (a public place being defined as a public road, car park or estate road) with two or more people (with the exception of immediate family members).'

Every single caveat in those above amendments has come about following a successful challenge in court over apparent vagueness of wording, and some terms are still being discussed. One area of ambiguity remains as to whether being in a car on a public road means you are in a private place or not. On the one hand, it's your property; you can lock the doors and you're allowed to stop people from getting in, so a car must be private. On the other hand, the car itself is in a public place and police don't need a warrant to search it if they have reasonable suspicion that drugs or weapons are present. So it must be public, right?

Our perpetrators have a vested interest in choosing to believe their car is a private place and have employed barristers to argue this. I have offered a counter-argument to our barristers that they have declined to use, which states, 'If the judge says a parked car is a private place, I'm going to find out where they live, sit in a parked car outside their house and start energetically masturbating.'

Injunctions can also have positive requirements – things the subject has to do rather than things they are forbidden from doing. These have to relate to stopping the bad behaviour, so will usually require the subject to do things like attend drug counselling or speak to a youth worker.

It would be nice if I could get an injunction to make a drug dealer who has been threatening people on my estate stand there for one hour every day with a sign saying 'I wank off dogs', but I imagine the bench would take a dim view of this.

If you breach an injunction, the entry level for sentencing is prison. Realistically, unless you have breached it in a grotesquely awful way, the likelihood is you will get a suspended sentence and a stern warning from the judge about coming before them again.

They do work, sort of. I would estimate that about seventy-five per cent of the injunctions I've been granted are never breached. Of the ones that are breached, about seventy-five per cent are only breached once. I'm realistic enough to understand the difference between 'injunctions that were breached' and 'injunctions we caught them breaching', but it is still a fairly robust deterrent.

But ultimately, it's a bit of paper. And if you're amoral, shitfaced, insane, a career criminal or merely profoundly stupid, a bit of paper isn't going to stop you.

4 February

To paraphrase Lou Reed, I'm waiting for my man, set of court papers in my hand.

Iain had previously worked for the council until it became apparent he was terrible at his job and becoming increasingly abusive towards his colleagues. Despite what certain newspapers might have you believe, that can actually be enough to get you fired as a council officer.

He had taken his P45 with neither equanimity nor good grace and had started harassing his former colleagues: waiting outside his former workplace, sending abusive emails, that sort of thing. This had led to an injunction being taken out against him, which had basically asked him to stop being an arsehole, but in more legally-appropriate language.

Arsehole is as arsehole does, however, and Iain had continued his pattern of behaviour by, amongst other things, texting a former colleague to let her know he was sitting outside her family home, waiting for her to get back from work.

Iain had also branched out into threatening and harassing a local vicar. Vicars are often the unsung heroes of local housing, as part of their pastoral care includes listening to residents' concerns, pressing authorities for minor improvements like better street lighting, attending endless evening meetings and drinking more lukewarm tea than is advisable.

Iain had decided to start messaging Samuel, even though Samuel wasn't his local vicar, had never met Iain and had no idea what he was talking about. Iain said he knew Samuel was taking bribes from local politicians (he wasn't) and that he'd tampered with a recent election (he hadn't).

We were lucky enough to count Iain amongst our tenants. For this reason, we were taking him back to court. We wanted to show that he had breached his injunction and might require a little spell in prison to reconsider his life choices. And we wanted the existing order amended to protect the vicar specifically. Samuel had confessed that the stress caused by Iain's entirely unwarranted abuse towards him had made him consider moving parish altogether to protect his family.

When we take somebody to court, the judge likes to be certain the perpetrator was given all the papers we will be relying on for our case. Well-funded private organisations would have a firm of process servers they would employ to ensure this was done. We are not a well-funded private firm.

This means I am standing outside a small block of flats in the rain, waiting for Iain to come home. Even in a blaze of August sunshine, seen through the slightly fogged eyes of a Saturday afternoon spent in a beer garden, surrounded by good friends and with a song in your heart, this area would in all probability still look a bit rubbish. In the February drizzle, Ken Loach would think you were overdoing the grimness just a touch.

Iain does not answer his phone, or the buzzer to his flat, and there is no letterbox on the main door, so I can't serve the papers. I try again later that afternoon without success before posting them. Judges don't always trust Royal Mail to deliver items (and having worked for them many years ago, I can't say I blame them) but it will have to do.

6 February

Simon has quit, having somehow secured a better job elsewhere. Our loss is the stationery budget's gain. We are back to being understaffed. Let the joy be unconfined.

8 February

The court hearing date for Iain.

First things first, we know he definitely got the court papers because he has shown up. You would be surprised by how often people don't show up for court hearings, especially when the hearings might see them have an injunction granted, a breach of injunction accepted as proven, or an eviction agreed. The fact they could end up homeless, in jail or both is actually so terrifying it discourages them from coming. I think for many people the legal system can seem so intimidatingly Byzantine that they prefer to stay at home and pretend it isn't happening.

Iain is not intimidated by legal action, though. In fact, he's so chilled out about it he is choosing to represent himself. Before the hearing, he proudly mentions the degree he has in law as proof he can handle this, which is like volunteering to be dropped into the war in Syria because you're really good at *Call of Duty* on the Xbox.

That said, representing yourself isn't always the terrible idea it might seem. Judges tend to be extremely forgiving towards litigants in person, guiding them through the process, allowing them time to decide what point they're trying to make. They can be like a parent teaching their kid how to ride a bike. Only it's a bike that will land them in jail if they fall off.

I have a cheap black suit that I use for court appearances. Seeing as an average court hearing can consist of listening to our tenant tell the court that I, the police and several of their neighbours are all mistaken in their belief that the tenant keeps racially abusing people, a Primark suit seems the right level of spend for the occasion.

Unfortunately, I've forgotten to wash a shirt ahead of this hearing, and the only suitable clean one I have is also black. Black suit, black shoes (obviously, I'm not a savage) and a black shirt. I look like Johnny Cash's probation officer.

We have half a dozen witnesses who dutifully repeat their witness statements saying they have received abusive emails from Iain. On each occasion, Iain's defence pivots on the fact that anyone could have created an email account in his full name, so how do they know it was him? One by one they admit that yes, it is theoretically possible somebody else could have sent the emails.

This is where witnesses and victims can be very frustrating. They mean well. They've been through a rotten time. They want to make clear they're telling the truth. But something about standing in front of that little lectern and swearing allegiance to the judge tends to shave eighty IQ points off most people.

Rather than telling Iain, 'The only people who received

emails were your former colleagues, you mentioned things that happened while you worked there, and nobody else I know has any reason to send me or all your former co-workers abuse, so I'd say it's pretty unlikely it could be anyone else,' they meekly accept that his far-fetched-sounding defence might hold water.

And so does the judge. She repeatedly tells our barrister that she could set up an account as Bugs Bunny but that does not make her Bugs Bunny. I'm tempted to tell the judge that her ears bear a striking resemblance, but I don't.

Iain has been careful in his campaign of abuse but not, ultimately, careful enough. One of the messages was sent via WhatsApp from his own phone. A phone, he tells the judge, that the police recently seized on an entirely unrelated matter, so he can't disprove it was his number.

All the allegations regarding the abusive emails are found to be not proven thanks to Iain's 'maybe somebody is out to get me' defence, but the judge finds the abusive message to be proven. She tells him, 'For the message, I'm going to give you a suspended sentence but let me say this: while the applicant was not able to prove to the criminal standard that you sent those emails, I'm pretty convinced on a personal basis that you did. Don't appear in front of me again.'

I know that I will be dealing with more and more cases in which, like Iain, the defendant represents themselves – not due to planet-sized egos like Iain's, but because getting legal-aid-funded representation is becoming more and more difficult. It's not financially viable work for solicitors, and the rules governing who qualifies baffle even the solicitors themselves, so their potential clients have no chance of understanding.

A quick example: an injunction is a civil order – that is, a court order granted in a civil court rather than a criminal court. Civil courts deal with less serious issues such as bankruptcy, evictions and divorces. A civil court order is a judge telling you to do certain things. But if you're accused of breaching the order, it's dealt with as a criminal matter. I've heard numerous defendants tell the court that they couldn't get a solicitor to defend their alleged breach of injunction. Why? Because the solicitors who deal with civil matters say they don't do criminal work, and the criminal solicitors say that an injunction is a civil matter, so they won't represent the defendant either. Confused? Join the club.

We are given our additional clauses to protect Samuel, and Iain is told he will have to pay the costs we incurred in bringing this hearing to court. As a public body we try to keep our legal costs to a minimum but even so, our bill – which is now Iain's bill – runs to about £1,500. He will have to pay that back to us with payments spread out at £70 a month. Justice, in a way, is served.

11 February

The battle over the office heating is in full swing. Lines have been drawn in the sand. No quarter will be accepted, no quarter offered. It, like all the radiators, is *on*.

Paul sits directly under the main heater for the office. For nine months of the year he likes to have it on full blast, as well as occasionally checking all the radiators in the office to make sure they are also hot enough to smelt iron. I have often wondered whether he is some new hybrid creature: half gecko, half orchid. He still wears a cardigan on top of all this. I decide to confront him.

'Paul, I've just checked what temperature you've got the heating set at. And well, look. It's 31 degrees in here. Thirty-one. Do you know where else it's currently 31 degrees, Paul? Singapore. If I was on holiday in Singapore and it was 31 degrees I'd be in shorts and an open shirt. I'm sure neither of us wants to see that, do we? Could we maybe just turn it down? From 31 degrees? Just a bit? 20-ish, maybe? How about Cairo? Could the office be the same temperature as Cairo, maybe, Paul?'

'It's freezing in here.'

And that, it seems, is all the compromise Paul is willing to make.

I'm not proud of what I did next.[1] As an adult approaching middle age, I should be above setting the heating to 15 degrees, hiding the remote in the gents' toilet and going out on visits for the rest of the day, but apparently I'm not.

14 February

Another GP appointment. The Salvador Dalí dreams have died down somewhat, but I still spend most days with my stomach lurching around the place like a pissed sailor in a hurricane. It's an acid mix of panic, unfocussed fear of being fired for not doing my job properly and a general cold, wet duvet of depression flung over the top. You'd think it's impossible to be both bored and anxious at the same time, but it isn't.

The GP doubles my dosage and that's that. I don't resent her, though. I recognise somebody trying to deal with other people's dramas and not having the time or tools to do it properly. And unlike in my job, she can't shuffle me about on an Excel spreadsheet until I go away. Here's hoping my brain chemistry can stop fucking about.

---

1 I could not be prouder if that remote control was my kid and I had just attended its graduation ceremony during which it had received a double first from Cambridge in Ninja Studies and Astronautics.

15 February

Speaking of drugs ... When people ask why somebody would become a drug dealer, here's the job advert I would pitch to them.

Role: drug dealer – mobile venue
Location: various
Start date: ASAP following recent imprisonment of sales staff
Salary: £40,000 basic + commission + percentage on stolen items fenced + company car

Introduction
Can you drive around an inner-city borough for eight hours a day? Threaten drug addicts with a baseball bat if they're short on their money? Be trusted not to start smoking the merchandise? Do you like stabbing people? If so, you may have a promising, if brief, career in our tight-knit team of drug dealers.

The role
Our dealers are the backbone of our operation. In this role, you will be expected to service our ever-growing existing customer base, as well as developing new sales

leads amongst the exciting youth market. We believe our range of products – heroin and crack cocaine – are the best in the marketplace. And even if they're not, our customers will buy them anyway.

If you choose to join us, you will. . .
Move from location to location dependent on police raids, working both indoors and outdoors.

Use your powers of negotiation and people skills to convince local residents not to report you to the police if they want their windows unsmashed and their cat alive.

Ensure every interaction with customers leaves them wanting to come back for more, as long as they have £20.

Who we're looking for
Ideally you will have no educational qualifications, a family with a history of drug and/or alcohol misuse, and a proven track record of living in grinding poverty.

While we will consider all candidates, anybody with a cohesive family unit and functioning support network may find their application unsuccessful. Female applicants will not be considered for frontline roles, but may be suitable for non-sales positions such as hiding drugs/weapons/cash and being sexually exploited by other staff members.

Previous experience of petty violence and theft preferred but not essential.

We are especially interested in hearing from you if you have psychological issues that are undiagnosed, ignored or untreated.

Entry-level roles in our team are also available for people aged ten to seventeen, with a competitive starter package and your own pushbike.

What's in it for me?

We like to consider our team to be one of the most feared around and are willing to prove that by putting a zombie knife where our mouth is. Employees will feel a level of belonging and safety that they have not previously experienced. If it's misguided respect you're after, we are second to none.

Perks include:

- Hire car changed on a monthly basis to avoid ANPR detection, typically an Audi or BMW.
- 0 days of holiday each year. Crackheads don't take Christmas off, why should we?
- Generous sick leave allowance – if you are assaulted, stabbed or shot, we will make every effort to maim the person responsible. Or their friends. Or somebody who looks like them.

- A burner phone to be changed monthly.
- Plentiful promotion opportunities, due to imprisonment, death or the last guy fucking up by leaving all his supply in the glove compartment. Man like that can't be trusted, y'get me?
- Great offers and deals on TVs, games consoles and whatever other things we steal on the side.
- Possibility of foreign travel with condoms full of cocaine stuffed up your arse.

About us
You've seen our gang tags around. You know who we are.

Equal opportunities statement
Nah.

Things to consider before you apply
You must be willing to move to another city at a moment's notice to deal with problems occurring there, so meaningful relationships are discouraged.

A career with us will usually last less than a decade for the reasons listed above.

If you mention any of this to anybody, we will kill you. No, seriously.

Good luck with your application!

18 February

Training day.

The manager from MAP (the multi-agency panel) is here to tell us how it's doing since its inception twelve months ago. The MAP meets once a month to discuss cases that are multi-storey pains in the arse. The idea is that a coordinated approach will produce better results than everyone working on their own. Apparently, muttering about those lazy bastards in (insert the name of any team that isn't yours) isn't the MAP way.

Things that make a MAP work well: a fully-funded police force that has strong links with the local community due to a functioning 'Safer Neighbourhood' team; a mental health service that has trained, experienced community psychiatric nurses who can make regular visits to their clients because their workload is manageable; social services that can run the same way; drug and alcohol intervention teams that can support vulnerable people via timely and readily available treatment programmes; homeless outreach teams that can offer accommodation to rough sleepers to enable their re-introduction to mainstream society; ASB officers that aren't knackered all the time.

Things that our MAP has: none of the above.

I currently have a vested interest in how effective the

MAP is. That's because I referred a case to them a few months ago, after Lynne tried to shove me down a set of stairs.

Lynne, in official parlance, is a 'challenging client who presents a varied set of symptoms and requires a bespoke approach to her case management, which should be responsive to her changing needs and robust enough to react to problematic behaviour in a joined-up manner'. Or what you or I would refer to as a 'right annoying bugger'.

Since she moved into her flat last year, she has pissed off her neighbours in a variety of exciting and innovative ways. She started with the trusted classics of playing loud music and having lots of drunk visitors. She quickly moved on to the more esoteric approach of running around waving a broom over her head like a cleanliness-obsessed Gandalf, or peering through people's letterboxes demanding to know if they had ever seen a giraffe close up.

Last year the council issued her with a noise abatement notice,[2] which seemed to have calmed her down. It's normally a good indicator of exactly where on the mad:bad

---

2 A noise abatement notice is a bit like an injunction. Council officers are given powers to serve them on anyone creating statutory noise nuisance. This is any noise caused by power tools, musical instruments, stereos or TVs. So DIY parties accompanied by a thrash metal group at 3am with *Homes Under the Hammer* on in the background are strictly verboten.

Noise officers are trained to assess how loud is too loud. If you breach the notice, you can be fined, or the council can confiscate whatever it was that was causing the noise (i.e. the stereo, not you. Local authorities haven't been given the power to kidnap rowdy tenants. Yet).

scale people sit if they can comply with orders, and Lynne had complied with this. More likely to be bad rather than mad, then. But last year, I was informed about some 'offensive signs' she had in her window, so I went to take a look.

Lynne's kitchen window looked like the comments section under a YouTube clip about JFK and 9/11. Her posters said that the Pope was actually an eight-foot lizard, which would make the Vatican the world's largest reptile house, and that microwave ovens could be converted into time machines.

This in itself was no problem. People are allowed to believe in whatever bite-your-own-ear-mad stuff they like. But in addition to these were two posters we couldn't ignore. The first was a barely coherent screed that claimed Muslims were part of a shadowy worldwide cabal that was stealing Lynne's used tampons in order to extract the blood in them to make chemical weapons. (I suppose to make dirty bombs.)

The second called her neighbour a 'known gangster' and said that I was part of a 'crypto-Islam cabal' coordinating to harass her. I've never been called a crypto-Muslim before, showing that even after all these years, the job can still throw up surprises. I took a couple of photos of her window and started to make my way out of the block. Lynne ran out of her flat after me, repeatedly asking who I was and what I was doing. She blocked my entrance in the stairwell, making it clear she wouldn't move until I answered her. 'I'm from the landlord. Can you let me past, please?' I said several times, to no avail.

At one point, she moved slightly to one side so I tried to walk past. She shoved me, nearly causing me to fall down the stairs, telling me I was going nowhere. Only when I gave her my full name did she let me go.

Fortunately, in our team we have a process for dealing with members of staff who have been assaulted. It's called 'going out for a fag (if you smoke) then going back to your desk and carrying on with your job'. The organisation as a whole is very good at dealing with such incidents in a robust manner, but ASB officers tend to just take them as another day in paradise.

I've been threatened and jostled numerous times over the years and have never had any post-incident counselling for them. To even ask for it is to open yourself up for the question, 'Are you really cut out for this?'

I've managed to recognise the post-adrenaline crash that follows something like this and I can usually avoid the worst side-effects of it by not speaking to anybody until it's time to go to bed.

So, time to go to court. We got an urgent injunction asking Lynne not to be aggressive or abusive, or to threaten anyone visiting the block. However, the judge was not minded to grant the clause we suggested, asking that she take down the offending signs. 'This may be viewed as a freedom of speech issue,' said the judge, kicking the issue down the line for another judge to deal with. Which is easy enough to say when it isn't you who's been called a crypto-Muslim tampon-stealer.

Lynne, it was clear, had 'mental health'. Speak to any-body who works in the council or the NHS and this is the phrase they'll use when talking about those for whom brain chemistry and rational actions are on a collision course. It's not meant to be derogatory or insulting, it's just quicker. Technically, we all have varying degrees of mental health, but 'they have a history of mental health issues which may or may not impact on their behaviour' takes ages to say. If you get a report of somebody taking their binbags to the rubbish chute in the nude or gesticulating wildly at clouds, the first thing you'll ask in our profession is 'Have they got mental health?'

Historically, Lynne's mental health had been a person-ality disorder, a diagnosable but untreatable illness. Broadly speaking, it's a psychiatric term for 'they're obviously crack-ers, but tablets and talking therapy aren't going to help so ... [shrugs] dunno.' People with personality disorders are deemed to know that their actions have consequences and it can't be used in court as a defence when applying for an injunction or eviction. Lynne had worked with the same set of doctors for years and they were quite happy to go on record saying that if Lynne was acting up, she knew what she was doing. Her consultant even chipped in with some suggestions for what the injunction should include. The consultant was an expert in psychiatry but not in civil law, so a lot of the suggestions, such as insisting Lynne was not allowed to raise her voice in a public place or go into a GP's office without an appointment, were inventive while also legally unworkable.

But just before the main hearing could take place, Lynne managed to employ an independent psychiatrist who, on the basis of a one-hour chat, wrote a report that said Lynne might be schizophrenic. When I relayed this back to the CMHT dealing with Lynne, the officer said, 'Well, she's paying him, so of course he's going to give the diagnosis she wants.' If you think this opens up the possibility for two-tier access to justice to avoid sanctions, you would be quite right.

This essentially knackered our application. If Lynne was schizophrenic (which she wasn't), it could be argued she wasn't in control of her faculties when she very carefully printed out those posters and sellotaped them to her window. When she assaulted me, she may have been experiencing a schizophrenic episode (she wasn't). And if there is any doubt about a person's mental health status, the courts are loath to grant an order that may later be overturned. Judges hate being told they did something wrong.

Our application for an injunction was set aside pending an independent (i.e. not a shrink for hire) assessment to establish whether Lynne's lift went all the way to the top floor. I told the mental health team the outcome and left them to it. And then, nothing happened. Over and over again. The assessment the court asked for was never arranged by the CMHT. When it eventually was, several months later, Lynne just didn't bother turning up. Nor to several meetings after that.

So when our MAP training is over and we are asked if we have any questions, my first one is, 'Is there any point to this existing? How many times can I come back to the same meeting, with the same people, and ask the same question – has Lynne been assessed yet? – and get the same negative answer? It seems that you can do whatever you want as a tenant just as long as you act mad and don't answer your door.'

To be honest, I think she'd been hoping more for a 'Can you email us the PowerPoint training slides?' type of question.

20 February

Let's talk about the other main tool for people working in housing: the notice of seeking possession, or NOSP.

If you have a tenancy with the council and the council would really much rather that you didn't, the first thing they need to do is serve you with a NOSP. This puts you on notice that the council wants to go to court and ask the judge to kick you out. The NOSP will have all the necessary jargon about which Housing Act it depends on and what grounds the landlord is relying on.

It's far easier to think of a tenancy agreement as a contract. You sign it, the council signs it and if you do something that breaches the contract (like not paying rent, deliberately burning the place to the ground or growing a forest of cannabis in it), the council goes to court and asks for it to be annulled. With the side-effect of making you homeless.

There's an assumption that evicting tenants is a straightforward thing for the council, but from experience, it is exceptionally difficult to convince a court to kick somebody out. I have known tenants to be in rent arrears to the tune of £8,000 and the court has granted a suspended possession order. This is basically the court saying, 'The council have proved you've messed up, but we won't let them evict you just yet, so long as you do the following. . .' The proviso in this case was that they paid their £8,000 arrears off at £5 a week.

Yes, that *is* over thirty years to pay back what they owed. Well spotted.

Despite the fact that a lot of my job is reminding people we can evict them if they don't behave themselves, I think it's absolutely right that it should be difficult to do so. Social housing is, as my dear old mother used to say, rarer than rocking-horse shit these days.

While it would make my job a lot more manageable to make evictions easier, the weight on my conscience wouldn't be worth it.

21 February

Operation Poland Part 2: Day of Action. Or, rather, inaction, as will become clear.

When there's a risk of resistance or violence, police drugs raids happen in three stages. Several years ago, I attended a 5am police briefing for a series of visits police were intending to make to our properties, in which they went through the plan of action.

Officers in the first team are built along the lines of Easter Island statues. Their job is to force the door open, secure the property, and scare the shit out of everybody who wasn't expecting eighteen stone of copper in their face at 6am. As one riot gear-clad behemoth said as I sat next to him in the police van en route to the raid, 'I fucking *love* this part of the job.'

Team two enters and arrests everybody in the property, just to be on the safe side. This can often include trying to stop the occupants from swallowing whatever drugs they have on them, without the officers getting their fingers bitten off. People are then de-arrested where appropriate.

The third team in this kind of drugs raid then goes into the property to look for, y'know, the drugs. It's important to separate out the three roles, because a massive copper dripping with adrenaline from smashing a door in might not conduct the most nuanced of searches.

While it may look gung-ho, there's a good reason to go in mob-handed. Drug properties are often heavily guarded and the immediate risk to officers can be serious. Not in the raid that I attended all those years ago, though. After police battered in the door and secured the address, the lone occupant – a single drug addict on a thin mattress – awoke to find a rugby-scrum's-worth of coppers staring down at him. Which no doubt counteracted heroin's constipation-inducing side-effects.

That approach hasn't been deemed necessary in this instance. When the list of targeted addresses for Operation Poland II (This Time It's Still Not Personal, We're

Professionals) came in, only four of the forty addresses treated to a dawn visit from Her Majesty's constabulary were managed by us. None of them have the grilles on the doors and windows or CCTV camera outside that tend to indicate a thriving drug den. The people the police want do their dealing out on street corners, so it's unlikely they'll have mountains of crack or guns to protect them. The drugs raids are effected by knocking politely on the door. This happens more often than police dramas would have you believe.

Only two of these four are in at the time, so we serve them both with NOSPs. The first is served on a dad whose son, when police knock on the door, throws a bum bag full of cash and drugs out of the window, then scarpers. There is something almost disarmingly childish about the way this bloke, a known drug dealer with previous convictions, acts like a toddler holding a bag of sweets he isn't allowed when police arrive. *Throw it away! Run!*

The second is a habitual crackhead who is being employed by the dealers to bring in new customers in exchange for crack (they were never going to be offering National Trust vouchers or Nectar points, were they?). In his fifties, he lives with his mum in a flat that is immaculately tidy, except for his bedroom. His bedroom is immaculately crackhead-y: burnt foil, empty wraps, lighters, makeshift crack pipes. The works.

When I serve the NOSP on his mum, she genuinely cannot understand why I am there.

'We're serving the notice following the recent police raid.'

'They never found any drugs, though.'

'Yes, but your son's bedroom was full of evidence he's been taking drugs in your flat, and that's a breach of your tenancy.'

'But he's an addict.'

'Yes, I know. He's an addict that takes drugs in your flat. With your knowledge. Which is a breach of your tenancy.'

'. . . but he's an addict.'

People can have planet-sized blind spots when it comes to their kids. This is a woman in her seventies, living with a son in his fifties. She hoovers her living room, dusts the knick-knacks on her mantelpiece and gives the net curtains a good bleach once a month, all while living with a crackhead. She's somehow pretzelled her worldview to accommodate this.

Her son isn't a teenager who's spiralled out of control, remember. After a day's hustling on the streets, every night he kisses his mum on the forehead, wishes her a good night, then goes to his bedroom to smoke crack.

The rest of the Operation Poland Day of Action involves wearing a hi-viz tabard with 'ASB Team' on it and looking like a fluorescent tit. We knock on hundreds of doors in the neighbourhood to reassure residents that We Take the Issue of Drugs Very Seriously. We also ask if they have any information on drug activity on their estate.

As with every door-knocking exercise of this nature, we come away with dozens of complaints about outstanding repairs and queries about parking spaces, and absolutely no information on drug dealing of any evidential value whatsoever.

I go home and have several very large drinks. The largeness and the severalness of the drinks I need after work have slowly inched up in recent months. The irony of cracking down on substance abusers at work, then drinking myself numb of an evening, is not lost on me.

25 February

Monday. I book a day off as emergency leave as I managed to spend all of yesterday lying in bed, wide awake, in a funk of despair and palpitations. I've started dreading Sunday evenings in a way I've not experienced since I was a kid. Back then, *Antiques Roadshow* presaged another week in a school where bullying and substandard teaching worked their heady magic on me.

I spend the day staring at the TV, cursing myself for wasting the time, but too tired and terrified of tomorrow to actually do anything useful.

27 February

I check on the database and Albert's – the poor old guy with the cats – flat is now marked as 'void'. When a council flat becomes empty ('void'), the pressure to get it ready for a new tenant is immense. The organisation relies on rent revenue and every day a flat isn't making money is viewed as a day wasted.

Forty years will be dumped into a skip. New cupboards and doors will be fitted, and a coat of paint applied. Once it's deemed habitable, it will go to whoever currently sits at the top of the waiting list.

The new tenants will stand on the spot where Albert spent a fortnight seeping into the carpet, wondering where to put their sofa. Half a lifetime scraped off the walls and floor and sent to landfill. Albert is no longer the tenant of flat 12. Albert is now Void.

Goodbye, Albert.

March

Password: Knackered101
Medication: Mirtazapine 30mg

1 March

The first job of the day is taking down some signs because somebody broke their foot. I'm aware that might need some clarification.

The team were granted several premises closure orders three months ago on a number of properties. Another new power introduced in 2014, premises closure orders give local authorities the power to restrict access to any definable space they manage. In theory, this can be anything from an entire block of flats to an individual phone box (you may or may not be aware of this, depending on your age, but those boxes in the street that people piss in and use to shoot up heroin used to have the facility to make phone calls).

A premises closure order can either close down an area completely – so that nobody at all is allowed into the area it covers – or it can be partial (a partial premises closure order, or PPCO), so that nobody is allowed in that area except for specifically named individuals.

In practical terms, we use partial premise closure orders in one of two ways. The first is to stop our stairwells being used as hang-out spots to eat fried chicken, smoke weed, fuck, defecate, or perform any other of the various activities people like to do in such a semi-public place. If they manage to combine all of the above then that's a hell of a night out.

A PPCO on the communal areas of a block of flats means that unless you live there or have a really good reason for being there (you're a postie doing a round, a health visitor seeing a patient, or a firefighter stopping it from burning to the ground), you can be arrested. Needing somewhere to pass out next to a puddle of your own vomit is not deemed to be a good enough reason. Residents can get a bit confused about these orders, as evidenced by the audibly upset person who phoned me and asked whether his aunty could still come round to see him.

Anyone breaching a PPCO is arrested and dragged before the magistrates' court for a telling-off, fine, prison sentence or some combination of the three. This combination will always include the telling-off because magistrates like telling off people who've been found guilty more than kittens like a dangled strand of wool.

The second way we use PPCOs is to control the visitors

to a problem address. Getting an injunction on each of the three dozen heroin addicts who visit a flat that's being used as a shooting gallery isn't a realistic solution. So a PPCO limits who can go into a property without having to individually name who can't go in.

The order can even include the person whose flat it is, turning your PPCO into a PCO, or full premises closure order. However, if you get a PCO on your flat banning anyone from entering, including you, you've not been evicted. You still have to pay your rent. You still have a tenancy with us. You just can't use your flat for living in for three months. Or, if the court grants an extension, six months.

You can defend the application, of course, but you'd better be quick about it. We can spend as long as necessary building a case. We then notify the tenant, and within forty-eight hours, the case is heard in court. If granted, the PPCO is effective immediately. Oh, and if you want to defend the application, it doesn't qualify for legal aid. There may be drug addicts in social housing who can afford to hire a firm of solicitors at a moment's notice, but I've yet to meet one.

If you think this all sounds draconian and fatally weighted against tenants, you'd be absolutely right. The law as it stands needs amending in light of the obvious inequalities that came to light once people started using the legislation. It's a frequent problem that laws are written without consulting the people who will end up using them, and inevitably without consulting the people on the receiving end of them.

There are checks in place to make sure closure orders aren't being abused, as they need to be signed off by people in senior positions of power and agreed in court by magistrates. But even so, it often feels as if not enough has been done to give people a voice when it's their home that might be closed down.

That said, given it's one of the very few methods of enforcement where the ball is in the court of the ASB officer, my sympathies are sometimes strained. Especially when you have dozens of people coming to you to say their daily lives are being ruined by the actions of a single household.

Anyway, when the order is granted, notices are put up to make anyone visiting the block of flats aware of it. It's equally important to take them down once the order has expired, because a short-sighted copper might mistakenly believe the order is still valid and arrest somebody for breaching an order that doesn't exist.

A caretaker was working a late shift and noticed that some heavy signs were still in place for an expired order. In the process of taking the sign down, it fell on his foot, breaking a couple of bones.

So we were asked in very strong terms to make absolutely sure any expired notices were taken down. Carefully.

4 March

If you manage the same housing estate for any length of time, you end up having your regulars. These are people who view the rest of humanity as a potential issue to be complained about. No issue is too small to be ignored; no perceived slight can be overlooked. Thirty years ago, they kept the entire green-ink industry in business with the letters they wrote. Now they have your number on speed dial. The official descriptive term for such individuals is 'vexatious complainants', because the more accurate 'fucking nightmare' is deemed rude.

I once made the mistake of calling an FN resident using my personal phone rather than my work phone. The final straw was when they called at 2am. With my characteristically chipper outlook, I assumed this meant a family member had died. Instead it was the FN calling me to tell me the person upstairs was dragging their wardrobe around their bedroom. The fact they remained unsworn-at is testament to my consummate professionalism.

Today's FN is Colin. When he first moved into his flat, he asked me whether the estate was a bad one. I answered honestly, saying that it was a relatively quiet part of the borough. Little did I know that my definition of ASB (drug dens, violence, threats) was markedly different from his (literally anything you could possibly imagine).

Colin, it quickly became apparent, was terrified of and appalled by everything. The kids playing football on the patch of grass outside his flat could be potential burglars. The family upstairs were allowing their newborn baby to cry on purpose just to annoy him. The woman next door would sometimes be away all weekend, which was definitely a bit suspicious.

Police have monthly meetings to decide how to prioritise their resources and they use 999 and 101[1] calls to produce 'heat maps' of crime hotspots. One month, they were puzzled to see a massive red circle in an area beat officers didn't consider to be problematic. Further investigation

1 It's possible you've never had to call the police. Many people think that if you call the police for something they don't deal with, you'll be immediately thrown in jail. Not so. If anything, people don't call the police about ASB issues enough, so it's often hard to get a true picture of what's actually going on.

In theory, the two numbers work like this: 999 is for immediate risk of safety or for crimes currently in progress, and 101 is for everything else.

In reality, if you live in an inner-city borough and call 101, make sure you've been to the loo first, and have food and refreshments handy to keep your strength up. They're not answering the phone any time soon. Waiting on hold for forty-five minutes is not unheard of. Even when they do answer the phone, don't expect to see a response in the near future. I once called 101 to report a breach of an injunction. I told the call handler that the tenant was in his flat now so if they could get there soon, they'd catch him. They arrived four hours later, by which point he'd cleared off. When I told the police officers this when they eventually arrived, they shrugged their shoulders and cleared off too. It's not as if police are sitting in their cars eating doughnuts and reading the newspaper. The blue line is the thinnest it has ever been, and sadly, a neighbour acting up will often be pretty low down in their priorities.

showed that the circle was right over Colin's flat. At the time, Colin was the third-most-frequent caller to the police in the whole of London.

Life had been unkind to Colin. Plagued by various health issues, he looked twenty years older than he actually was. A difficult person to get along with, he appeared to have few friends and his most regular visitor seemed to be his aunt, a smart, efficient-looking former GP who wore the pain of the person her nephew had become like crow's feet on her face.

In addition to this, Colin clearly had unaddressed mental health issues. This is so common a factor with the people I meet, I sometimes wonder whether it would be quicker to point out the times when they *don't* have mental health.

Colin treated all interactions with authority – police, his local councillor, his landlord – like a child who believes everyone is just being mean. He was infantile to an alarming degree. Whenever challenged on his complaints – like the time he claimed the woman upstairs was shouting profanities all through the night when the woman in question was resident in a prison cell fifty-two miles away (admittedly, she *was* screaming obscenities throughout the night in her cell, but Colin could hardly claim to be hearing her from that distance) – he'd reduce himself to a tantrum of tears and recriminations that everybody was against him, this wasn't fair, and we'd all be happy once he was dead.

Asking whether he'd like a visit from somebody in the community mental health team also brought on a similar outburst. It was meant as just another offer of support, but that's not how he heard it. He wasn't mad and any suggestion otherwise was disgusting. How could I say such a thing? And so on. So whatever was causing him to call 999 every day and yell at the skies for deliberately raining on him would have to go untreated.

So a visit to Colin's flat – cluttered, dingy and filled with the sound of his ever-yapping dog (Colin abhorred any kind of noise from outsiders but seemed immune to the furry, shitting car alarm in his own flat) – is never going to be fun.

We leave the dispute as we always leave our disputes: Colin promising to fill out diary sheets we both know he'll never fill out, me promising to ask neighbours if they've also heard the noise he's completely invented, and the whole process being kicked a couple of months down the line, when we'll carry on where we left off.

5 March

A quick word about those diary sheets Colin won't ever fill in, if history is any judge.

Diary sheets are the main weapon of choice for the ASB officer, as they serve two completely different purposes. The first, obvious purpose is to gather evidence. Left to their own devices, tenants will document nuisance from their neighbours in all manner of unhelpful ways. Writing 'He's at it again' over and over again has very little evidential value, and commenting, 'I just wish he'd be evicted or die or something' might show the court the complainant is being less than reasonable.

Diary sheets help focus people on the who, what, where, when and how it made them feel. They can be incredibly powerful evidence in court: day after day of sleepless nights, frayed nerves and being called a cunt can really help to convince a judge to grant the order you're after.

The other purpose is for going-nowhere cases. Experience has told you that the case is a complete waste of everybody's time, and you also know that tenants *hate* filling in diary sheets, especially when their claims are less than honest. They'll chafe at the inconvenience and accuse you of asking them to do your job for you, ignoring the fact that they live on the estate and you don't; you're not there when the nuisance happens, and they are.

You'll occasionally be surprised by the return of detailed diary sheets with compelling evidence that will prompt further investigation, but often, if the complaint seems a little thin, they won't get filled in. You're then within your rights to see this as a lack of cooperation on behalf of the complainant and the case can be closed.

When using diary sheets, every ASB officer has, or at least should have, Fiona Pilkington's name in the forefront of their mind. Fiona Pilkington's case fundamentally changed the way so-called 'low level' ASB and nuisance were dealt with. In 2007, Fiona Pilkington killed herself and her disabled daughter after enduring years of abuse from local youths. She had reported the problem over and over again, to police, the council and social services, but nobody seemed to care. In the end, it became too much.

There were multiple failings from a number of agencies in dealing with her complaints, but in essence, each complaint was treated separately as a standalone incident, rather than being viewed as part of a cumulative effect, and none of the agencies involved talked to each other. One egg thrown at your window is no big deal. One kid weeing against your fence is annoying but hardly the end of the world. But what the Pilkington family endured was constant and targeted, and went on for years, and nobody seemed to be listening.

The 'have some diary sheets' approach was a contributing factor to what happened to Fiona Pilkington, but this was because nobody did anything with them. She was allowed to keep filing reports that sat on a desk until she couldn't bear to file another report.

As an ASB officer, you might think the case is going nowhere or the complaints are trivial. Years of experience allow you that. But what you cannot do is ignore what comes back from your complainant. There's a phrase I've had drilled into me for years, and while it might sound callous or heartless, it's as good a guiding principle as you could hope for: 'What will you tell the inquiry?'

Every single case you deal with could go horribly wrong at any moment, and there's no way of predicting which ones those will be. You could evict a violent criminal without a hitch, and then have a complaint about noise nuisance erupt into physical violence. Humans are messy, complicated and strange, and don't always act the way you expect.

Let's say somebody ends up injured or worse, and a public inquiry is called to find out how the tragedy was allowed to happen and to avoid such a tragedy happening ever again. You're called to give evidence about your involvement and the actions you took or failed to take. There's the possibility of the sack, or public vilification, or prison for negligence. The nation's press is waiting to hear what you have to say. So... what will you tell the inquiry?

And that's every single case you ever deal with, every single day.

No pressure.

11 March

Ashley wants a transfer to another house because he doesn't feel safe in his current property. A few months ago, four masked men burst into his home and set about him with metal pipes. His injuries required hospital treatment and he is worried they could come back again at any time. He was good enough to provide photographs taken at the time of his injuries, and sure enough, they were pretty serious. He looked like somebody mistook him for a piñata.

As always in cases like these, I submitted an information request to the police to verify his claims and to try to put what happened into context. Coincidentally, Ashley's neighbours had previously made complaints of multiple visitors coming and going from Ashley's address, as well as a strong smell of cannabis. Based on the initial evidence, my guess was that Ashley either had drugs that the masked men would have much preferred to have instead, or that Ashley had taken possession of drugs that didn't belong to him and the masked men rather wanted them back.

My cynicism was misplaced in this instance, though. Ashley didn't deal drugs and it was wrong of me to have suspected that he did. He beat up his partner. His criminal record shows a non-molestation order from his now-ex-partner following a series of incidents. Ashley used to live with his partner and her only son Hamish, who was in his late teens. After a prolonged spell of domestic abuse, witnessed by Hamish, she managed to get away from Ashley and get a court order to keep him away. Ashley had decided to ignore this court order and pay her a further visit so he could threaten her some more.

Hamish hatched a cunning plan to teach Ashley a lesson. He and three friends would wear balaclavas, break into Ashley's house, and give him a hiding. The fact that Hamish is due in court shortly for the assault showed that the 'nobody will know it was us' part of his plan had somehow backfired.

So what gave him away? Fingerprints? Nope. A tell-tale shoe print in Ashley's blood? Nope. A painstaking search of Ashley's flat, producing a set of fibres matching Hamish's balaclava which was only sold in one particular shop near to Hamish's home? Not that, either.

Hamish came to the police's attention because while he and his friends were beating Ashley up, he'd repeatedly shouted, 'Leave my fucking mum alone.'

Ashley is granted his place on the transfer list so he can start bidding for a place where Hamish can't find him and can't carry out any more fiendishly brilliant acts of violence.

13 March

Our team has been nominated for an award for partnership work. A lot of ASB teams seem to think they can do this job on their own without the assistance of social services, police, and drug rehab officers, to name a few. To them, I say 'good luck'. So me and a fellow officer get to dress up, eat free food and drink at a nice hotel. Or 'represent the team and act as ambassadors for the important and difficult work we do for our local community', if you prefer.

Despite what you might read in certain newspapers, council workers don't live a life of constant jollies and away-days scoffing smoked salmon and drinking champagne *paid for with your tax money*. I think the last meeting I went to with biscuits was sometime back in 2012.

My friends who work in the private sector often enjoy telling me about the latest jaunt their company has put on – gig tickets for the O2, a boozy day out at the seaside or whatnot. Occasionally, I'll accidentally bring home a biro from work that I decide to keep.

So the majority of the other award nominees at the ceremony are like me: people who do thankless jobs for not much pay, who are glad of a night out on somebody else's dime. Unfortunately, our table is also being shared by Important Local Dignitaries so it would not go too well if news filtered back tomorrow that I'd necked all the booze on the table or thrown bread rolls at the other nominees for our award. As a result, I have to pretend I only want glass (rather than two bottles) of wine and politely applaud when it's eventually announced that we haven't won.

And to think, I missed watching Liverpool win by three goals for this.

14 March

The awards ceremony taught me one thing, and that's that people don't really understand what I do for a living. People I spoke to the night before – and these were people who work in housing and local government – seemed to think I was a social-working copper who moonlighted as a solicitor-cum-caretaker. The job is exhausting but it's not that exhausting. So what do I do, when I'm not out at swanky functions and failing to win awards that we definitely should have won and were frankly robbed of?

The best way to visualise my job is not by picturing me as a hard-boiled, gritty investigator who isn't afraid to get his hands dirty and risk his neck to secure a slice of justice for the underdog in a world gone crazy. Although if anybody wants to picture me as such, and possibly picture me being twenty years younger and three stone lighter too, I have absolutely no problem with this.

The best visual metaphor would be an incredibly confusing Venn diagram, with circles of various sizes bumping up against ovals, triangles and squiggly shapes that look a bit like a pork scratching. These shapes represent the various agencies my job interacts with on a regular basis. A far-from-exhaustive list of these would include social services, mental health teams, drug and alcohol rehabilitation, probation, police, the fire brigade, places of worship, youth offending teams, environmental health, prisons, courts, counsellors, councillors and dog wardens.

Each shape, representing each agency, has an edge where their responsibility for a problem begins to blur and, they could reasonably argue, disappears completely. This is the point at which they can invoke the magic mantra: Not My Job.

Not My Job. Say it loud and there's music playing, say it soft and it's almost like praying, as Stephen Sondheim once wrote (about Maria in *West Side Story*, admittedly, and if I managed the estate where the Jets and the Sharks lived I'd have them all on non-association injunctions and be asking Officer Krupke the sergeant whether he was cut out for community policing, but I digress).

When you have more work than hours in the day to do it, you invoke NMJ whenever and wherever possible. I understand why they do it; I'm guilty of it, too. For instance, our team investigates household noise (shouting, banging doors) but not statutory noise (loud music, TVs) – the logic being that there is a different team that investigates statutory noise (the environmental health team), so why should we? So if somebody is complaining about their noisy neighbour, I will ask – never insist, never cajole, merely ask – if their blaring stereo really is the main issue and not the fact that they sometimes slam their doors.

The answer is often 'yes', and then NMJ can be invoked, and the complainant advised to contact my colleagues over in environmental health who deal with loud TVs but not slamming doors. If you think I sometimes feel bad for handing people off like this, you'd be right, but if you think I feel bad enough to take on work that might completely overload me, you'd be wrong.

Each agency has their own set of questions to ask when their NMJ antennae start twitching: 'But your neighbour's dog appears well-fed?'; 'And nothing was actually stolen?'; 'So you're not actually ill this very second?' – and they're all designed to define the problem as something somebody else should be dealing with.

This, in essence, is where the job of an ASB officer comes in. We're defined by what we're not. I'm not a police officer: I can't arrest people or investigate crimes or kick people's doors in (well, I can, but then I'd be arrested by somebody who actually is a police officer). I'm not a social worker: I can't put children into care, I don't make regular visits to homes to make sure they've washed up in the last month and I don't look for warning signs of kids or the elderly being neglected. I'm not a solicitor: I don't have right of audience[2] in court, I have no formal legal training and I

2 The right of audience is, in general terms, the right to carry out proceedings at court. Barristers have ROA in all courts and solicitors have ROA in 'lower' courts (magistrates' and county courts).

What this means in practice is that in court, I sit behind our solicitor (or barrister if it's a more complex case. Barristers can charge a grand for a day in court so we use them sparingly. This isn't to say they don't deserve their fees because they do – a day in court for them might mean several days' preparation beforehand, and might make the difference between getting the result we want and having a whole community continue to suffer at the hands of the person we've taken to court. You don't spoil the ship of your case for a ha'p'orth – OK, £1,000 – of advocacy tar). The solicitor or barrister is the person who communicates directly with the bench. The bench is typically a judge in most proceedings, but may be a magistrate, or three magistrates, if the case involves a youth or you're applying for certain types of order.

They will translate the thrust of your case into the arcane language of the court, which has bent and morphed over the centuries like a bonsai tree tended by a psychopath, and would be difficult to follow for most lay people. Simply saying, 'This person insists on continuing to act the twat and we would like an order forbidding him from acting the twat in public for at least twenty-four months' won't cut it.

They will lay out our case, question any witnesses we or the respondent (the target of our legal action) may have brought, and will argue why the injunction or eviction or whatever it is we're asking for is absolutely necessary.

The reason I'm seated behind them is that they are not the person applying for the court order. I am – or rather, the social landlord I work for is. So if the bench wants to ask us a question, such as whether we want the respondent to pay our costs, the solicitor or barrister can't answer directly even if they know what the answer will be ('We would like the respondent to pay our costs, even though the likelihood of a rough sleeper with a penchant for begging with menaces being able to do so is slim.').

One quirk of ROA is that the respondent can directly address the bench, and often does when he or she has been unable to get legal representation, or hasn't bothered to look. So you can sometimes find yourself listening to a barrister with twenty years of experience cite case

can't decide to jack it all in and earn a quieter living by handling divorce proceedings for the wife of a mob boss. I'm not a mental health worker, a fire safety officer, a child exploitation worker or anything else.

But an ASB officer is a tiny bit of all of the above. It's a job that's nestled on the very edges of all those jobs and many more, and when it's done properly, it knits all of those services together to make people's lives a bit better.

In very basic terms, the job is defined as follows. If a person is the victim of, or the perpetrator of, anti-social behaviour, and is the resident of a property we manage, then I will investigate this. If there are elements to the case that are criminal offences, the police will investigate these, but if people are convicted of criminal offences that took place in their homes, we can use that evidence to take action against their tenancy. My investigation might be something as straightforward as listening to somebody who needs to have a bit of a moan for half an hour but doesn't want any further action taken. Or it might take eighteen months, involve every ancillary service under the sun, go nowhere and not appreciably help anybody (hello, Lynne).

I gather evidence from whatever source is reasonably

---

law, legislation sub-paragraphs and legal precedent only to have the respondent counter their argument with, 'It's not my fucking fault.'

available to me. This may be the neighbours of the perp (using the word 'perp' might appear like an affectation to try and sound like a Noo Yawk cop but it's just quicker, especially when you're using it several dozen times a day) or it might be caretakers cleaning their block of flats, or the police.

Once I have as much evidence as I'm likely to get, the next step is usually to interview the perp to get their side of the story. Or 'let's see what load of bollocks they come out with', as it's often known.

As an example, I recently had a pretty standard complaint about Trevor, a man in a block of flats who was making a lot of noise and smoking copious amounts of cannabis, the smell of which was drifting into neighbouring properties. A surprising percentage of people think that if they can smell cannabis, they can get high from it. Which is like assuming you can get drunk from licking an alcoholic.[3]

Nevertheless, I interviewed Trevor about the complaints we had received, and he categorically denied ever behaving in such a manner. He was shocked – shocked! – that anyone could accuse him of such behaviour, and could only assume that the neighbours in question were jealous of

3 I would strongly recommend that you don't try licking homeless alcoholics, unless you feel your life is missing a black eye and hepatitis.

him for some unspecified reason, and this was why they were stating such baseless and pernicious falsehoods. This was the spirit of his denial if not the verbatim substance of it, which contained rather more references to 'lying cunts' and 'miserable old bitches'.

A few days later, I was walking past his block of flats when I heard the unmistakable dull bass thud of Music Being Played Too Loud. I went upstairs and knocked on Trevor's front door. As he answered the door I was over-powered by a wave of skunk (like unwashed armpit, which might explain the name) and ninety-odd decibels of Sean Paul (his 2002 hit 'Get Busy', which recommended I get both 'jiggy' and 'crunked up', neither of which I had any intention of doing. Not at 11am on a Wednesday, certainly.) Ninety-odd decibels of Sean Paul is at least eighty-eight decibels too many, I feel.

I asked Trevor how it was that people complained he was noisy and smoked weed, he denied being noisy and smoking weed, and yet here we were, with Trevor irrefutably being noisy in a flat that stank of weed.

'Yeah, well, it's a coincidence. It's the first time I done this,' he said.

Bearing in mind the odds of such a thing happening, I bought a lottery ticket on my way back to the office to write Trevor his warning letter.

Once the perp interview has been done, and once I have as much evidence as I'm likely to get, I then make a decision about what the right course of action is.

Sometimes the answer is 'nothing at all'. There may be insufficient evidence to proceed, contradictory evidence or even evidence that the complaints were malicious. (Like all those horrible people ganging up on Trevor.) Or it might be that the behaviour was an indicator of vulnerability, such as an unmet substance abuse problem or undiagnosed psychiatric disorder, for which treatment rather than punishment is the answer. In these instances, the duty of care is always to notify the relevant agencies such as mental health teams.

Increasingly, cases of ASB reported to me involve people whose lives have somehow got away from them and they're not coping any more. Support services have to run on an absolute-necessity basis these days, so you're less likely to get the help you need and are more likely to be left to cope on your own, no matter how dysfunctional your coping mechanisms are and how often they involve pissing off everybody around you.

Dragging somebody to court for noise nuisance because their abusive partner shouts a lot when he's committing acts of domestic violence isn't the answer. If a mum is trying to raise four kids in a two-bed flat, one of them is severely autistic and another incontinent, and she occasionally loses her rag with the neighbours, evicting her will not help.

However, sometimes some form of action is required, and this can range from a quiet rebuke all the way up to closing down their house for three months and evicting them. There is no flowchart or tick-box form that tells you which is the right course of action. A mixture of experience, training, consultation and gut instinct will tell you that *this* person needs a strongly worded warning letter, whereas *that* person needs a court order with a power of arrest.

Us ASB officers are both the bad guys and the good guys, depending on who you ask. To the person we put in jail or evict, we are the worst human beings they have ever met. And if we have been unable to put somebody in jail or evict them because the evidence doesn't warrant such action, then to the person who has to carry on living next door to the problem tenant, we're also pretty lousy specimens.

When we do solve problems, when a home or a block of flats or even an entire neighbourhood has been browbeaten by the actions of a few people (it can even be just one person; I can genuinely think of a few cases where the actions of one chaotic, aggressive individual made the lives of a whole housing estate a misery) and we make that problem go away, the relief is overwhelming.

You know when you've been swimming and you get water trapped in your ear and, eventually, it runs out? Imagine that feeling of relief, only instead of a few centilitres of chlorinated water, it's a group of people threatening your nan and shooting heroin into their groins behind your bins.

There are even times when you get thanks from the people you take action against. Never at the time and seldom immediately afterwards, of course, but people have thanked me for the intervention of a court order, or even a suspended prison sentence, as it was the wake-up call they needed and the first step towards sorting their lives out.

By and large, though, I'm the person people shout at because they're unhappy with an aspect of their lives. It's like being a priest hearing confession, only unlike priests, we're expected to go out and actually solve their problems. Also, unlike priests, we don't even get free wine. Unless we're at an awards ceremony, and even then we can only have one glass.

18 March

Another delay in dealing with a case because an email from a tenant I received was blocked by the work profanity filter. This understandably discourages colleagues from sending potty-mouthed messages to each other, but is less than useful when residents contact us about, say, verbal abuse from a neighbour.

I've asked our IT department several times if our team can have the filter taken off, but apparently it's company policy that it applies to everyone.

What a bunch of fu— **Blocked By Profanity Filter – Please contact IT**.

20 March

In court for a hearing. I've managed to get my metal detector preparations down to about fifteen seconds. Everyone entering the building has to empty their pockets into a used ice cream tub (it's *always* a used ice cream tub for some reason) and pass through a metal detector.[4] If you go to court often enough, you can finesse this down to seconds rather than the minutes of frantic fumbling you see at airports.

As I'm looking at the noticeboard to see which judge has our 10am hearing, I hear a slight commotion at the security gate I've just passed through. A woman has been told she can't take her almost-full bottle of wine into the court building, so she'll have to dispose of it. She steps to

---

4 An abiding memory of my grandmother's funeral was the fact that the dirt to toss into her grave was given to us by the priest in a three-litre Walls Raspberry Ripple tub. He hadn't even bothered to steam the label off. I won't say my enmity towards organised religion stems entirely from this, but it didn't help.

one side to allow others to pass through and rapidly gulps down the entire contents of the bottle.

Thankfully, she wasn't our barrister.

22 March

Colleagues in the office are discussing Britain leaving the EU because the government was compelled to trigger Article 50 (they weren't) after a referendum nobody wanted produced a clear mandate (it didn't), because the majority of the country want to leave the EU (they don't) for reasons that were clearly explained (they weren't) following a campaign that was run fairly, honestly and legally (it wasn't).

Given the problems people face every day of their lives (and given people continue to want education, need benefits, fall ill or become victims of crime), Brexit has been a tragic, terrible waste of time and energy, even setting aside whether it's a bad idea or not. It's like having your hair cut while your crotch is on fire: whether you need a haircut is not the burning issue.

Since the vote, I've noticed a gradual decline in tolerance towards others, whether that's somebody playing music slightly loudly or a neighbour having the effrontery to speak their native language in their own home rather than English. In a crowded part of a crowded city, this intolerance soon leads to people making poor decisions. These poor decisions can spill over into damaged homes and damaged people. And with each passing month, it feels as if they're making those decisions more and more often.

25 March

A week off somewhere hot and sunny and relatively cheap, where the only difficult decision to make is when to have dinner and whether my next drink should be a beer or a gin and tonic. A week's holiday normally guarantees me three days of actual relaxation. The first two days are taken up by decompressing from work worries and slowing my walking pace down to a leisurely saunter.

I've always stomped everywhere since I was a kid. My dad kept a brisk pace and expected us to be able to keep up, so I inherited it from him. Also, on the housing estate on which I was raised, it was often desirable to get from where you were to where you needed to be in as short a time as possible. It can take time to stop myself from marching between beaches, bars and restaurants like a health inspector with a quota to fill.

The final two days of a holiday see a steady ramping up of the stress and worry that I've come away to avoid. It's like my brain is getting into its usual 'ohshitohshitohshit' state of moderate panic in readiness for work. I can feel it slowly building, like clouds on the horizon, and knowing that's what my brain is doing does nothing to stop it from happening. But the middle three days are good: blue skies, plentiful food and reading books I've been meaning to read for months.

One night, I get talking to an older couple who have moved permanently abroad for just this kind of relaxed life. The conversation eventually turns to work, much as I'm trying to pretend my job doesn't exist. I tell them a potted version of what the job can involve, as I've learned over the years not to be too honest about it. What I think is an amusing anecdote that ends with '. . . so it turns out they hadn't cleaned the blood off the walls from when he killed himself' can often kill a conversation stone dead.

'It must be important to get support for the mental health side of things,' the husband says, seeming genuinely troubled by what I've told him. I'm in the middle of talking about how hard it is to refer our residents to get help, to diagnose when our tenants have reached crisis levels, NHS shortages, and so on, when he interrupts.

'. . . no, I meant for you.'

The fact that my job meant that maybe *I* might need help for my mental wellbeing had never occurred to me. I smiled, went to the bar, and this time I ordered a beer *and* a gin and tonic.

April

Password: Resignation101
Medication: Mirtazapine 30mg

1 April

I almost make it to my desk. Seriously, from the front door of the office to my desk is about twenty feet, and I get about ten feet of the distance with some of the relaxed feeling from my holiday before it all turns to shit.

To give some background: Immanuel House is a block of flats we manage, and over the past year I've been told by a number of residents that one of the teenagers living there likes to have their friends round to sit in the stairwells to have a bit of a socialise. The problem is, their version of socialising includes, but is not limited to,[1] smoking weed,

---

1 'Includes, but is not limited to' is a phrase you end up using a lot doing my job. Human ingenuity is a boundless wonder, and if you can imagine it, somebody has probably done it outside a neighbour's bedroom window at 2am with a bloodstream full of amphetamines. Using the phrase when drafting the terms of an injunction can save a lot of legal wrangling further down the road, when some imaginative defence solicitor argues that their client's court order doesn't expressly forbid them from, say, shitting in a bin cupboard. We therefore

spitting, urinating, playing loud music, painting graffiti, setting off fire alarms, shouting, threatening residents, vandalising the lift and littering.

I know somebody has been doing it, because I've seen the repair bills and the weary look on the face of the caretaker who has to clean the block after each of their little soirées. And I'm pretty sure the teenager in question is responsible, having been named by at least half a dozen neighbours as being amongst the group. What I haven't been able to do is prove it.

There is a world of difference between what you know and what you can prove. This isn't some abstract philosophical exercise, like trying to prove the existence of God or whether armchairs are left-handed; it's about being able to justify taking action against somebody if and when it ends up in court.

'Everyone round here knows what they're like' is a common phrase from witnesses, but I've yet to meet a judge who's willing to take that as sufficient evidence. They tend

---

need to show, they will then argue, that bin cupboard defecation is conduct 'likely to cause harassment, alarm or distress to any person'. (It is.)

So your injunction will list the stuff you've proven they do already and you don't want them to do (spit, play loud music, and so on) but you'll preface it. A typical injunction clause will read, 'The Defendant must not behave in a manner likely to cause harassment, alarm or distress. This includes, but is not limited to...' to insure against the time they find new and interesting ways to get on the local community's collective tit.

to pedantically insist on elements such as times, dates, descriptions and so forth.

Nobody in Immanuel House is willing to be a named witness; they will only give hearsay[2] statements. I had previously spoken to Mr Rashid, the dad of the teenager in

2 Hearsay isn't just the band that unleashed Myleene Klass, Kym Marsh and, to a lesser degree, Danny Foster into the wild. In essence, a hearsay statement is one where the person making it is willing to say it's true, but they don't want to be named, almost always due to fear of repercussions. Hearsay evidence is almost always inadmissible in criminal cases but permissible in civil cases. This is because the two courts are looking for two different levels of proof.

In criminal cases, the offence needs proving beyond reasonable doubt. This is not, as some may think, the same as saying, 'It's impossible to suggest they didn't do it.' Reasonable doubt means just that: a doubt that a reasonable person might have. 'There were three men in the bar at the time wearing the same clothes so maybe the defendant isn't the guy caught on CCTV with his dick in the fruit machine' is a reasonable doubt. 'Multiple universe theory suggests people from alternative timelines can appear in this reality, so it might have been a traveller from another universe with his dick in the fruit machine' is not.

In the civil court, the level of proof required is 'on the balance of probability', or the 51:49 test, as it's sometimes called. If the judge is just fifty-one per cent satisfied that something might have happened, you've proven your case. So if there's no photographic proof that the defendant stuck his dick in a fruit machine and no physical evidence (although I'm not sure forensic evidence has explored the possibility of dusting for dick prints) but two witnesses say they saw him do it, that will probably be enough.

When using hearsay statements, I will present the evidence in court in my statement by saying, 'The witness did not wish to be named due to fear of repercussions and will hereafter be referred to as Witness A', with each subsequent witness named as Witness B, Witness C, etc. (I've never had a case with enough hearsay statements to be able to call somebody the exotic and mysterious-sounding pseudonym 'Witness X', sadly.)

While admissible, hearsay evidence carries less weight in civil proceedings than direct evidence from a witness in person. The defence can't cross-examine hearsay statements ('Are you sure it was 10pm?', 'Is it possible it was somebody who just looked like the defendant?') as I'm just telling the court what somebody told me. Also, judges tend to think that if somebody is willing to put their name to a statement and take the time to come to court to assert it, they're either telling the truth or they're a really committed liar.

It's not an exact science but one live witness is worth several hearsay statements. Pure and simple. (Sorry.)

question, and he employed the standard technique of blanket denial. It couldn't possibly be his kid, his kid was well-mannered, the neighbours had it in for him and there's another kid in the block who's identical to mine so they must be getting the two mixed up. (I knew the alleged doppelgänger the dad was referring to. He stood a good four inches taller, weighed 3 stone more and had hair twice the length of that of Mr Rashid's kid. A blindfolded mole couldn't mix up the two.) Mr Rashid really threw in the kitchen sink of excuses when I interviewed him. The claim that they were a good, strict Hindu family, when a half-empty bottle of Teacher's was visible on the kitchen counter behind him, was a particular favourite.

All I needed to tip the case over into enough evidence to proceed to court was one confirmed sighting of the poor, misunderstood kid with the local lookalike. So as an option of last resort I had CCTV [3] installed in the communal area of the block in early March.

3 Despite the UK having more CCTV than almost any other country in the world, and despite growing concerns about a surveillance state from human rights groups, offer some cameras to ninety-nine per cent of ASB victims and they'll whip them out of your hands quicker than a shoplifter running out of PC World. ASB complainants *love* CCTV, and when you refuse to install it for the most minor of cases, they can act like a toddler being dragged past a funfair by their skint parents. 'My friend's landlord lets *him* have CCTV,' they'll pout, and will bring it up every time something else goes wrong. ('See? That pigeon wouldn't have crapped on my car if you'd let me have CCTV.')

A basic installation – two cameras and a hard drive to store images – can cost about £1,000, and that's before the ongoing cost of maintaining it. If the problem is in a big block of

Just before I left for my holiday, I reviewed the footage to see if it had picked anything up. I managed to capture a dozen or so pictures of youngsters hanging around in the stairwell, and I'd emailed them to local police to see if any of them were familiar. The plan was that when I came back off holiday, I would visit the kids identified, along with their parents, with the police, and politely request that they knock it off if they wanted to avoid being taken to court. And ten feet from my desk, the following month, I learn it has all turned to shit.

My colleague is standing, on the phone to the police,

---

flats with multiple entry points, you can multiply that several times. And all this technology can be undone by wearing a £10 hoodie off a market stall.

CCTV does have its uses, and it can help resolve issues, but it's not the panacea many complainants assume. Not least because when we do install it, we almost always have to use overt cameras rather than covert. The Regulation of Investigatory Powers Act 2000 (RIPA) goes into great detail about covert surveillance – that is, CCTV that you don't know is there. The short version, because God knows you don't want the long version, is that it's allowed for really serious matters like human trafficking or large-scale drug dealing, as long as you get a court order giving you the go-ahead. So Doris from number 12 dumping her used nappies on the landing won't really justify it.

'Overt' doesn't mean the cameras themselves have to be visible – technology now means that detailed footage can be obtained from a camera the size of your thumb that can be hidden in light fittings or smoke alarms – but there has to be clear signage in place warning people that they are entering an area in which cameras are in operation. You still get people doing stuff they'd rather not get caught doing in front of the cameras – urinating, selling drugs or injecting heroin into their knackers, for example – because they assume the signs have just been put up as a deterrent.

Overall, I have mixed feelings about CCTV. I've never had a case in which it was the only form of evidence. Human beings giving statements will always trump camera footage. When I'm not at work and I'm allowed my own opinion on this sort of thing, I worry that as a society we're giving up a great deal of our personal privacy for a misplaced sense of safety. But when you can show the court the same person making exchanges with two dozen drug addicts in the same stairwell over a twenty-four-hour period, you have to concede they have their place.

and frowning and swearing a lot. When I ask if everything is OK, he puts his hand over the receiver and says, 'It's all kicked off at Immanuel House.' I see numerous printouts on his desk, full of my case notes from the last few months, and I can see he's asked police for information, and that he's in the middle of writing out an MG11,[4] and everyone is looking at me like a person who doesn't know he's been fired yet, and I learn that somebody had a knife brandished at them over the weekend in Immanuel House and arrests have been made and questions are being asked about how things have got this bad, and I'm asking what I need to do and I'm having to collate months' worth of complaints and the documents need to be ready for court the next day, and the family that were threatened with a knife are in a Travelodge somewhere because they're too scared to go home and it's suspected that my teenager with the lookalike might be part of it, and if we're lucky the mayor won't get involved, and I'm racking my brains to think how this could have been resolved sooner and we're getting calls from all the neighbours asking what the hell has gone on, and I'm meticulously searching the CCTV footage to see if any of the suspects were captured on camera and we have to get

4 An MG11 is a form used by police to take statements. If we have to give a statement that the police are subsequently going to use, we'll put it directly onto the MG11 form rather than giving the statement, and the officer then having to transpose it onto the form and get us to sign it.

premises closure notice signs ready to place on the block by the end of the day, and I have 117 unread emails after my week off and six new cases while I've been away that could all explode in exactly the same way, and I just want to be by a pool again but I'm not, I'm here, and I wish I wasn't, but I am, I'm here and this needs dealing with now and I was just ten feet away from my desk.

The thought does occur to me that it's 1 April and this may be the world's most elaborate April Fool's joke. It's not. Welcome back, dickhead.

3 April

Return hearing for Mr Smith. Last month Mr Smith was sent a letter by a colleague of mine asking him to remove the cage outside his third-floor flat, and to take the dog that lived in the cage inside rather than leaving it out exposed to the elements. The letter suggested we might consider further action should he fail to do so.

Mr Smith responded by phoning our call centre and telling the audibly shaken call handler (the call was recorded for training and monitoring purposes, just like every call centre tells you) what a pussy the letter's author was. Did the letter-writer, Mr Smith asked, know who he was dealing with? He would come to our office and slap this person's jaw left, right and centre. Mr Smith knew people who could get the letter-writer's details at a moment's notice and he would wait for him outside his home. He would be sorry he ever wrote that letter, if Mr Smith had his way.

To a lay person this might not be obvious, but to a trained eye like mine, saying things like this can be construed as threatening behaviour. The court agreed with us and granted a without-notice injunction ordering Mr Smith not to threaten our staff or come to our office, even if he had no intention of slapping a jaw in any direction. Today is the return hearing.

Mr Smith says he intends to fight the application. He does not need to seek legal advice as he's 'been in court loads of times, innit?' The court adjourns the hearing to give both parties time to prepare their cases and serve full evidence. Based on my experience so far, I expect Mr Smith's submissions to be written in crayon.

4 April

Meeting with Mr Rashid from Immanuel House, who wishes to report that he is actually the victim of harassment, not the family who were chased away from their home by a knife-wielding friend of his kid. And unsurprisingly, he's alleging that the family who have fled for their safety are actually the bad guys here. He's made similar reports sporadically over the last twelve months, usually to coincide with the times his kid has been particularly problematic.

Any inference that may be drawn regarding the close proximity of the two reports is entirely yours to draw.

When Mr Rashid has made these complaints in the past, he's been given the opportunity to make a full statement. He has never taken advantage of these opportunities, and has either ignored letters asking him to get in touch, not responded to voicemails, or pretended to be out when I've knocked on his door and can hear him inside.

This time, though, he has followed through with his complaint, and we meet in a neutral venue, a nearby café. Given the kind of person I'm told hangs out in his flat, I decide not to interview him in his home,[5] so I listen to his

---

5 Safeguarding training advises you that you should never interview alleged perpetrators in their own homes. Psychologically, it can be traumatic to have a stranger sit in your living room and accuse you of things, even if they're true. There's the risk of physical violence and you're not in control of your environment in the same way that you are in an office or a public place.

It's a lesson I learned early in my career. In a small, eight-property block of flats, I'd been told the new tenant was inviting drunks to his flat. They would stay up late having parties, pass out in the stairwells and harass the other tenants. I decided to interview the new tenant in his home. It was sparsely furnished, and we sat opposite each other on two kitchen table chairs, the only pieces of furniture in the living room. The new tenant was a slim, diffident, quiet man who seemed to shrink into himself as I read out the complaints.

He admitted what had been happening. 'The problem is, I don't like upsetting people,' he said, about his unwelcome visitors. 'I'm just not a very assertive person.' I reminded him his lack of assertiveness could cost him his tenancy, and we ended the visit.

I updated his neighbours on the outcome of my visit, and one of them told me an outlandish story about our problematic new tenant. I usually dismiss rumours from residents, but I googled this one and it turned out to be true. A decade earlier, our new tenant had become involved in a religious cult that used hallucinogens as part of their indoctrination process. This had done odd things to his grip on reality, and one day he became convinced that the leader of this cult was the reincarnation of Hitler. Armed with this knowledge (and a bread knife) he went round to the leader's house and cut off his head. He was found not guilty on the

tales of woe surrounded by the irresistible smell of other people's toast. Oh, and strong lager.

The interview is hampered somewhat by the presence of Mr Rashid's mate, who has plonked himself in a seat behind Mr Rashid. It's 11am and the smell of alcohol from Rashid is noticeable from a distance of ten feet. His friend starts chipping in with helpful comments about me such as 'fucking pussyhole', 'fucking crackhead' and 'fucking racist clart'.

I advise Mr Rashid that either his friend leaves or I do, and we continue. In essence, Mr Rashid's version of events is that an entire block of flats has decided to invent a web of lies about his behaviour and the behaviour of his kid. This has been conducted at the behest of one particular neighbour during clandestine meetings and made worse by the racist abuse he has had to endure from this same neighbour. Some immediate questions spring to mind and I put them to him.

'Why would all these people make stuff up just because he asked them to?'

'I don't know.'

'Which neighbours has he talked into lying?'

'I don't know.'

---

basis he was madder than a shithouse rat when he did it. After ten years in a psych ward, he was deemed fit to go out into society again. And shortly after that, I sat with him in his flat, on my own, telling him off because he wasn't 'very assertive'.

While I'm not saying it's a good way to show it, I'd say that beheading somebody is *fairly* assertive, isn't it?

'You say they all met to work on their stories – when was this?'

'I don't know.'

'Where did they meet?'

'I don't know.'

'You said you know all this because a neighbour told you. Which neighbour?'

'I'm not telling you.'

'When this neighbour verbally abused you, did anyone else witness it?'

'No.'

'Has he done it to anybody else?'

'I don't know.'

I tell Mr Rashid I will follow up on the many leads his statement has provided.

5 April

Met with a resident complaining about his neighbour living below, who is named Carrie. Carrie has a bad habit of combining vodka, cannabis, loud music and standing in her garden shouting that she's going to get everyone in the flat above killed because she 'knows people'. Most people know people. The Pope knows people. But it's safe to assume this means, 'I know people who could have you killed.' Carrie, I mean, not the Pope. Well, possibly not the Pope.

I've known her for a decade and I know which part of the cycle we're in. She grew up in care homes and was eventually given a tenancy aged seventeen. Domestically violent predators can spot people like Carrie a mile off and she had a history of being the victim of abusive relationships. These had produced a couple of kids that were taken into care when she couldn't look after them, show any signs of turning her life round while they were in temporary foster care, or even remember to visit when she was meant to. The fathers never managed to stick around even until the kids were born, so were free to go and look for the next Carrie.

It's hard to say whether her schizophrenia was there from birth or exacerbated by the blows that life (and her boyfriends) had dealt her, but her current chaotic lifestyle certainly did nothing to help her condition. At the peak of her mental health cycle, Carrie was a caring, quiet young woman who genuinely wanted to knit together the loose strands of her life. She had real insight into how she'd behaved previously. But then she'd decide she didn't need her medication any more, and then alcohol would become a factor, followed by cannabis, followed by the erratic and violent behaviour.

Which is where we were now. Her neighbour had called the police and unusually, the police had actually turned up. Carrie continued to threaten her neighbour but started threatening the police too. The neighbour was told, 'Well, there's nothing we can do, she's clearly not well, what good would arresting her do? You should call your landlord.' Then they left.

I would never criticise a fellow frontline officer and have no intention of doing so now, but when I heard this, it made me say the kind of words you're not meant to use in front of the Pope. Carrie was sectioned the following day. Once she's well enough, she'll be released back into the community and we'll spin the wheel once more. But ten years of working with Carrie made me see one thing that troubled me: the amount of time between wheel spins was getting shorter with each passing year.

I went home, had a Carrie-sized dose of booze, remembered to take my medication and hoped the combination would send me to sleep before I could dwell too much on the day I'd just had.

8 April

Set aside a few hours to Deal With Red Cases. Dealing with red cases basically means looking at any case that has been open for more than six months and trying to think of any inventive reasons for closing it.

Printouts of active cases use the traffic light system: red, amber and green. Red are over six months old. Amber are three to six months. Green are less than three months. If a case is in the red, you need a good reason, and 'because I'm too busy to adequately give each case the time and attention it deserves' isn't generally considered good enough. If it's amber, unless there's pending legal action it's probably gone a bit stale by now. Green means it might still be possible to do something with the case while the situation is ongoing and the evidence is fresh.

Like most jobs, we have key performance indicators (KPIs). Mine is a difficult job to measure accurately using numbers, because what success looks like to one person might look like failure to somebody else. For example, some places might want to see how many evictions you've done in a year, as that feels success-y. But in reality, success is having nipped the problem in the bud before it gets to the point where somebody needs kicking out. It's like measuring the NHS on how many lung removals (lungectomies?) they have performed rather than how successful they were in stopping people from smoking.

One infuriating KPI we're measured on is the final question a resident is asked once their case is closed: 'Are you happy with the outcome of your case?' Because unless you evict the problem neighbour within a fortnight, erect a security wall around the complainant's house manned by armed guards, and bake them a cake, the answer will almost certainly be no. I've read numerous questionnaires where the answer to all the previous questions has been 'yes' and the final question still gets a 'no'. Were you contacted promptly? Did they keep in touch with you? Was the officer knowledgeable? Do you feel every effort was made to deal with the issue? Would you recommend the service to others? Yes, yes, yes, yes and yes. But I'm still not happy with the outcome. Because reasons.

It would be nice if realistic questions could be asked instead. 'Was this just an excuse to get back at your neighbour?', 'Did you have unrealistic expectations of what life would be like when you bought an ex-council flat in a gentrifying area?', 'Is anything on fire or hitting you in the face?'

One of the KPIs we're measured on is how long on average we take to close a case. Literally no other mitigating circumstance is taken into account when looking at how long a case has been left open. Taking eighteen months to deal with a one-off tiff and taking eighteen months to coordinate a dozen witness statements, psychiatric reports and input from several support agencies, consulting a barrister for advice, and enduring several adjourned court hearings and bailiff delays are equal.

I hate red cases.

12 April

Going to court is a quite exceptionally boring experience.

Every procedural TV drama carries with it an inherent level of inaccuracy by virtue of the fact it depicts being in court as exciting. Nobody bangs on a gavel. You don't get to call a surprise witness that walks into the courtroom at the eleventh hour to the gasps of the shocked crowd. You don't get people in civil courts who are just there for a nosey, anyway. You don't get to shout 'Objection!' I've never seen somebody browbeaten into a full confession by the fiendish cross-examination of a grandstanding barrister.

The best way to describe going to court is that it's like paying a visit to a run-down hospital where nobody gets better.

If it's your first time at court, here's what it's like. You'll be given the address of the court and its opening times. If you have any enquiries about specific facilities at the court, don't expect to be able to call them to find out. Sure, it will have a phone number you can call, in the same way you probably have an old Nokia mobile buried somewhere in your spare room under a pile of old bank statements and electrical leads for gadgets you haven't owned since Jude Law had a full head of hair. Your old Nokia has more chance of being answered than the court's enquiries number, and in any case, I can tell you what facilities your local court has: an overpriced vending machine and toilets with angry messages scraped into the walls. That's it.

When you arrive, you'll notice that the décor and standard of repair is similar to the kind of hotel they use to house people who just got out of prison. You're fairly sure that nothing will fall from the ceiling and kill you, but you're also fairly sure you've just stepped into an ex-Soviet country in the eighties. You will have to go through a metal detector that is so erratic it would beep if you flew a paper plane through it but would remain silent if you drove a tank through it. This will be staffed by security guards that look as if they would struggle to quell an uprising in a nursery.

Your case will be listed on the daily-typed list of cases on the noticeboard. Probably. If not, there will be a front counter that is staffed between the hours of 10.15am and 10.27am. This is largely irrelevant in any case, because they cannot see you unless you have an appointment, which can be booked by calling the main number. Yes, that one.

If you're lucky enough to know which courtroom your case is due to be heard in, you will go and sit in the relevant waiting area. The wait will seem endless but there is the potential for entertainment as people are remarkably unguarded in court waiting rooms. I think there's an assumption that we're all in the same boat because we're all there for bad reasons. Somebody did something bad to you, somebody said you did something bad, or you made a bad career choice that meant you spend a lot of time in court waiting rooms. The things you will hear in one day in a court waiting room could keep the entire drama department of the BBC busy for a year. Infidelity, fraud, assault, bankruptcy, lies, secrets and self-delusion: it's all there, and it's all due to be heard in Court 3.

You may hold the mistaken belief that it's magistrates and judges that are in control of courts. This is a serious error. In the whole of the legal system, nobody holds quite as much power as the usher. To the casual observer, the usher simply announces when a case is due to be heard, and makes sure all the involved parties go into the right courtroom and that everyone has turned their phones off.

Incidentally, if you want to feel the full weight and terrible majesty of the court, let your phone start ringing while the judge is speaking. The first ASB case I took to court was before Judge Chapman, an old-school martinet of a judge who demanded respect bordering on reverence and whose mood of an afternoon depended largely on whether he'd enjoyed the half-bottle of claret he'd had with his lunch. He was midway through talking when my phone started ringing. He glared at me over his glasses while I hurriedly retrieved it, babbled apologies and turned it off.

He continued to glare at me for a full ten seconds of silence like a dyspeptic basilisk, then resumed pointedly, '. . . as I was saying. . .'

Anyway: while moving people into the right courtroom is the most visible part of an usher's job, their role of making sure the courts run smoothly can massively affect what kind of day you have. They can also make sure your court order gets typed up quickly, or sometime in the next fortnight. If a judge has an oversubscribed list, they can try to get you moved to a judge who's in a good mood, or you can sit there until 5pm before being told your case is going to get adjourned.

Bringing well-presented and reasonably argued cases to court will, over time, garner you a good reputation with the bench if you're often in front of the same judges week in, week out. But a good relationship with the ushers, via the odd borrowed fag or a box of ice lollies when the air conditioning in the building breaks down during a heatwave, is worth its weight in gold.

Today we're in court for the PPCO hearing for Mr Rashid of Immanuel House. What we're asking the court to do is grant an order that would only allow Mr Rashid, his kid and their immediate family members into their flat. Anyone else entering would be arrested.

The logic behind this is that if Mr Rashid's place stops

being the go-to hangout for his kid's friends, the rest of the block won't have to suffer when they decide to take the party into the stairwell. It is a serious restriction on a family's life, but then so is living in a Travelodge because somebody pulled a knife on you near your home.

Our case is being presented to the bench of three magistrates by a police officer attached to our team. Marshalling various reports, witness statements and explanatory maps is all an important part of presenting a case to court, but when you have a copper giving evidence, making sure they're wearing a neatly ironed dress uniform gives the evidence a little bit of extra gloss.

Mr Rashid's friend from the café is also here. He audibly sucks his teeth and shakes his head in an exaggerated show of disbelief during the officer's statement, but in his defence, he manages to respect the dignity of the court enough not to call him a fucking pussyhole.

After we present our case, Mr Rashid presents his. It's largely a rehash of the statement he gave to me in the café, but he garnishes it with as many mitigating factors as he can reasonably think of that require no evidence to support them. I almost suck my own teeth when he refers to himself as being a well-respected member of the community. It goes on a bit. It's not so much a rambling statement as a five-day trip to the Lake District, taking in many of the region's finest vantage points. It makes Wagner's 'Ring Cycle' sound like a Ramones song by comparison.

Our police officer refutes several parts of Mr Rashid's statement, prompting him to stand up again, addressing the bench to announce he has something else to say. It's often difficult to predict whether you've convinced the court of your case, but when the head magistrate says, 'I trust this won't take another forty-five minutes, Mr Rashid?', I am pretty sure we'll get what we've asked for.

This hunch turns out to be on the money, and after some short deliberations, the court grants the closure order, effective immediately. While Mr Rashid is visibly upset, his friend seems almost relieved to be leaving the court. It is nearly 1pm and the pubs have already been open for a couple of hours.

17 April

Our company has introduced an IT system for recording all monthly one-to-one meetings, yearly reviews and so on. It's the part of the job I like least, as performance review-type meetings often seem divorced from the job you actually do. The old form for monthly one-to-ones used to have two questions – 'What did you do over the last month?' and 'What do you plan to do in the next month?' – and my line manager at the time seemed unimpressed when I answered 'my job' to both.

Anyway, they've been scrapped in favour of this new IT system because, as we all know, computers = better. The only problem is that they've called it 'PerformanceHub' and whenever I see out of the corner of my eye a word starting with P and ending in Hub on my work computer screen I feel a little jolt of alarm.

26 April

Mr Angstrom can smell something. For quite some time now, Mr Angstrom has been able to smell something and he's not happy about it. He lives halfway up a block of flats and in the flat below, they are making a smell that is causing Mr Angstrom no end of distress.

In the beginning, it seemed a fairly straightforward case. Mr Angstrom had lived in his flat for years, and I'd dealt with low-level complaints he'd made during my time managing his estate. They were standard complaints – the main entry door to the block was being vandalised, kids were hanging around in the stairwells – and they formed the kind of background noise, bread-and-butter cases that make up the majority of my workload.

So when he said he could smell cannabis from downstairs, this seemed like another one to add to the list. A little niggly, maybe, but something I would look into. But this time, Mr Angstrom really, *really* complained about it. It would be an unusual week in which I didn't spend half an hour on the phone with him while he detailed the dizziness, nausea and sleepless nights this smell was causing him.

I don't know if there's a medical term for this, but when certain people say certain words, it causes my entire body to shudder and all of my skin to try to leap six inches upwards. Just something about the way they form the word in their mouths, the horrible wetness of the noise it makes when they say it, I don't know...

Pungent. Whenever Mr Angstrom used the word 'pungent', and by God he loved that word more than nuns love Jesus, I held the phone receiver away from my head as if it had just tried to lick me. Even remembering it and writing it down makes me feel icky.

Mr Angstrom really had a problem with the pu**ent smell from downstairs. And as my efforts to trace this smell intensified, the more hyperbolic his complaints became. I did the obvious stuff first: an unannounced visit to the flat in question. A young Hindu family with three kids lived there, and the flat was a neat family home with absolutely no hint of cannabis[6] odour.

They knew why I was there and who had made the

---

6 If you smoke weed in your home, your home smells of weed. And no amount of incense, scented candles and Febreze will change that. Yes, it does. Yes, even yours.

complaint, as Mr Angstrom had frequently knocked on their door to remonstrate with them, to the point they'd stopped answering. I spoke to neighbours in adjoining flats and they confirmed what I thought: the family didn't even smoke cigarettes, let alone cannabis.

Hearing this, Mr Angstrom upped the ante. He said the smell was so bad that of an evening he and his wife had taken to walking the streets rather than staying at home amongst the fug. They were not a young couple, so clearly something was upsetting them.

I tasked our evening patrol officers to walk by the door of the neighbour below and see if they could smell anything. I asked the caretakers in the block to do the same. When this produced no result, Mr Angstrom said he had taken to staying in a hotel on occasion to get away from the smell at home and he had the receipts to prove it.

We had the use of a sniffer dog one evening to patrol areas known for dealing, so I asked if they could just swing by the 'problem' flat. If it was causing Mr Angstrom such distress the dog would go nuts. It walked past the flat without a flicker.

Mr Angstrom said the smell had changed. It was now more of an acrid, chemical smell (and, thankfully, no longer pu**ent) and he had read somewhere that this was the smell of crack cocaine. He believed it was possible the smell was coming up via the bathroom so he'd been keeping the plugs in the bath and sink as a precaution, but to no avail.

I tentatively enquired whether he had ever had any neurological issues. Mr Angstrom hit the roof at any suggestion that he was crazy. I tried suggesting that some medical conditions can cause auditory or olfactory hallucinations. He reiterated he wasn't mad, he didn't need a GP, he just needed those people downstairs evicted.

I did a police check on the family below and neither of them had been so much as arrested. By this point Mr Angstrom had contacted his local councillor, local MP, the mayor, our chief executive, the local coroner (nope, me neither), police and environmental health to ask for help with this smell that assailed his nose as soon as he walked into his flat.

He had an open offer: if he smelled this cannabis/crack cocaine/chemical smell in his property during 9–5 office hours, he could phone our team and we would drop everything to try and witness it. We had sent evening patrol officers to go into his flat in the past, but when they had said they couldn't smell anything, Mr Angstrom simply said, 'They both had a cold, I could hear they were bunged up.'

Today he called to say he'd just returned to his flat and the smell was overpowering. My colleague and I jumped into a car and hurried round. We met him and his wife outside the flat. His wife had previously confirmed that yes, she too could smell the same thing as her husband. (In less than convincing terms, admittedly.)

Mr Angstrom let us into his flat. After we made no indication, he confirmed that no, the smell wasn't as bad in the hallway, but in the living room it was unbearable. My colleague and I entered the living room with Mr and Mrs Angstrom. He looked at me expectantly. We both took a chest-swelling deep breath through our noses. And there it was: the unmistakable, undeniable smell of absolutely nothing at all.

And by that, I don't mean his property just had the usual household smells you'd expect – air freshener, food, drying laundry. It just smelled of nothing at all. An absence of smell. I even gave my own armpit a surreptitious sniff to make sure I hadn't suddenly been struck down with anosmia but no, I smelled armpit.

'See?' asked Mr Angstrom. 'Can you smell it?'

I had to tell him that no, I couldn't. I looked to my colleague for confirmation. Nope, neither could they. Mr Angstrom's look – a mixture of exasperation and disbelief – is one I'll never forget.

Imagine if, one day, you came home to find a six-foot dildo in the shape of Abraham Lincoln in your living room. Then imagine that after months of complaining, you finally convinced somebody from the council to come out and take a look at it (although which department would deal with six-foot presidential dildos I've no idea). Then imagine the council officer walked into your living room, stared straight through Lincoln's vibrating hat, and asked, 'What dildo?'

That's the look Mr Angstrom gave me. Then he asked me to leave if I was just going to lie to his face. We never ended up solving the Case of the Strange Odour in Flat 22, and he stopped contacting us about it, meaning he either stopped smelling what wasn't there or he's sitting at home right now with a ball of cotton wool up each nostril.

27 April

I make enquiries to see how Carla is getting on and whether we should expect to see her back in her flat any time soon. The news is that there is no news, and we should watch this space for further developments. Given that 'further developments' might mean a very angry woman returning to her home to cause further havoc, I certainly will.

30 April

The GP has agreed to up my dosage of antidepressants, on the basis I still feel as if every day is an unendurable slog, totally devoid of any meaning. She says it might make me more drowsy. Right now I'll take drowsy.

May

Password: Sodthis101

Medication: Mirtazapine 45mg, Omeprazole 20mg

1 May

Picked up my prescription for Omeprazole to deal with my chronic indigestion. The stress and depression increase how much stomach acid I produce and I tend to eat food which isn't so much 'junk' as 'the kind of thing that should be dumped in the Atlantic encased in concrete', which doesn't help. I've had indigestion since my twenties, with the first serious attack resulting in my having a barium meal to check for ulcers.

For the scan to work properly, they make you eat a cup of sodium bicarbonate crystals followed by the barium fluid, then a large glass of water, which causes your stomach to inflate like Mr Creosote. You're not allowed to burp until they finish the scan, which seems to take an eternity. Once you're given the all-clear, you will make a noise like an enraged foghorn.

Oh, and it's likely that the first dump you take after-wards will make an audible clank as your dark grey, barium-enriched poop hits the bowl. Many are the ways in which depression and the related problems it causes will rob you of your dignity.

2–3 May

A brace of domestic violence cases. As an ASB officer, I can put a case together for the victim with a view to getting an injunction to keep the abuser – which, while it can be a wife, child or other family relative, is almost always a male part-ner or ex-partner – away from the address.

In addition to this, we are also encouraged to signpost people to the various agencies who can help them: Victim Support, Shelter and so on. The logic behind it is that the victim can get legal advice and support to take out any necessary court orders themselves. I definitely Have an Opinion on whether this is a good idea or not, given that I often find it difficult to navigate the legal system and it's part of my job.

Legal remedies aren't always the most effective. Either the evidence isn't there, or the victim isn't mentally strong enough yet to face going to court. In instances like this, we have to be inventive in our approach. Once, a tenant came into the housing office with her friend. The friend could speak English and Sylheti (a commonly spoken language amongst our Bengali tenants), and Monwara, our tenant, only Sylheti. Monwara had told her husband she had a problem with her rent card and this was the reason for being in the housing office; he knew a number of people in the local community and it would get back to him if she was seen anywhere other than shopping or at home.

Monwara lived in her mum's house with her husband, who was assaulting and threatening her on a regular basis. She did not feel able to report the assaults to the police and take the matter through the courts. Given the conviction rate of domestic violence (DV) cases in this country, I could hardly blame her. She just wanted him out of the house, but had no idea how to make that happen. Her husband was at work but would be back home by 5.30, she told me. At this point, it was about 3pm. So I got cracking.

By the time he got home, there was a letter, drafted by me and signed by Monwara's mum, basically saying, 'It's my name on the tenancy, I say who lives here and who doesn't, and you don't any more. Get out.' There was a locksmith changing the locks to the front and back doors. There was a suitcase ready with his clothes, toiletries and other immediate essentials (I'd told Monwara to pack the bag for him so there was no reason for him to stick around when he got home or to come back to the property for his stuff).

There were also two coppers from the local Safer Neighbourhood police team, who advised him that they would be regularly swinging by the address for the next few days just to check in. The property would have an alert put on the system for an urgent response to any calls from the address. Police told him it would be best for all concerned if he stayed with friends or relatives if he wanted to avoid arrest for kicking off at his wife again.

The husband looked as if somebody had told him that Scooby Doo had just been elected the next Prime Minister of Australia. 'Shocked' really did not do it justice. Monwara separated from him shortly afterwards and, to my knowledge, he never laid a finger on her again.

Sadly, such a resolution is an exception rather than the rule. Domestic violence is still massively misunderstood, even by frontline workers who deal with it regularly. To view it as a straightforward issue (bad person doing bad things) with a straightforward solution (leave them) does not begin to take into account the multiple-competing factors involved in most DV cases.

Victims often don't view themselves as victims. They can minimise what is happening. They may rely upon their abuser as a carer, for financial support or for childcare. It may be a mutually-abusive relationship. There are often cultural and religious factors as to why people tolerate (or at least don't wish to report) abuse. As mentioned, the criminal justice system is utterly inadequate and unfit for purpose when it comes to bringing abusers to justice.

It's estimated that on average, victims will leave an abusive partner half a dozen times before they make the permanent move. This can result in a 'cry wolf' response from the overloaded services they depend on, sadly. In previous jobs I've heard colleagues say, 'Oh, again? Yeah, right,' when a tenant says they plan to leave their partner, and I would be lying if I said that that tenant got the level of service they deserved from that former colleague.

It is impossible to guess what will trigger somebody to leave an abusive partner for good. I've known victims of repeated serious violence finally leave their partners because they forgot an anniversary. Ultimately, if somebody tells you they are suffering from domestic violence and they want to escape their situation, you have to take them 100 per cent seriously, regardless of whether it's the first or the twentieth time you've heard them tell you that.

It's not always easy. Another aspect of domestic violence seldom covered by the media, and a difficult subject to broach, is that some victims of DV aren't very nice people. It should, I hope, go without saying that this in no way excuses the abuse they're suffering, or means they are any less deserving of support. But it does real-life victims of DV a disservice when soap operas and Hollywood portray them as one-dimensional victims, rather than rounded human beings with complex personalities, which can sometimes mean they can be arseholes themselves. Nobody working in frontline services will tell you this unless they know you well enough to trust you won't judge them, but it's always easier to help the nice ones. For this reason I always ask myself if I'm doing all I can for the ones who aren't.

For the first case I receive this month, the number of complaints the victim has made to us is zero. Like many DV cases reported to us, this was classified as a noise nuisance issue. The shouting, screaming, door slamming and crockery flinging was interrupting the neighbours while they were trying to watch *Love Island*. When a victim does not report DV to us (and you cannot force support on victims who aren't ready to accept it; it doesn't work, and can actually place them in further danger), dealing with the associated noise nuisance is often the only option open to us.

Beth is a crack addict and Chris is a crack dealer. A marriage made in heaven, you might think, but Chris has been both physically and verbally abusive on a regular basis. In the midst of this is Beth's twelve-year-old daughter Jade. Jade's attendance in school had been nosediving as she took time off to look after her mum. As well as the detrimental effect of living in a home environment like this, teenage girls with a home life like Jade's are prime candidates for exploitation from criminal gangs.

Child exploitation usually happens when somebody shows a modicum of attention, kindness or generosity to somebody who receives none of those things at home. It's then that the exploitation begins – which can be using the child to store drugs and weapons at their home, sexual exploitation, and more.

I really want to help Beth and Jade (I couldn't care less about Chris's wellbeing, to be brutally honest) so I want Beth to work with me rather than against me. The idea is to get an injunction banning Chris from the block. If Beth gives a supporting statement for the injunction, it will show me, as a representative of her landlord, that she is willing to maintain her tenancy. It will also show social services that she is acting in Jade's best interests. A meeting is arranged, during which we can all put our cards on the table, work out a plan of action, and listen to Beth's concerns and try to address them, as well as offering her neighbours some uninterrupted reality TV viewing. But Beth doesn't turn up for the meeting. *Shit.*

The second case involves a pair of heroin addicts who routinely knock the shite out of each other, beg for money from other people in their block of flats, invite the local class A fraternity round for early-morning smack shindigs and generally make people living in their block feel as if they are living in a skip.

Emma had told us many times that she couldn't go home because she was afraid of what her partner would do to her when she did. Many times she was given temporary accommodation (a mixture of hostels and local Travelodge rooms). Many times she was kicked out of this temporary accommodation for smoking in the room or filling it chock-full of heroin users. And many times she was seen arm in arm with her abusive partner while we were still trying to find her somewhere safe to live. As a result, there had been many times when we had torn up all the help offered to her and waited for the next time.

This time, he has put her in hospital. She isn't in the best of health anyway – she has a heart condition and years of heroin use have made her look twenty years older than her actual age – but this latest episode has really taken its toll on her. She wants help, she tells us. Next time he might kill her. She wants to live somewhere else.

I believe her. I always had to believe her in the past, but this time I believe-believe her.

6 May

A bank holiday. I spend it in the taproom of a brewery near where I live. Over the years, I've developed a fondness for good food and good booze, and I have the physique to prove it. This often means spending time in pubs and restaurants with people who wear braces, have interesting facial hair, and have kids called Salinger who take tai chi lessons and have never been told 'no' in their entire lives. Wankers, basically.

Over the years, I've come to terms with the fact that I am no longer the dirt-poor council estate kid I used to be, and that I have a decent standard of living and middle-class tastes. I too am a bit of a wanker, and I'm learning to make peace with that. So much so that if I see a review of somewhere I like the look of, I'll tell my wife there's 'a new wankers' place' we should try out.

8 May

Meeting with Mr Rashid and social services. I explain that if we are satisfied that Mr Rashid is accepting responsibility for his actions and the effect it's had on his neighbours, if he works with social services to try and improve matters, and if he abides by the order we got last month to stop anyone from coming into his flat, we won't consider evicting him.

After the twentieth shouted minute of him saying none of this was his fault, it occurs to me that he might not be showing the level of contrition one might have hoped for.

I suspect it will be a case of when, rather than if, he breaches the court order.

9 May

A resident calls to say they have a very serious complaint they wish to make. They recommend that I should stop whatever it is I am doing to help them. Given that I was trying to dislodge a seed from a back tooth after having eaten a bagel for elevenses, this seems fair enough.

The caller says they are being harassed by a member of staff. This immediately grabs my attention as it has the potential to seriously damage a colleague's career. The main thing to concentrate on in the early stages of a complaint like this is to make sure you get all the relevant information down at the beginning so there's no chance of a misunderstanding later down the line.

I ask how the harassment has manifested itself: have they been phoning? Visiting their address? Bombarding them with emails or letters? The caller says they would prefer not to say at this stage as it might help identify the member of staff they're complaining about. This pulls me up a bit short. I ask whether I'm right in thinking that the caller doesn't wish to identify who it is that's been harassing them? They confirm that I am right in thinking that.

Serious harassment can be a very traumatic experience

and victims can be re-traumatised by having to describe what happened. Bearing this in mind, I consider that the caller may not want to have to go over the experience repeatedly, to me on the phone, then again to whoever ends up investigating.

I explain that if they're not comfortable going into detail over the phone that's fine. If I can just take a name and telephone number (I assume they won't want to give their address as this could also potentially identify them and their tormentor), I will get somebody senior in the complaints department to call them back to arrange an appointment to take a statement.

'No, I'm not giving you that information, sorry.'

Another basic skill in initial complaints investigation is to repeat back what you understand to be the situation to the complainant so they can agree or make modifications.

'If I've understood you correctly, your complaint is that a member of staff you won't name has harassed you in a way you won't discuss, and you don't wish to give any details so someone can call you back to discuss this any further?'

'Yes.'

I promise the caller their complaint will be passed on to the relevant team, and get back to the more pressing issue of the recalcitrant seed lodged under my molar.

10 May

Canvassing residents of Worthington House to see if they've had any problems with people congregating in the stairwells. This kind of issue is as standard to an ASB officer as you can get. It's like a taxi driver answering a question about how busy they've been today, or a doctor in A&E removing something unusual from a person's rectum.

One person has suggested it's the friends of the kid living at 11 Worthington House, and given my experience of working with that family over the last decade, it's not entirely beyond the realms of possibility.

Marta has lived in 11 Worthington House for twenty years, slowly filling the flat with kids she has become gradually less able to control. Five in total, with four having come to the attention of police, social services, me, or some combination thereof. It's a fairly common glitch that in a household in which petty crime, alcoholism and the absence of boundaries is the norm, one kid will somehow manage to emerge unscathed.

Jakub was Marta's middle child, which made his feat of achieving escape velocity from the family all the more remarkable. With unruly older siblings to learn bad things from, younger siblings to pick on if he so chose, and a mum watching on in a fug of booze and weed, he diligently passed exams, attended after-school activities, gained a university place far away from his home and never looked back. It must have been like trying to play chess in a tumble dryer.

The rest of Marta's brood hadn't managed to break the gravitational pull of her parenting and had caused varying amounts of strife in the last ten years. When I first spoke with Marta about one of her kids and the problems he was creating on their estate, she treated me with the knee-jerk aggression and suspicion with which she treated anybody in any position of authority. One of the main accusations she levelled at me was one I hear all the time: that I had no idea what it was like living on an estate like hers. This could not be further from the truth.

For the record, I grew up on a 1960s-built council estate in the north of England – the kind of estate that wins design awards, then has to be demolished fifteen years later because chunks of concrete are falling off the buildings. The kind of estate where people throw themselves out of windows (at one point in the seventies, mental illness was so rife on the estate it earned the nickname 'Valium Valley').

I grew up with the kind of poverty that required occasional visits to the food bank (this was before the current government made food banks so *de rigueur*), a school uniform provided by the council and a practised line in deception when answering the door to the rent man. No central heating or double glazing, and coats on the bed during the winter months. Always one financial setback away from disaster. Second-hand everything. Grinding, boring, quotidian poverty that never leaves you, regardless of how many layers of financial and social insulation you manage to accumulate later in life.

If this sounds perilously close to the 'Four Yorkshiremen' sketch, then I absolutely and wholeheartedly don't apologise.

When it became clear that I wasn't going anywhere regardless of how often or how loudly she shouted, Marta and I managed to build a functional relationship as landlord and tenant. She began to see that none of this was personal, and when I came to her door with a fresh batch of complaints about her kids, I was giving her the chance to give her version of events (even if it often strayed so far from the truth, it dipped over the horizon). She eventually thawed, and we actually got to the point where she trusted me. I got a cheerful 'hello' if I saw her on the estate and a rueful 'OK, what have they done now?' when I knocked on her door. I'd arranged for her to get help – with her debt problems and with how run-down her flat had become – and counselling for her gambling problem.

Marta was never going to feature in a Waitrose advert smilingly waving her kids off to school with a healthy packed lunch prepared in a gleaming kitchen, but we could work on issues without her flying off the handle, and in situations like hers, that counts as an absolute win. In fact, it had been a few years since I'd had to speak with her before today, so I wondered whether the worst excesses of her kids were now a thing of the past.

Instead of the usual sight when I knocked on number 11 – Marta in pyjamas, fag in mouth, a gravel-throated 'hello' – it was her eldest kid who answered. When I asked for Marta, instead of the usual shout back into the flat of 'Mum! It's the council!' – I was taken into the living room.

In the space of a few years, Marta had aged twenty. Several stone lighter than when I'd last seen her, her skin was the colour of a faded bruise, a pall of yellow, spotted with faint patches of purple and black. She was sitting up in a hospital-issue bed in her living room, with a pharmacy of medication on a bedside cabinet. The TV that would once have been blaring a music channel was silent.

My shock must have been apparent. 'I know. I look a right fucking state, don't I?' she said, her Tom Waits growl now a whisper.

One day eighteen months ago, she had woken up on her sofa unable to move and unable to shout for help. She had to wait until one of her children came downstairs to get them to call an ambulance. Tests, scans and a barrage of medical interventions followed. Paralysis remained down most of one side of her body. Therapy and medication was helping but not curing. She looked up to the left side of her head, a peach fuzz of hair growing back after a recent operation on her brain. 'Might shave the other side off. Be a skinhead,' she chuckled.

I explained why I was there, hard though that was. Marta said her son stayed home all the time since her illness, so it wasn't him. She said she knew who was causing the mess in the stairwells. She used terms to confirm the ethnicity of the boys in question that I won't repeat here and that I rebuked Marta for using, as I had done every time she had used them in the past.

She lit a cigarette and exhaled the smoke with a shadow of her former chuckle.

'I know, Nick. I know. Too late to change now, though, isn't it?'

16 May

The allotments on the Cambridge Estate have been a great success. Large open-space areas that had previously served no purpose other than giving dogs somewhere to shit and mattresses a final resting place have been transformed into little fortresses of greenery amongst the concrete. Residents can look out of their flat windows many floors above onto patches of kale, carrots and cabbages. A simple change that has made a massive difference.

Recently, though, residents have reported robberies from the allotments. Not the mindless vandalism one might associate with bored teens – the gates into the allotments, the frames and bamboo canes hadn't been broken. But their veg had very specifically been harvested and carried away.

Locals have named a culprit and police have confirmed that they have caught him. It is not, as you might suspect, a rogue gang of rabbits. If anything, the culprit is even less likely. A heroin addict known to locals, who had often been seen sleeping in the bin chambers that held the huge hopper bins for the bin chutes, has been seen selling bags of still-muddy fruit and veg to nearby corner shops. He was then taking the money to the opposite street corner to buy smack.

Drug education in schools warns of the perils of addiction. It can lead to crime, homelessness and death. What they fail to mention is that it can occasionally lead to greengrocery.

20 May

I have a Members Enquiry. Stop sniggering, not that kind of member. If you live in a local authority (and unless you're reading this from one of those weird World War 2 forts off the coast of Britain that people buy and declare to be the

Independent Duchy of Tiresome of which they are the Grand Wizard, I assume you do live in a local authority), you have the opportunity to go to your local councillor, your local MP or your mayor (if you have one), and tell them that the local authority has not done its job properly. This gets logged. This gets given a number. And this gets given to the poor sod who apparently hasn't met the standards you have set in your own head, so they can provide an explanation.

In a charitable frame of mind, this is grassroots democracy in action. It is the mechanism by which locally elected representatives exercise their function in order to ensure that services reasonably expected by their electorate meet the required standard. Accountability and all that. I'm all for it. Yay. Go the people.

In a less-charitable-and-more-busy frame of mind, the Members Enquiry is a way for people to circumvent the usual channels of reporting an issue because they think reporting it to a politician will somehow magic a different answer out of thin air. It also gives a politician the opportunity to make a show of doing their job.

A phrase I've heard a thousand times goes something like this: 'Just to let you know, I'm recording this conversation and I'm going to inform my councillor/MP/the press/ the Prime Minister/whoever I can think of that might scare you.' This is meant to make me leap out of my chair and marshal all the resources that clearly I've always had access to but have withheld from them out of a mixture of laziness, malice and the kind of whimsical caprice that's rampant in local government.

The actual response it elicits from most officers experienced enough, and therefore immune to this kind of not-a-threat-but-it-is-a-threat, is a shrug of the shoulders. My view has always been that if you text message Jesus himself about your case, I could not summon a single ounce of a shit if you force-fed me figs and coffee for a month. If I know what I'm telling you is right – and I do – then knock yourself out, because the answer is not going to change.

This does not stop Members Enquiries (the catch-all term for complaints via local officials) coming in. To be fair, there are valid reasons why people go down this route. They may not know how to report stuff, so they go to their local official instead. We do get things wrong, so it is a way of highlighting this so it demands a formal response. Or it may be that they're just not happy with the way the various agencies are dealing with their complaint (although there are other ways of making this be known[1]).

---

1 Another way is the community trigger, a little-known but accidentally powerful bit of legislation introduced in the 2014 ASB Crime and Policing Act. If there have been three or more complaints made about the same issue and you don't feel that enough has been done, you can enact this trigger, like somebody shooting a flare gun into the air.

The system can be, and is, abused, though – especially nearer to election time. Local councillors and local MPs are measured, in part, by how many Members Enquiries they submit. On more than one occasion near election time, I have received multiple Members Enquiries in the same day from the same local politician about the exact same thing.

Opening the first one, I see that the issue is that Flat twentyblah has a problem with kids congregating in Skibbityboo House. No problem, I'll look into it. Then the next Members Enquiry I get from the same politician is about the resident from twentyblah+1 Skibbityboo House about kids congregating in the etc and so forth. The record for a local councillor boosting their numbers about the same issue is six people all complaining about the same problem.

Your local council has to have a written-down policy for dealing with community trigger requests which you can refer to when they don't know what you're talking about (like I say, it is a widely ignored bit of legislation) and the remit is really quite broad.

To be clear, when I say 'three or more complaints', this can be three different people complaining about the same incident (persons A, B and C complaining about the same loud party) or the same person complaining to three different bodies (council, police and their landlord, for example) about the same single incident (same single loud party. I know, right?).

If your complaint qualifies for the Community Trigger, a meeting has to be convened, at which all agencies have to turn up and say what they have done about this issue. The answer may very reasonably be, 'It was a one-off birthday party that happened on New Year's Eve and ended at ten past midnight, and we were dealing with an infestation of radioactive salamanders at the time, so we were a bit busy,' but you still have to turn up to give that explanation.

It was clearly introduced to increase accountability to make sure local agencies were doing their jobs properly, but for whatever reason it seems to have been forgotten. If it was more widely known and widely enacted, it would massively increase the workload of people doing jobs like mine. So let's pretend I never mentioned it, OK?

It's like ordering your groceries online and Asda making six visits to deliver the same box of eggs.

So, today I deal with a Members Enquiry. I cut and paste the standard 'No, we have not investigated this person's allegations because this person has never told us about them and despite our best efforts we have yet to develop the power of mind reading' response and send it on its merry way.

I am not feeling my usual sunny, upbeat self today, I must confess.

21 May

I'm called about a party that has been going on since 2am, though sadly it's not an invitation to join it. It's 10am now, and the stressed single parent on the other end of the phone has decided that they've probably heard enough of their neighbour in the house next door for one day. This is not the first complaint I've had about Colleen, the neighbour in question. Far from it. A handful of anonymous complaints from nearby residents was enough to secure a temporary injunction in court a couple of months ago forbidding Colleen from behaving in just such a manner. We're due back in court next month for the full hearing.

The statements taken were anonymous because the neighbours were frightened of what Colleen and her friends might do if they knew they had complained. 'I wish to remain anonymous due to fear of reprisals from this person and/or their associates' is a standard phrase at the bottom of such a statement, and in this case it was understandable.

On the few previous occasions on which officers had visited Colleen and asked her to keep the noise in her house below the level of an industrial steel mill, the visitors had waited for the officers to depart, then marched up and down the road making it clear that they intended to 'kill the fucking grasses' who had reported them. Given this, I didn't bother asking the caller whether she'd asked Colleen to keep the noise down. Instead, I grabbed my work bag[2] and headed over to Colleen's house to see if I could witness the noise myself directly.

There is a hierarchy of witness evidence in civil courts.

---

2 My work bag contains all the things I might need on a visit: pre-printed interview sheets for taking statements; attack alarm; disposable rubber gloves in case something unpleasant needs disposing of in a hurry; and drop keys.

Drop keys are the nickname for the keys fire and police officers use to access buildings that have a security door. The next time you go past the security door of a block of flats, you'll notice a square metal panel with a round hole just above the entry door keypad. This is where the drop key is inserted and turned to bypass the main door lock.

Technically, this is to allow the emergency services (and housing officers like myself) quick access to buildings without need of a bunch of keys for every building they cover. In reality, they are easily available online if you know where to look (or for a couple of quid if you know which dodgy pub to drink in), and are often found in the possession of rough sleepers as it allows them to shoot up/smoke crack/take a shit/vomit in some degree of privacy and warmth.

On more than one occasion, I've accidentally gone out of a weekend with a drop key in my pocket and without my work ID, which could, if I were searched by police, be potentially deemed as 'going equipped'. I won't go into the politics of why it's highly unlikely I'll be stopped and searched, but I'm white and middle-aged and vaguely middle-class, so you can probably work out the rest.

Technically there shouldn't be, but there is. A hearsay (anonymous) statement may be largely ignored unless it's accompanied by other supporting evidence. A resident giving a statement in person is deemed fairly credible but still open to question, as they might have ulterior motives (such as a previous grievance or a counter-allegation) for giving their statement. If a uniformed officer gives a statement, it's a brave barrister that will attempt to call them a dirty great big liar.

In terms of credibility, my evidence falls somewhere between that of a resident and that of a uniformed officer. I'm unlikely to risk losing my job by inventing stuff in my statement, but it's not taken as gospel to the same degree as a police statement. If I witness Colleen breaching her injunction, it has a power of arrest attached, so I can call the police and ask them to pop along and nick her.

I turn up half an hour later to find the party is still in full swing. Several people can be heard in Colleen's house shouting in that drunk/aggressive way that people have when they've mixed booze, drugs and being dickheads. The six simultaneous conversations the three people are having are all in a tone that denotes 'No look, right, I'm just saying, right, no, shut up, right, listen, I'm just saying.'

I stand nearby and carry on listening, so I can confirm in my eventual statement that it was continuous noise and that it was audible from a considerable distance (I'm about 100 feet away). Along with the shouting, there's the deep bass throb of reggae–Toots and the Maytals' cover of 'Louie, Louie', to be precise.[3] I record a clip on my phone as evidence and call the police to advise them there's an injunction breach in progress.

The police arrive just as Colleen is sitting on her front step enjoying a brunch of Superking cigarette and can of K cider (a brand of strong cider I cannot imagine ever having been drunk out of a glass). They explain why they've been called and that she's about to be arrested. Her friends drift out of the house, aware that the party is very much over, and that anyone lingering behind might have their pockets searched for the weed which an educated guess and a basic sense of smell suggests they probably have in their possession.

One friend decides on the very different tack of going absolutely fucking ballistic, though. He stands between Colleen and the police officers, calling them pussyholes and telling Colleen she should go back into her house because

---

3 As a kid, I had a friend whose older brother was a massive reggae fan. Sessions playing on a ZX Spectrum were often soundtracked to late seventies/early eighties reggae from the adjoining bedroom. This has resulted in a deep and abiding dislike of reggae,[4] but experience has taught me not to bring this up in company as you will usually be looked at as if you have just expressed an admiration for the works of Oswald Mosley.

4 Yes, even Bob Marley. Especially Bob Marley, in fact.

she doesn't have to talk to these pigs (presumably due to them being pussyholes). He then spots me, and bounds over to enquire who the fuck I am. His body language is textbook Gobby Bastard: on the balls of his feet, moving constantly, making quick, sudden movements to try and provoke a flinch, subtle invasions of personal space to assert dominance.

In the meantime, police have called for backup as the situation looks like escalating beyond something two officers (I don't have the training, the authority nor the inclination to physically intervene myself) can safely deal with.

I tell Mr Pussyhole that I'm from the council, and he points out that I don't fucking live around here, so what the fuck has it got to do with me? Something in his manner leads me to believe he's not interested in a breakdown of my job specifications, nor my relief that I'm fortunate enough to live a good thirty miles away from him, so I stay silent.

The police ask if I still wish for Colleen to be arrested, in a manner that suggests they would rather be doing anything else than deal with the mess this is spiralling into. I confirm that I do, so they continue speaking with Colleen, explaining calmly what's going to happen next, while Mr Pussyhole bounces between me and them like Skippy the Bush Wanker. Mr Pussyhole goes back into Colleen's house and slams shut the front door. Police have not much authority to enter the house and turf him out, and it's decided between the six officers now in attendance that the best way to avoid the situation deteriorating any further is just to leave him in there.

Colleen is arrested, cuffed and led to a waiting van to be processed. They let her finish her can of K and her fag first, though. This is more than just a courtesy. Deny a heroin addict their smack for twenty-four hours and while they'll want to die, they probably won't. Deny a chronic alcoholic booze for any length of time and the shock to their system can kill them.

22 May

In court to deal with Colleen's injunction breach. If somebody is arrested for breach of an injunction, the law states that they must be produced before a judge within twenty-four hours of the arrest. This is immutable and quite literal. In the past I have had somebody arrested at 2.35pm and been waiting in court the following day for a spare judge to hear our case. By 2.20pm, we still had not been allocated a judge. By 2.25pm, we were hectoring the usher to try and find somebody. We walked into court at 2.33pm and thirty seconds. Literally ninety seconds longer and the case would have been thrown out.

The breach hearing is almost always adjourned, as the

defendant will want a chance to get legal advice, so the thinking behind the law (to fast-track injunction breaches) ends up just adding another unnecessary hearing to the already-overburdened court lists.

Today's hearing is adjourned for a very different reason, though. In the police cells overnight, Colleen complained of stomach cramps. As I've mentioned, police custody sergeants really don't like having to explain why there's a dead body in one of their cells, so they tend not to take any chances. Colleen was transported to hospital for tests which would take much longer than our deadline.

So the court hearing to decide whether Colleen was playing loud music with a house full of people shouting – that was witnessed by a neighbour, then witnessed by me, then filmed by me, then witnessed by police – will have to wait for another day.

I hope Colleen is feeling better soon and that the illness she definitely was suffering from – which naught but a mean-spirited cynic would suggest she was inventing – isn't too severe.

23 May

On the morning news, reports of a fatal stabbing of a teenage boy. No arrests made yet, no indication of motive. Whenever a story like this occurs, the first thing I do is find out where, specifically, it happened. And when it's clear it's not on my patch, I breathe a sigh of relief. And then I hate myself for a while that this is my first response and this is the sort of person the job has turned me into.

Nobody wants kids bleeding out on the street due to some petty grievance, some perceived slight, some tawdry offence taken or given. But doing this job has shown me just how easily it has happened in the past, and will happen again, and that the odds dictate that sooner or later it will happen in a case in which I've had some involvement.

Every time a teenager is stabbed to death, somebody, somewhere, will look to a moment in time in their job, and ask themselves whether a different decision they might have made could have created a different fork in the road for that teenager to walk down, in which they lived to see at least twenty at the end of it.

It may be that there was nothing anybody could have done. Or nothing one single person could have done, at least. It's likely that there was an accumulation of things we all could have done, as a society. But it won't stop that one person spending the foreseeable future haunted by the kid who's now dead.

Tomorrow, that somebody might be me. Today it wasn't me and it was probably somebody else. The tiniest tick in the positive ledger. And so we carry on.

June

Password: Anfield101

Medication: Mirtazapine 45mg

3 June

In an attempt to raise staff morale, a radio has been installed in the office. Given the wide range of people working here, a radio channel has to be chosen that won't offend anybody, and as a result we have a soundtrack nobody really enjoys listening to.

As with all middle-of-the-road commercial radio stations, it has a daytime playlist of half a handful of songs. Because of this, I have total recall of a very thin slice of popular music from the last eighteen months, and can probably recite every lyric from the top fifty. I know exactly who loves it when they are called señorita and who considers themselves to be titanic.

At least with my current job, I'm often on the phone or out of the building visiting residents, so I can escape the repetitive barrage. Many years ago, I worked in a warehouse. My job was to stack boxes into the trolleys that would be wheeled onto the delivery vans at the end of the shift. After a while, I developed a 3D-Tetris eye for which boxes should go where, and to this day, if you ever need somebody to pack the boot of your car, I'm your man. The work was physically rather than mentally challenging, meaning I was in as good health as I've ever been, and the lulls in workload meant I could fit the odd half-hour in here and there to sit and read, much to the bafflement of one of my colleagues. On one occasion, he approached me while I had a paperback in my hand.

'You read a lot, don't you, Nick?'

'A bit, I suppose, yeah.'

'So... do you read at home as well?'

'Yes.'

'...even though you've got a telly?'

If I'm being honest, if the warehouse job paid what my current job does, I'd go back to it in a heartbeat. Badly stacked boxes didn't keep me awake at night, nor did I worry about their fate once they left the warehouse. The one downside was the radio, permanently tuned to Magic FM and played at a volume impossible to ignore. Headphones were banned from the warehouse, as getting a forklift you didn't hear in the small of your back could ruin your day.

At the time, Toploader were in their mercifully brief

pomp, and their version of 'Dancing in the Moonlight' was on a heavier rotation than a load of hippos' washing. I once did the mental arithmetic to work out how often I had heard the song during my eighteen-month stint, and the conservative estimate was about 1,300 times. Even now, the opening keyboard trill causes a reaction in me like that of a Vietnam veteran accidentally walking into an unexpected firework display.

The current office radio situation isn't making my eyelid twitch to the same extent yet, though. Yet.

4 June

Today was one of the reasons I do the job and one of the reasons I'm not sure I want to do it any more.

I was told there was a tenant in reception who needed to speak to somebody. They didn't have an appointment but it was urgent. 'It always *is*,' I muttered tetchily to myself, but I agreed to speak with them.

In a small side room was a social worker and Phoebe, a Greek woman in her early forties, who looked so nervous that I made sure the door closed softly behind me to keep from startling her. The social worker explained that she'd worked with Phoebe for a few years now. Phoebe had some learning difficulties, but was able to live more or less independently.

Her care worker had become concerned about Phoebe's wellbeing over the last few months, and today Phoebe had told her something that alarmed her. While this was being explained to me, Phoebe was agitating the sleeve of her coat and looking increasingly anxious, nervously glancing at the door to the room. She interrupted the social worker and suggested that she should just forget about it, and asked if they could just go home now.

It's a cliché but it works: I asked Phoebe if anyone had offered her a cup of tea yet. Making sure I made it the way she liked (three sugars, not too strong) I left them in the room with a promise I would see if I could rustle up some biscuits as well. The time it took to boil a kettle was enough time for Phoebe to regain her confidence slightly, and an apology for the poor quality of biscuit on offer (rich tea. Seriously, who actually likes rich tea biscuits?) cracked the ice ever so slightly.

After some more small talk about the terrible tea and biscuits, I nudged the conversation gently back towards the reason Phoebe and her care worker had come in. She took a moment, then began with a prolonged apology for bothering me with this, she understood I was busy, and she was probably making too much of it. After further reassurances that I was happy to spend as long as she needed, she told me what life had been like for her for the last few months.

Phoebe lived in a ground-floor flat in a local housing

estate. She had no family living nearby but she was on nod-
ding terms with neighbours, and the staff of the local shops
and post office. With occasional visits from social services
to make sure she was managing all right, she lived a quiet
life on her own, bothering nobody and being bothered by
nobody in return. She knew about the druggies on the
estate, she told me, but she just walked a different route
when they were hanging around outside the blocks of flats
so she could avoid them. Druggies scared her, she said, and
she didn't even like it when people were loud and drunk.

Phoebe had begun noticing a young woman who sat in
doorways on the estate, and she worried that the woman
always looked freezing cold. The woman, Caitlyn, had started
saying hello to Phoebe as she passed, and this had developed
into small chats whenever Phoebe went to the shops or collected her benefits from the post office. She started inviting
Caitlyn into her flat to have a hot drink and something to eat.
She felt sorry for Caitlyn. Like her, she seemed to have
nobody else in her life, but Caitlyn didn't even have a social
worker keeping an eye on her.

At some point, Caitlyn moved into Phoebe's flat to sleep
on her couch. I didn't press too hard on whose idea that
was, but I could guess how that conversation would have
gone. Caitlyn just needed somewhere to stay to get back on
her feet, and Phoebe was happy to help and happy for the

company. I asked her whether she'd ever seen Caitlyn take drugs. 'No,' she quickly answered. After a moment, she clarified, 'Not in my flat, anyway, she knows I don't like it.'

One day, Phoebe came home and alongside Caitlyn on the sofa was Frank. Frank was Caitlyn's boyfriend, who'd been away for a while for unspecified but easy-to-guess reasons. He was just stopping to say hello and he'd be on his way, Caitlyn explained, apologising for not asking if it was OK for him to be there. Over the weeks, Frank visited more and more often, and one day it was decided it was all right for them both to stay in Phoebe's flat. Again, Phoebe was cautiously vague about whose idea that had been.

To begin with, they helped Phoebe. Tidying the flat. Going on errands for her. Giving back what she was pretty sure was the right change. This developed into going to the shops for her all the time to save her having to leave the house at all. Once it was established that Frank and Caitlyn did all the shopping for her, it made sense, Phoebe said, for them to have her bank card to pay for it.

One day a few weeks ago, Phoebe wanted to go shopping herself, and asked Caitlyn for her bank card back. Frank had it, Caitlyn said, but he'd give it back when he came home. (Phoebe's flat was now 'home' for the couple.) When Frank returned later that evening the subject wasn't raised, and Phoebe felt awkward having to ask again.

The last few pretences of civility from Caitlyn and Frank fell away in quick succession once the couple felt they were no longer required. The bank card was theirs now, so she should stop asking about it. If they had friends around, and they often did, Phoebe should stay in her room if she didn't like the way they acted. She was constantly reassured that if she repeated any of this to her social worker, the social worker wouldn't believe her. And even if they did, it would prove she was too stupid to look after herself and she would end up in a home. Phoebe had always feared having to go and live in a home.

The verbal taunts about her learning disability turned physical. A fist raised as a threat, an open-handed slap, a shove to the floor. Nothing that would leave too much of a mark, but enough to leave her in no doubt that worse was in store if she complained.

They started referring to her as their pet dog. Dogs eat off the floor, they explained, so the little food she was allowed was dropped onto the kitchen floor for her to eat. They laughed as they watched her eat, Phoebe said.

She wouldn't have said anything, Phoebe explained as she held onto her mug of tea like a life jacket, but the other night, 'they went a bit far.'

Caitlyn and Frank had 'come home drunk or stoned or something', Phoebe explained. After shouting at her for a bit, Frank unplugged an electrical extension lead from the wall and wrapped the flex cord twice around her neck, pulling it tight. Caitlyn told Frank what they should do. 'We should chop her up and leave her in bins all around the estate,' she'd said.

Phoebe tried not to cry when they taunted her, as it usually made it worse, but she was really scared this time and started sobbing. Frank released his grip on the extension cord as she sobbed, and told her it was only a joke. They were only having a laugh. She was such a child, Caitlyn agreed.

This was two nights ago, and today was the first time the social worker had visited sincc it had happened. Phoebe was more subdued than usual during the visit, and had finally admitted to her social worker that Caitlyn and Frank were starting to scare her.

Two things needed to happen very quickly: we needed to get a court order to keep Caitlyn and Frank away from Phoebe, and Phoebe needed somewhere else to stay tonight, because the second the pair realised their meal ticket had reported them, Phoebe's risk of harm would go from extremely serious to an absolute certainty. Two ASB officers needed to work on this simultaneously for it to get dealt with properly.

What didn't need to happen, and I made sure it didn't, was for me to process any of what Phoebe had just told me or to try to visualise it in any way. Somebody too emotionally invested in a problem lacks the professional distance to be of any use to those involved.

My colleague dealt with the legal side: a formal report for theft was made to the police (both Caitlyn and Frank were known to them), and an urgent, same-day injunction application was made to the court, using their previous criminal records for violent offences and Phoebe's statement taken that morning as evidence.

I was told later that an ashen-faced judge readily granted the order, banning the pair from a two-mile radius around Phoebe's flat, with the exclusion area drawn out on a map. They were also forbidden from trying to contact Phoebe by any method. They would be immediately arrested if they tried either. A copy of the court order was emailed to the police and they served it on the pair, having found them in Phoebe's flat, awaiting her return. They also decided to take them into the police station to have a little chat about obtaining money by menaces.

While this was happening, I sat with a bewildered Phoebe in the waiting area of the HPU,[1] reassuring her that

1 The homeless persons' unit, or HPU, is the office a person will go to in order to apply for housing from the council. Some applications are less urgent, like when a child in a crowded family home reaches adulthood and wants a place of their own. Others more so – like Phoebe's.

Depending on where you live, your personal circumstances and what kind of place you need, your wait for a council property can vary from a matter of weeks to several years. The

we were going to get this sorted, and making sure she didn't lose her nerve during her numerous trips outside for a cigarette and go straight back home to the lion's den.

I helped her fill out the kind of Kafkaesque application form that local authorities are justly famed for and waited until an officer could see us. When they eventually did, a few hours later, I made it clear in a calm, measured tone that Phoebe would be sleeping tonight in safe accommodation far away from the despoiled sanctuary of her home, and that I would cheerfully burn every bridge of goodwill I'd built with this department over the years if this did not happen.

After a chat with a manager, and a manager's manager, Phoebe was given an address where a room awaited her until somewhere more permanent could be found. I walked to a minicab office with her to make sure she wasn't tempted to go home first to pick up her things. We would arrange that tomorrow, I assured her, so she'd just have to rough it for one night. I watched the cab drive her away to what I hoped would be the first decent night's sleep she'd had in months.

---

reason for such long waiting times could fill another book all by itself. (Not one written by me, as such a book would mostly feature convoluted, baroque insults and a free 'Stick the Pin in the Margaret Thatcher' poster.)

Working in the applications department of the HPU breeds a level of world-weary cynicism that makes me look positively Pollyanna-ish. A life spent sorting through confected woes and genuine hardships to decide who gets first dibs in the woefully inadequate pool of available accommodation must grind your optimism down to a smooth obsidian nub.

When, eventually, this had all been sorted out, it was time for me to go home for the day. I even managed to make it all the way home before crying my fucking eyes out. Go me.

5 June

Happy birthday to me.

I spend my birthday not at work. One of the benefits of working in the same place for so long is that for every year you work there, they give you another day's annual leave entitlement. My long-term plan is to work there for so long I don't work there any more.

6 June

'So, talk me through what happened.'

'I was sitting at home, minding my own business, when I heard somebody kicking my door.'

'Was anybody else with you at the time? No? OK, carry on.'

'So anyway, I went and opened my door and it was my neighbour from next door.'

'Somebody was kicking your door and you opened it without checking to see who was outside first?'

'Yes. I asked what they were doing and asked if they could please stop, and they just started hurling abuse at me. Just terrible language.'

'Do you remember what they said? Any specific phrases or bad language used? You can just use the first letter of the words if you'd rather not repeat them.'

'Nothing specific, no, it was just abuse. I asked them not to use that language and I closed the door.'

'You didn't shout anything back? Use any offensive language in return?'

'No, I wouldn't do something like that. I just closed the door and this morning I called your office.'

'So, what led up to this? Have you had a row with your neighbour? Any falling out?'

'No, I've never said two words to them. I was really shocked.'

'So, they spontaneously decided one evening to start kicking your door and swearing at you.'

'Yes.'

'And you, in return, calmly asked them to refrain from speaking in such a manner and closed the door?'

'Yes.'

'And nobody else witnessed this? Nobody was at home with you, no neighbours came out to see what was happening?'

'No.'

I have heard a variation of this allegation literally hundreds of times during the course of this job: people leading quiet lives of simple dignity suddenly descended upon by the person they've lived next door to for a decade. This neighbour, for reasons no human mind can fathom, spontaneously decides to wreak a whirlwind of physical threats, verbal abuse and dogshit through the letterbox for no reason whatsoever. And these poor paragons of restraint turn the other cheek and do the right thing of informing the authorities.

This kind of report seldom stands up to even the most cursory of scrutiny. Usually a long-standing feud over a borrowed hairdryer or a borrowed spouse is at the bottom of it. A simmering argument has graduated from dirty looks to muttered insults to (with the help of a Friday night on the ale) a size-eleven foot to the front door.

In fairness, there can come a point in a neighbours' feud when one party goes too far and it's only right we try to intervene. A story like the one above can come about after weeks or months of sniping back and forth. It's unusual that both sets of people (because you'd better believe they will drag anyone into the argument that they can: every neighbour, relative and auntie's best mate's second cousin who knew a bloke who used to piss down their grid) are equally as bad as each other.

The problem comes when people think they're helping their claim by painting themselves as entirely innocent, as it calls into question the veracity of every other part of their statement. When somebody makes a statement like the one above, my first instinct is to assume there is something they're not telling me. While it's not unheard of for a neighbour to suddenly kick off, it's overwhelmingly more likely to have started somewhere.

So let's say the same person reports the same incident as above, but they report it like this:

'Me and next door haven't got on for years. He thinks he's better than everyone else because he buys a new car every two years. He's always complaining about the slightest thing I do – if I have friends round, if I'm playing with my grandkids in the back garden, everything.

'Last night I'm at home watching telly, and I've got the volume turned up a bit but it's not stupidly loud. The next thing I know, that dickhead from next door is kicking my front door. I know it's him because I can hear him shouting "Keep the fucking noise down" outside.

'So I open the door and he carries on calling me a noisy bastard. So I call him a baldy old twat and tell him to fuck off back to his own house and I close the door. I reported it to you because there's no need for him to be kicking my door.'

I am more likely to believe this account because they haven't held back the parts when they've been less than saintly themselves. I might advise them against retaliating or using offensive language, but I'm also going to feel that when they make further reports, those reports are likely to have at least a grain of truth in them.

This isn't the only way of testing the solidity of a statement. Another easy way is to get somebody to tell the story they just told you again, only backwards. Start with the last thing they told you, then ask what happened immediately before that. A lie seems to sit in a different bit of the brain to a memory, and will usually only be rehearsed in forward chronological order.

Another way is to walk down a side-road of their story which isn't strictly relevant. Again, they will have furnished a lie only with the details they thought were important. So they can confidently tell you what time it happened and what the person looked like. Ask them what show they were watching on TV or whether it was raining.

Conversely, another sign of a lie agreed upon[2] is when a series of statements all fit together as neatly as well-made flat-pack furniture. Asking several people about how their neighbour has been behaving over the last few months, what I would hope to find are very different accounts.

One neighbour doesn't hear the noise in the evening because they work shifts. This neighbour hears more noise

2 This would be a great opportunity to appear erudite and say I'm quoting Nietzsche, Voltaire or Napoleon (depending on who you attribute it to), but in the interests of honesty, I first heard it as an episode title from the majestic TV series *Deadwood*.

because they live right below them. That neighbour heard nothing for a fortnight because they were in Magaluf, the lucky things. He notices a smell of cannabis but she doesn't. Everyone hears the stereo but only one has heard the swearing. And so on.

When I'm presented with half a dozen witness statements from half a dozen neighbours who all heard the same incidents on the same days stretching back weeks or months, they can all probably be discounted as entirely useless. Human memory is messy and unreliable, so you should expect statements to be similarly ragged around the edges.

At the bottom of the evidential pile are petitions. Tell me you're going to get a petition signed, and all you're presenting me with is a list of people I have to contact separately to find out what they actually saw or heard.

Anyway. I tell our blameless victim of door-kicking that I will knock on a few neighbours' doors to see if anyone heard or saw the incident, or if they know of any issues caused by this danger to carpentry. This is greeted with something that falls far short of enthusiasm. I don't see this one going anywhere, truth be told.

10 June

Return date for Colleen's injunction hearing. The interim injunction has been in place for a few months. To get an interim order, the court needs to be satisfied that, on the face of it and without testing the evidence, it looks necessary to grant an order for now. This is the day that all the evidence is put before the court and a final decision is made as to whether to make the temporary order permanent.

Ahead of the 10am start for the trial, Colleen is on time, smartly dressed and clearly slightly shitfaced. If you've ever had the misfortune of walking into a nightclub during the daytime,[3] that's the smell we're talking about. I've had previous dealings with Mr Stangersen, the barrister assigned to represent Colleen in court, and remember he can be somewhat combative.

Apart from a couple of visits from the police, all the other evidence we're relying on is from residents who have asked to stay anonymous. I give their evidence on their behalf. My lengthy statement basically consists of me saying 'Witness A told me (x), Witness B told me (y)'. This means the overwhelming bulk of the evidence relied upon will be mine.

---

3 I worked as a nightclub glass collector while I was a university student and can confirm that nobody would set foot in such a place while sober unless they were being paid to do so. Other things it taught me is that you'll always find loose change on the floor by the bar, people can fall down an entire flight of stairs holding a pint without spilling a drop, nobody ever won a fight with bouncers – there's more of them and they're sober – and that the popular singer Shaggy doesn't like being asked to grab a broom and help sweep up when he does a two-song personal appearance that starts forty-five minutes late, causing the staff to be forty-five minutes late finishing up (to pick an example entirely at random).

Mr Stangersen starts by asking me who else lives in Colleen's estate, one house at a time. 'So, in number 12, there live two Portuguese people and their single male child, isn't that correct?' I fail to see the relevance, but realise it's not my place to ask, so I confirm I've no idea. After the third or fourth household whose occupants I'm unable to list, I interrupt him by saying, 'Sir, I manage about three thousand properties, so I'm afraid I'm unable to accurately recall who lives in every single one of them.'

Asked by the judge why these questions are being put to me, Mr Stangersen asks whether I have met 'Witness A' and whether I attest to their good character. Again, I have to point out that drawing up 3,000 detailed character assessments would be a little time-consuming and I have to assume, given the lack of inconsistency or exaggeration, that Witness A (and B, and C) is telling the truth.

Most of Mr Stangersen's other questions are of the 'Isn't it possible that this didn't happen?' variety. I'm unable to give any answer to these, other than to say, 'I don't know, I wasn't there.' He eventually runs out of ways of getting me to say, 'I can neither confirm nor deny what happened as I was not present at the time of the alleged incident,' so I'm allowed to stand down. Now it's Colleen's turn.

When asked by our barrister about the various complaints made against her – the noise, the shouting, the threats to neighbours – she denies all knowledge of anything of the sort. She is so well-drilled in denial, in fact, that when asked about the smell of cannabis coming from her property, she replies, 'What's that?'

Not, you will note, 'When was that?' Or 'Who said that?' The barrister is quick to notice this and clarifies to Colleen, 'I am talking about cannabis. Marijuana.' Colleen sticks to her training. 'I don't know what that is.'

'Miss ___, just for the record, and I apologise for asking again because I need to make sure that I am understanding you correctly: are you telling the court that you have reached the age of fifty-six, having grown up on a housing estate known to have a serious drug problem, and regularly play reggae music, yet you have no idea what cannabis – marijuana – even is?'

'Yes.'

Judges have very good poker faces, and the slightly raised eyebrow of the district judge hearing our case is the equivalent of a lay person tipping the desk upside-down, standing in front of Colleen furiously scratching their chin and shouting, 'Oh, chinny-*reckon*!'

We are granted the injunction.

11 June

No further news about Carla. Her neighbour hasn't been back in touch to complain so I assume she hasn't been allowed back into her flat. Given her condition, it seems unlikely that she has suddenly started behaving herself and is quietly getting on with things. I check her housing record and her tenancy is still active, so she hasn't moved away anywhere either.

The only explanation is that she is still in hospital. Still ill and still beyond help. I don't proactively ask, because something in the pit of my stomach tells me that I won't want to hear the answer.

12 June

My manager is away for the day, but has asked that we have a sit-down tomorrow. She's booked out a room and an hour in both our calendars. I immediately think that this will be The Bad Thing.

My depression has always been accompanied by what cognitive behavioural therapists have told me is 'catastrophising' – assuming that the worst will happen – and in the absence of any available data, I fill in the blanks with steaming piles of awful. In work, this has led to me always assuming that The Bad Thing is just around the corner – The

Bad Thing being that I have been found out as a fraud and will be asked to leave. I will be unable to pay my bills, pay my mortgage, things will become so untenable that. . . well, you get the idea.

To a catastrophiser, 'Can I have a quick word?' is like the low growl of a lion to an antelope. An unexpected meeting of a whole hour sounds like the entire cast of *The Lion King*. Is this going to be The Bad Thing?

13 June

It's The Bad Thing. I walk into the meeting and already printed out is a list of my cases, the older ones coloured an ominous shade of red. Also in the room is a computer logged into Resolve, the database we use to log, update and cross-reference our cases. What's absent from the room is a relaxed atmosphere.

In short, I have been living in my emails. This is the term I use to explain the situation in which the work-load becomes so overwhelming that you can only function on a reactive basis. If somebody emails asking for an update, or to report an issue, or for some immediate action, I can deal with it there and then. But anything longer-term or anything that needs revisiting has slipped. Urgent matters like Phoebe's case I'm fine with. The more mundane day-to-day stuff that makes up the bulk of the job, less so.

Worse still, I haven't been updating Resolve with the actions I have been carrying out.

If you looked at my cases on Resolve, it would look as if I haven't done anything for the last six months, which is not entirely accurate. I have frequently been frozen by stress at my desk, staring at the screen in a kind of silent horror at the sheer volume of work that's piling up. Because I can't possibly clear the backlog, I often find myself not feeling able to do anything. Which in turn causes the backlog to get even worse and my stress levels to rise.

It's been going on for months, with me sitting silently screaming at my desk, feeling unable to admit to the amount of help I need or how much I'm drowning. The logical part of my brain knew that the situation couldn't continue indefinitely and that at some point somebody would notice. Sadly, the logical part of my brain tends to get locked in the boot of the car when stress and depression take over, with the illogical part of my brain taking the wheel and driving the car at 115mph up the wrong way of the motorway with its eyes shut.

After taking the bollocking I richly deserve, I'm asked a simple yet complicated question that I've been asking myself for a long time: 'Do you even want to do this job any more?'

It's a question with several answers, none of which are 'yes' or 'no'. I'm not qualified to do anything else, certainly not anything that would pay even a fraction of the relatively modest wage I currently earn. On the days when it feels as if I'm helping people, it's a job I still enjoy, but those days feel as though they're becoming more of a rarity. I can't afford to get fired as I have a mortgage and bills like anybody else. Coming to work each day feeling like my head is going to explode will, at some point, become too much. Then there's the arrogant part of me that refuses to acknowledge that it's a job I'm no longer capable of doing.

I don't feel that any of these answers are what's required of me at this juncture, so I simply say 'Yes'. A structured approach to clearing the backlog is agreed, and I'm confined to my desk, meaning no out-of-office visits for the foreseeable future. It's clear I will be closely monitored to make sure things don't deteriorate again. It's basically as close as you can get to being fired without being fired. It's humiliating and torturous, and entirely necessary given the circumstances.

The worst part is that when the meeting is over, the catastrophising part of my brain whispers, 'Told you so,' and chuckles to itself.

14 June

A minute's silence is observed in the office to mark the anniversary of the fire at the Grenfell Tower which claimed the lives of seventy-two people: an entirely avoidable tragedy that was the logical conclusion of what happens when mismanagement, neglect, unchecked capitalism and greed intersect.

18 June

An unexpected letter from the solicitor of a former tenant, Mr Donaldson. A couple of years ago, I visited one of our high-rise blocks to speak with the concierge to see if there were any outstanding issues. Sitting in her office in the ground-floor lobby of the block, she saw a lot of what went on and was often a good source of information. Although things had been quiet recently, she mentioned that a few months ago, police had come into the block and left with Mr Donaldson in handcuffs. She hadn't seen the tenant since.

I was dubious that this was any cause for concern, as he had never come to our attention before, but I sent an information request to the police about Mr Donaldson, assuming it was some minor misdemeanour and he had been lying low ever since. Not quite.

Undercover police had visited Mr Donaldson's home a few times before his arrest, posing as people that wanted to buy a gun. This was something that he could help them with, because Mr Donaldson's living room was equipped with a library of books about guns, machine tools for making guns and guns that he had made.

He was given five years for making and selling illegal weapons, and was currently in prison, which was why he'd not been seen about the place for a while. Taking the not-unreasonable view that our properties were meant for people on low incomes who needed a home rather than arms dealers, I wrote to Mr Donaldson in prison.

The letter gave him the choice we often give tenants found guilty of serious crimes in their home, which can be summarised as follows: 'You've got two options. We can go to court for an eviction, which we will win, and when we do, we will ask for you to pay our legal costs, which usually run into four figures. Or you can sign this bit of paper relinquishing your tenancy in twenty-eight days, give us the keys back and we'll say no more about it.'

Mr Donaldson chose the second option, and his tenancy was terminated, making me think this would be the last we heard from him. But now he was suing us. He alleged that we had not given his agents sufficient time to clear his flat before we changed the locks, and he was therefore suing us for the suspiciously neat sum of £9,999.99. It's suspiciously neat because you can sue people or organisations via the small claims court for sums up to £10,000. I've had to do it myself once.[4]

---

4 When I bought my house, there was a missing garden wall the sellers had promised the neighbour they would rebuild before selling. There was no mention of it during the sale, and now I was

Amongst the effects he claimed had been thrown away were his collection of books on how to make guns, and the work bench on which he made his guns. I do wonder what his probation officer would make of him wanting this stuff back.

So now I can add 'being sued by an arms dealer' to the long list of 'really weird shit that happens to you in this job'.

21 June

More news on Mr Rashid and Immanuel House. After a brief period of relative calm, problems are once more being reported, and Mr Rashid's household is being pinpointed as the source of the problems again.

People have apparently been going in and out of his flat, contrary to the court order obtained back in April,[5] and the

---

bound to get the wall built myself, which would cost about £3,000. I tried several times to politely ask the previous owner to pay up, even offering to accept a payment plan, all of which was met with variations on 'tough shit'.

So I put together a claim for the small claims court, with a formal statement, evidence exhibits, references to possible further legal action for fraud, and so on. Basically, I treated it like an ASB case I was taking to court.

One week later I received a cheque for the full amount. It's not often my job has transferable skills but this was one of those times.

5 I say 'apparently', because despite the great effort in obtaining the court order, despite the signs clearly displayed in the block explaining the court order, and despite the letter everyone received explaining how to report breaches of the court order, people had not been reporting breaches of the court order.

This is not uncommon. Neighbours often think that getting a court order is the end of the process, when it's usually about halfway through the process. A determinedly recidivist neighbour will require their breaches of a court order to be proven (and proven, as previously

visitors have been hanging around on the stairs. Whereas you or I might consider the threat of being made homeless reason enough not to hold any dinner parties at our homes for three months, Mr Rashid was clearly too free-flying a social butterfly to be constrained by such considerations. I could only assume he was friends with charming racon-teurs like Stephen Fry, Barack Obama or the ghost of Peter Ustinov, and could not live without the pleasure of their company[6] for a moment longer.

We receive a call from a neighbour saying they could hear somebody was in the flat, so we ask police to attend. They have the power to enter the property, even without a warrant, if they suspect the order is being breached. When the officers arrive, cannabis can clearly be smelled coming from the flat, as well as the sound of two voices: those of Mr Rashid's kid and a teenage boy, Max. It is clear they are

---

mentioned, beyond reasonable doubt), and without further evidence, that's not going to hap-pen. As far as the court is concerned, the order has done its job.

Residents of Immanuel House were telling each other that they'd heard people in Mr Rashid's flat. They told caretakers that they'd seen kids loitering in the stairwells. What they hadn't done was phone the police so they could come and arrest people or tell the ASB team so they could increase police presence in the block.

The best analogy I can think of is working in an office that didn't have fire extinguishers. Staff quite reasonably clamour for their installation and they're installed. Three months later when the building bursts into flames, none of the staff actually use the fire extinguishers, assuming their existence was somehow enough.

6 I am not for one second suggesting Messrs Fry or Obama are in the habit of pissing in stair-wells or gouging the word 'cunt' into walls using a screwdriver. Their autobiographies certainly make scant mention of such behaviour.

getting ready to leave, so rather than knocking on the door and giving them the chance to hide anything that needs hiding, the officers wait.

When the two open the door to leave the flat, the officers escort them back inside and explain why they're there. Mr Rashid is also in the flat, so they decide to have a chat with him while they're at it. Trying to come up with an alibi is made more difficult when you're confronted by coppers, have had no time to prepare, are stoned, and are a bit thick to begin with.

Mr Rashid says he had no idea Max was in the smallish two-bed flat, despite the fact that the police could hear him through a heavy, fireproof front door, there was no music or TV playing to drown it out, and the hallway in which the teenagers had been heard directly connects to the living room in which Mr Rashid was sitting. He also had no idea that either of them were smoking cannabis, despite the smell similarly having penetrated the front door, and the remnants of a smoked spliff being visible in an ashtray on a coffee table in the living room.

Max has no idea he isn't allowed in the flat, despite the fact the court order has been in place for nearly three months, and a copy of it is glued to the front door of the flat.

Mr Rashid's son has no idea Max isn't allowed in the flat either, because he's dyslexic and can't read the notice, despite it having been explained carefully to him and his mum by both me and the police when it was granted.

In any case, it is said, Max had only just arrived in the flat when the police turned up, despite the fact that the neighbour called to report the noise forty minutes before police got there, and when they did arrive, they stood outside for a few minutes before the door opened. The only thing they didn't try was pointing over the officers' shoulders, shouting 'Look, it's Beyoncé!', then leaping out of the window.

Mr Rashid is informed the breach will be reported back to our team and Max is arrested (the way the court order is worded, it's the visitors who are in breach rather than the occupants). While being arrested, Max tries to pass his cigarettes to Mr Rashid's kid. Unfortunately, this is not the arresting officers' first day on the job, so the packet is intercepted and opened, and the inevitable cannabis inside put into an evidence bag.

As Max is a minor, police take him home to inform his parents of the arrest (which is now for breach of the order and possession of cannabis). I learn of the details of this visit via the official police statement.

Police statements don't conform to the old cliché ('Hie was proceeding hin a northerly direction when hie apprehended what appeared to be a scrote what was up to no good', etc) but they're often possessed of a dry understatement. This one reads, 'When I informed Mrs ___ of her son Max's arrest and the reasons behind it, she sought to remonstrate with her son by slapping him across the back of the head. I advised her against committing any further assaults against her son while in the presence of two police officers.'

The upshot of all this is that we now have to consider evicting Mr Rashid and his child. It is an option of last resort, but every other reasonable step has been tried without success. This will not be fun for anyone concerned.

24 June

I've had to print, laminate and Sellotape to the wall in the gents' toilets at work the following sign:

'To whoever it is that keeps urinating on the toilet seats:

Please stop urinating on the toilet seats

Thank you.'

Apparently this is something that needs pointing out as less than desirable behaviour. Because I'm a professional, I didn't add, 'If I find out who it is, I'm going to piss on your head when you're at your desk.' I might bring this level of restraint up at next month's one-to-one during the section about personal development.

25 June

Nearly two weeks of being desk-bound and having to ask permission to leave the office for meetings or visits. Nobody knows this has been asked of me, but everybody knows, I convince myself.

26 June

Child protection meeting about Jade, her mum Beth and contender for 'Britain's Most Capacious Arsehole' Chris. This follows on from the meeting Beth didn't attend last month.

Police advise that they have managed to get a CPW[7] against Chris. This means I can tell all the other residents in the block that if they see or hear him about, they can call the police. I remember how closely the residents of Immanuel House followed this advice and ponder how effective this will be.

A representative from Jade's school says her attendance is just above the threshold at which they could intervene,

7 The community protection warning (CPW) and community protection notice (CPN) are another set of tools available to local authorities and police. Essentially, a CPW is a warning to stop being a pain in the arse, with specific ways in which your arse-paining must cease, similar to the clauses you might see in an injunction. It's sort of like a yellow card coppers can hand out to people whose behaviour is a nuisance but not quite criminal.

If ignored, the CPW is upgraded to the red card of a CPN. Breach a CPN and you can be forced to do remedial works (like fixing something that's causing the nuisance), have items seized (like a stereo that's causing the nuisance) or get a fine of up to £2,500.

A lot of CPNs are issued against people on low incomes due to their personal behaviour rather than something they own causing a nuisance. When the only available sanction is a fine they can never hope to pay back, can you see where all this might fall down? Me too.

with most Mondays being missed after Jade has spent a weekend dealing with her mum and Chris.

While in school, she's showing signs of anxiety and has been frequently chastised for looking at her phone during lessons. Rather than being on Instagram, she's checking her text messages to see if her mum has been in touch. There have been occasions when she's not returned after lunch break and said the next day there was a problem at home.

The neighbours are telling me that Jade has started knocking on their door asking for small amounts of money, ostensibly for the electric meter or small amounts of groceries, which neither the neighbours nor I believe to be true.

The neighbours also say the rows between Beth and Chris are intensifying, and on one occasion at about 2am, Beth was seen following Chris out of her flat, across the car park and into the night so she could carry on shouting. Jade was seen traipsing after her mum, wearing a dressing gown, pleading for her to come back home. Given the tableau of misery this provides, the fact this happened on a Wednesday night shouldn't make a difference. But it does.

Social services tell the meeting they're keeping a very close eye on the situation and if further intervention is required due to the situation deteriorating, they will not hesitate to take action. The unasked question lingers in the room for the rest of the meeting: 'How much worse can it get?'

July

Password: Panicked101

Medication: Mirtazapine 45mg, Omeprazole 15mg

1 July

I just showed my sister-in-law a photo of a human turd. When you're out on visits on the estate you manage, you have to keep your phone with you at all times. One reason is personal safety. If an interview suddenly goes south and you need to get help, there are safety protocols in place to call the office and ask for help in a coded way. In one previous job, our code phrase was 'Can you look up the red file for (whatever the address you were in), please?' This was as subtle and difficult to decode as saying, 'Could you get Mr Police on the line so I can talk to him about buying some fruitcake?'

Whatever the angry tenant is demanding – a transfer to a bigger house, their neighbour to be evicted, Ewan McGregor's left bollock on a platinum platter coated in icing sugar – you nod politely and say you'll call the office to get it for them ASAP. GPS technology on smartphones also makes it handy for giving precise locations of where knives/drugs/etc have been found, or where you need extra lighting or security cameras.

But the most common use is for taking photos of the problems our residents are encountering. When you take a case to court, you can write as much as you like in your statement about the revolting condition in which the defendant left a stairwell, but nothing can match a few photos as exhibits to drive the point home.[1] As a result, I have numerous photos of piss stains, burnt tinfoil, smashed windows and fag ends on my phone in amongst photos I've taken on holiday or nice dinners I've eaten (yes, I'm one of those wankers).

And so it was today that when I went to show my sister-in-law a photo I'd taken of a lovely sunset from my recent holiday, I accidentally scrolled one photo back, which was taken at work the day before my holiday began.

---

1 Especially given that judges and magistrates tend to be drawn from a fairly narrow segment of society. This segment doesn't tend to be one that lives, or has ever lived, in a concrete tower block or a crowded housing estate.

Trying to make them understand the effect of a neighbour's ASB in already difficult living conditions is like trying to explain life on the International Space Station to a seventh-century dung farmer. For instance, noise nuisance is a frequent situation that's hard for them to fathom, given that 'the family next door' probably lives at least 200 yards away on the other side of a hedge.

I often wonder how the courts (and politics) would change if the people passing judgements or passing policies on people living on housing estates had to live on one themselves for six months.

'How awesome is THAT?' I asked, waving a picture of a turd in a bin shed under her nose.

4 July

In court for an urgent injunction application. Lizzie is thirty-two, homeless and inordinately fond of smoking crack. In order to get money to keep her love affair going, she frequently visits her uncle Ted, who is in his mid-seventies and whose biggest vice is the occasional pint in the nearby Wetherspoons, to beg for money.

When Ted tells his niece to go away, or tells her that he's got no money, or when he selfishly decides not to be at home, Lizzie reacts stoically and calmly walks away to reconsider her lifestyle choices.

Just kidding. Of course she doesn't, she goes berserk.

'Fucking bastard mean old fucking fat cunt of a fucking shithouse cunt it's only a few fucking quid you tight fucking wanker' is just one of the things Lizzie has been known to say to her uncle when he's withheld part of his pension from her.

Ted is understandably less than keen on being called a fucking etc and so forth, so he often relents and lets Lizzie into his house so she can at least have a shower and some-thing to eat. This is in the hope it will put her in a better mood. It doesn't stop the verbal abuse, but it keeps her indoors and quiet for the length of time it takes her to eat some toast. But pretty soon, the persistent begging starts again when he tells her he doesn't have money to spare.

He has tried calling the police (like the time he asked her to leave, so she took out her crack pipe, loaded it, inhaled deeply, blew the smoke into his face and told him to eat shit), but all they can do is escort her back outside and advise her to go away. Which she won't.

When Ted asks her to keep it down to stop disturbing the neighbours, she embarks on florid streams of abuse about them, with specific reference to their age, sexuality and race (amongst other things). Said neighbours have had enough, so they contacted our team to let us know what had been happening. I took statements from them (anonymous statements, because hell hath no fury like a crackhead snitched upon), combined them with a police report I obtained (Lizzie has an epic-poem's-worth of offences against her name, everything from the anticipated burglary/ shoplifting/theft to assaulting ambulance drivers for God knows what reason), and made an urgent application for a without-notice injunction.

Obtaining the order was fairly straightforward. It was obvious to the judge that the level of nuisance Lizzie was causing was excessive[2] and all we were asking for was the

2 'Nuisance' tends to be the catch-all term used to describe ASB in court, despite it being the kind of word you'd use to describe your corner shop running out of milk.

standard clause forbidding her from causing alarm, harass-ment or distress, and an exclusion map with a red square drawn around the row of houses in which Uncle Ted lived.

All we had to do now was find her. An injunction isn't active until it's physically handed to the subject. Posting it won't suffice (although in Lizzie's case we had no address to post it to anyway; we could leave copies in all the local shop doorways but that seemed a little slapdash). She was hardly a creature of regular habits, so a copy was put onto the PNC with an instruction to serve it on her when (the more hopeful 'if' seemed redundant) she was next arrested. The PNC is the police national computer, the database onto which every run-in with the police – searches, cau-tions, arrests, convictions – is stored. I imagine Lizzie's records probably have their own air-conditioned room full of whirring hard drives.

5 July

On my lunch break. Walked past some lads I'd had prior dealings with who were stood at a bus stop. One of them shouted 'Five-oh!'[3] to his associate across the road. Mate. This isn't *The Wire* and you aren't Avon Barksdale. You

---

3 A reference to the 1960s–70s cop show *Hawaii Five-0*, popularised in HBO's *The Wire* – a fairly incongruous reference when used in late-2000s Baltimore, but a positively surreal one when shouted at a short-arse Scouser near Lidl.

smoke weed in a kids' swing park and I'm a council worker armed with a dodgy knee and a biro. Let's not embarrass ourselves, shall we?

9 July

Sometimes you have to approach a case from a sideways angle. Today was a good case in point.

Artois Villas are a series of maisonettes that share a communal front door and hallway: two homes with one street door, their own front doors and a shared hallway. Ten Artois Villas has had problems with their neighbours at number 11 for several years, mainly because 11 is an HMO.

An HMO is a house of multiple occupancy. The official definition of an HMO is a property where at least three occupants who have no relationship with each other share amenities (such as a bathroom or kitchen) in a dwelling that is their principal place of residence, and have their own lockable rooms to sleep in. A less-official definition is 'a property that's been carved up into a shithole to extract every last screaming penny of rent from the available square footage'.

Another consequence of the disastrous 'right to buy' (RTB) policy is the proliferation of HMOs amongst the properties we manage. Purchase your local authority property for a discount, wait it out for five years (you have to live in the property for five years to avoid financial penalties), then you can move out and earn enough from rental fees to pay the mortgage on that place and whatever place you've moved into. Capitalism red in tooth, claw, brick and mortar.

Some RTB landlords feel a moral obligation to ensure their tenants have luxuries such as smoke alarms, functioning plumbing or a life free from mould. Others are less scrupulous and treat their tenants like a pop-up shop selling fireworks for a month in November: pile 'em high, sell 'em (relatively) cheap and don't worry if somebody loses an eye.

The two main customers for HMOs are students and migrant workers, as they are the most easily exploited due to their lack of experience in the rental market and their lack of alternatives. Room shares (i.e. more than one bed per room) are commonplace, and even bedshares (where two people working different shift patterns rent the same bed for twelve-hour stints) are not unheard of.

Managing ASB caused by these properties is like trying to nail a stretch of moving river to the pebbles underneath. By the time neighbours get fed up enough to report an HMO for nuisance, by the time you've taken statements, by the time you've tracked down contact details for the owner (they almost never inform us that they no longer live at the property, so warning letters have to be sent to the HMO, where they will be immediately binned by the occupants), it's a new set of tenants, either because it's a new university term or because the seasonal migrant workers have moved on. These new tenants have never caused a problem before, so you can't take action against them (not that you can anyway, because you have no idea who they are – a landlord who doesn't tell us when tenants have moved out won't tell us who lives there now), and so the whole process starts all over again.

None of this would be possible in a private rental market that wasn't based on a grasping race to the bottom, where even the scantest of regulations are viewed by many buy-to-let speculators as if you just took a shit in the manger during their kid's Nativity play.

In Artois Villas, there's the usual HMO litany of problems: slamming doors, shouting, transient occupants. The usual approach hasn't worked because the landlord keeps moving out one set of nuisance tenants and replacing them with a new set of nuisance tenants.

So instead of trying to tackle the noise nuisance head-on, we try to deal with the problem from a fire safety approach. Having been inside the property and seen what a slapdash job the owner has done to turn the two-bed flat into a three-bedroom HMO, I know that there are no smoke alarms and no fire extinguishers. The internal doors are so flimsy they would collapse if a French Symbolist poet collapsed against them in a laudanum swoon.

I inform our fire safety team that the property needs an urgent inspection as it could pose a fire risk in its current condition. To get it up to standard could cost the landlord thousands of pounds in fire doors, amongst other alterations. These will address the noise nuisance, because fire doors are fairly soundproof and are fitted with hydraulic closers which mean they're almost impossible to noisily slam shut.

The fact that the noise nuisance gets dealt with is, of course, my primary concern. The fact that I will cause the owner a significant amount of inconvenience and financial penalty when he could have just cooperated with me is merely a bonus.

10 July

At a certain point this afternoon, I realise I have been staring at the same screen on our Resolve computer system for the last twenty minutes. It is the main screen that gives an overview of who made the complaint, what the issue was, who they were complaining about and when the case was logged.

I've got myself caught in a feedback loop of panic and inertia, worried that I haven't called the tenant in ages, and worried that the problem could have got much worse, and worried that something awful might have happened because I haven't been in touch, and worried that my calling them would prompt them to report me, and worried that this would be it, this would be the one, this is the case, this one, this is the point where enough is enough and this is the case, this is the tipping point, this case is where they realise how badly I'm doing this and I'll remember this case because this is the case that made me lose my job.

I call the complainant and remind them of the problem they'd reported about their neighbour. There is a heart-lurching pause.

'Oh, them? No, they moved out months ago. It's all fine now.' The case can be closed, no further action is required. Relief washes over me.

'Oh, it's all fine *now*,' my stupid brain tells me. 'But it won't always be.'

11 July

Health wobbles. If an inventive and vindictive god wanted to put together a brace of conditions that complemented each other perfectly, they couldn't choose a better pair than ulcerative colitis and low-level OCD. I speak from experience.

The OCD has been around for decades to a greater or lesser degree, depending on my stress levels. I'm fortunate that it's never progressed to the crippling levels that completely dominate your life. For some people it crowds their every waking thought, but for me it's an annoying inconvenience – at most two out of ten – and for that I'm extremely grateful.

It expresses itself in two main ways: left/right balance and object checking. The left/right thing is about one side of my body needing to feel the same as the other. For instance, when I'm out walking I have to step on an even number of similar paving stones – nobbly/smooth, dark/light, wet/dry – with each foot. I'll keep a rough tally as I'm going along. If I scratch my left cheek, I'll reflexively scratch my right cheek. If one foot is out of the covers, the other one has to follow suit. It doesn't always work out. I broke my right femur when I was twenty-one and it's bugged me ever since that the left one is still intact.

The object checking is probably more familiar to most people: at night I have a routine of taps, lights and doors I have to check. If I'm not happy with the way I checked them, I have to start again from the first one (kitchen sink tap, fridge doors, back door, cat flap, front door, bathroom taps, lights as you go along, in case you're wondering).

When I leave the house, I check I've closed the front door more than is perhaps necessary. I also check a tap is switched off whenever I use one. I know everybody does, but by this I mean I hold my hand under the tap while I stare at it. My logical brain knows the tap isn't on and that my hand is dry and I can see no water coming out, but OCD isn't interested in logic. It can take several attempts to satisfy myself it's off properly.

If I get it 'wrong', I'm not plagued with the intrusive thoughts more serious OCD can produce, I just feel odd until I've done it 'properly'. And the object checking is entirely personal: if somebody else has turned off a tap or locked a door, I feel no compulsion to check that they've done it properly. I think it's partially rooted in self-esteem. I assume everyone else isn't the same level of unreliable idiot as I am and can be trusted to switch a light off properly. (I sometimes worry I'll develop photosensitive epilepsy alongside having to check light switches. If I had that and I flicked a light on and off sixty-seven times in a row I might never be able to leave the house.)

The ulcerative colitis is a more recent diagnosis, and was reached after a series of doctors placed a succession of larger and larger objects up my arse, starting with a solitary gloved digit and ending with what felt like a Pendolino train. The colitis means my daily visits to the toilet usually go into double digits (double digits is something I'm glad the doctor didn't try). And obviously after every visit I wash my hands because I'm not an animal. And every time I wash my hands, I spend a few minutes making sure the tap is turned off, and the toilet was definitely flushed and my hands were definitely washed.

I'm not sure what my work colleagues think I'm doing in there all the time but they must think I'm either doing great, fat, knobbly lines of gak off the back of the toilet cistern or I'm wanking like a teenage chimp. Neither of which has been the case since I was in my mid-twenties.

12 July

Return hearing for Lizzie's injunction. First, the judge asks whether the order has been served on Lizzie, making it an active order and meaning she's aware the order exists. We can confidently answer yes to this question, because she was arrested a couple of days ago and served a copy of the order in her police cell. She had been beating up another relative in the middle of the street for some unspecified reason that, based on what her conversations were usually like, was probably some disagreement on who was actually a cunt, and why.

The judge asks a second, perfectly reasonable question, 'Where is she now?', the answer to which is, 'In prison.' The previously mentioned assault constituted a breach of previously agreed bail conditions of which we were unaware, so she was recalled to prison to serve the rest of her sentence.

Arranging to have a prisoner appear in court is difficult

at the best of times, but when there is little or no notice to arrange a prisoner escort, it's more or less impossible. While the court likes to see defendants make an effort to appear in court when they're required, they don't expect them to organise an escape from prison, so the hearing is adjourned again for after Lizzie's release date.

15 July

The radio station in the office has a competition in which you can win a jackpot worth tens of thousands of pounds. The word 'competition' is taking a bit of a battering, though, as the competitive element extends to 'What pop singer were you just listening to thirty seconds ago?'

There's the usual office chat about what people would do with today's £30,000 prize if they won it, with 'treat my family' winning the honourable (and in all likelihood not entirely honest) top spot.

The radio station makes a big deal about what the winners will do with the money, though. There is a pathological insistence that the caller should say what a life-changing sum has been graciously bestowed upon them by the benevolent radio hosts and how humbly thankful they are. Cars will be bought, honeymoons booked and Disneyworld visited with the kids. We're paying for this, you pleb, so make with the grateful tears.

I'd like to think if I ever called the station and won the prize, I'd tell the hosts I needed the money to pay off some drug and gambling debts because those guys don't fuck around.

16 July

A member of staff has been verbally abused by a resident so I've been asked to take a statement from him and see what we need to do.

As part of his duties, he was using a slightly noisy piece of equipment to clean the stairwells of a block. A resident took offence at being woken up at the crack of afternoon by this noise (it was just after 1pm when the incident occurred). He approached the caretaker, asked him to turn the machine off so he could talk to him, and when he did, explained in graphic detail how far up his arse he would shove said piece of equipment if he woke him up again by using it. He then stomped back to his flat in his pyjama bottoms, tossing further profanities into the warm July air.

The caretaker doesn't want anything major done, just for the tenant to be spoken to and discouraged from threatening DIY proctology again. I arrange for our police team to pay a visit to the resident in the next few days to gently dissuade him from any similar outbursts in the future.

17 July

Injunction hearing for Mr Dane. Mr Dane has a hobby, and that hobby is to shout profanities at the top of his voice for no particular reason. He likes nothing better than relaxing in his flat with a nice cup of tea, sitting back in his armchair and shouting as if he's just jumped barefoot off the top of his wardrobe onto a paddling pool filled with Lego pieces.

Nobody really knows how Mr Dane got into his particular hobby or why he finds it so engaging. When it was investigated a couple of years ago, the usual referrals were made to mental health and social services to see if his tram went all the way back to the depot. Nobody could detect any underlying reason why he behaved the way he did, so we pressed ahead with legal action.

A twelve-month injunction had been obtained a couple of years ago asking him to refrain from shouting and swearing at the top of his voice at all hours of the day and night (for some reason, he believed that bellowing 'fucking whore cunt' took on an extra level of fun when it was done in the wee small hours of the morning). He had, more or less, abided by that injunction. So when it came towards its end, we had no justification or reason to ask that it be extended. And then a couple of months after it had expired, he went back to his hobby with gusto.

I had wondered whether Mr Dane had a similarly potty-mouthed friend that he was speaking with on the phone during his bouts of profane shouting, but neighbours said there were no tell-tale pauses in the tirades during which another person could be responding to him. Others had also seen him walking down the stairs in the communal hallway swearing his head off to nobody in particular, and they doubted he was talking into a Bluetooth headset (an invention that has made it much harder to guess whether the person you've just walked past is on the phone or having a schizophrenic episode).

So, we had notified him we were taking him to court, and advised him to go and get legal representation, and the day in court has finally arrived. Mr Dane, it appears, has chosen to represent himself. He has brought the bundle of papers upon which his defence relies (papers that he has not served to the court or to us, and as such, cannot be relied on in court) in a Tesco shopping bag. After the judge confirms that Mr Dane definitely wants to go ahead with this hearing by mounting his own defence (judges cannot instruct people to get legal representation but they can really very strongly recommend that they give it a try), the trial gets underway.

Our evidence is pretty straightforward: statements from a handful of residents all reporting similar, but not suspiciously identical, disturbances caused by Mr Dane. This includes a short audio recording of enough cursing to fill a swear jar, all in a voice that is unmistakably Mr Dane's. We add that he has a history of this behaviour, referring to his previous injunction, and ask that the court grants another injunction.

While our evidence is being presented, Mr Dane furiously rearranges the same six pieces of paper on the desk in front of him, as though the crumpled letters and handwritten notes are I Ching cards and a specific combination will somehow produce a workable defence. When it comes time for Mr Dane to give the court his version of events, it is clear that the plane of reality in which the rest of the court is operating bears little resemblance to the one Mr Dane is currently experiencing. Mr Dane's testimony is a rambling denunciation of the neighbours who had reported him, me as a representative of his landlord and the court itself.

His neighbours, he says, are in collusion against him, and are inventing these stories because they are jealous of him and the fact he has the nicest flat in their block. (All the flats in the block are of an identical layout and size, and they all face out onto the same busy main road.) Mr Dane asserts that I am not, as I claim, an ASB officer working for his landlord, but an agent working for the Department of Work and Pensions, and this case is a ruse to deny him benefits owed to him. I cannot prove I am who I say I am, says Mr Dane, and as such my evidence should be ignored.

The court itself is also working against him by trying to commit him to prison for something he has not done. He follows this up with a handful of vaguely legal-sounding words like 'subpoena', while the judge, with increasing impatience, tries to explain to Mr Dane that he has completely misunderstood why we are here today.

Given his lack of a cogent defence, the court finds in our favour and grants another one-year injunction banning Mr Dane from shouting or swearing loudly enough to cause a nuisance. This causes Mr Dane to redouble the ferocity with which he shuffles the papers in front of him (the papers to which he has never once referred during the hearing). He also begins shouting further allegations at the judge, ignoring requests to calm down, until he manages to make the judge do something I've not seen in a court before: he visibly loses his rag and shouts back at Mr Dane. The hearing is over, the judge tells Mr Dane, he will not listen to another word Mr Dane has to say and he is now withdrawing (there is still a bit of ceremony surrounding a judge entering or leaving a court. You're expected to stand whenever they do and it's considered good manners to ask permission to leave the room before they do).

Mr Dane glares at his bits of paper, hoping they might

contain a convincing and decisive argument. He angrily examines whatever was written on them before slowly placing them, carefully and one at a time, back into his Tesco bag.

We leave the courtroom and Mr Dane continues to glare at me in the waiting room, shouting that I am a fraud and he will see to it that I lose my job. As we walk away, he makes a sexist comment to the barrister who had represented us, and is asked to go into a side room by the court usher until he has calmed down. In short, he does nothing to dispel the idea he is a nightmare to live alongside.

Now, do I think Mr Dane was in the rudest of mental health and was fully aware of what was going on in that court? No, absolutely not. Do I think that a fully resourced mental health service would be able to work with him to identify which bits of wiring in his brain were faulty and maybe address his behaviour as a result? Definitely. But do I have to work in the world I've got, rather than the world I would like, and sometimes accept that people don't get the help they deserve, and it helps us win a case? Yes.

18 July

A colleague who has worked in our team pretty much since it started has announced they're leaving: a tenacious, dedicated and insightful ASB officer who regularly worked an additional twenty unpaid hours a week to try and provide the best service possible to our tenants. When somebody leaves the organisation, it's not just a job vacancy to be filled. It's not even the difficulty of trying to get somebody with the same level of experience. It's the encyclopaedia of local knowledge they take with them that is impossible to replace.

A few years ago, one of the housing officers that managed the same housing estates as I did retired. A housing officer manages the day-to-day issues that arise for our tenants. The specific duties change from organisation to organisation, but they will typically involve dealing with signing up new tenants and transfer requests (if a tenant's home is now too small or unsuitable due to medical grounds), visiting estates to make sure they're in a good state of repair, and so on.

To make a comparison with the NHS, if an ASB officer is like a cardiologist, a housing officer is like your GP. They're the first person you'll go to with an issue, and they will either deal with it themselves or refer you on to a specialist.

The housing officer who retired had worked in housing since the 1980s, and it had stretched him so thin the light was starting to shine through him. He cared a great deal for the tenants he looked after, and the fact that he was struggling to provide the right level of care for them troubled him deeply.

He had family back in the Caribbean, from which he'd emigrated as a child, and the prospect of spending his latter years with them in the sunshine rather than in the valleys of rain-sodden concrete in which he'd spent the last few decades had become too much to resist. When the organisation announced a need for redundancies, imposed on it by the latest set of austerity cuts, he grabbed at the opportunity as if he'd been kicked out of a plane and had just been offered a parachute.

I missed his company and his way with words (he once described a manager as being the kind of man who 'could give an arse a headache'), but I *really* missed the insight he gave me when dealing with my cases. He knew most of the families who lived on our estates, when they had moved in, where their kids now lived and the various relationships they had with other households on the estate. It was like an invisible metro map in his head of interconnecting associations, allegiances and animosities. He could tell you who was expecting their third grandkid and who was a bit of a sod when they got drunk. He'd notice if he hadn't seen an older resident on the estate for a while, or if an unfamiliar face appeared at somebody's window.

Whenever I was given a new case with a set of residents I hadn't dealt with before, I'd ask him if he knew anything about them. He wouldn't look at his computer. Instead he'd stare absently at the ceiling for a few moments, repeating the surname as if he was trying to get a jigsaw piece to fit in the right place. More often than not, he'd then be able to give a potted history of the people I'd asked about, as well as anything to watch out for.

This intangible information cannot be recorded on a housing file or cross-referenced in a database, not least because some of it was the kind of stuff people wouldn't like to have written about themselves ('He's usually pissed by late afternoon so I'd book to see him in the morning', 'Don't wear anything nice when you visit, her house is a right tip', and so on). When he left, all that knowledge left with him. It's now stored inside a grey-haired head, baked hot under a cobalt sky and within reaching distance of a glass of Guinness. I can't pretend I don't envy him, but if anyone earned it, he did.

And today we are losing somebody from our team with a similar level of irreplaceable experience. Somebody else will come in and that person will, I'm sure, give the job the same level of dedication and hard work. In truth, being an ASB officer is a hard job to do half-heartedly. It either consumes you, or you quit within a year because you fear for your sanity if you don't escape. But what the new person won't have are those countless little points of reference that allow you to do the job on the intuitive level that makes the difference between a competent and a good investigator.

Bugger.

19 July

Another HMO problem: a maisonette with half a dozen tenants who spend frequent evenings smoking weed and talking loudly in their front garden. Most people would prefer not to live near a household like this, but by some quirk of previous housing allocation, most of the nearby residents are older people. Not that I wish to stereotype, but older residents tend to worry that because somebody likes a spliff, they might also like to break into their house and play rugby with their cat, or worse.

I had previously sent out-of-hours officers to patrol the block, and they had confirmed the noise nuisance and cannabis smell that had been reported. Armed with this, I searched our database and got the contact details of the letting agents for the block. (The owner didn't rent the place out directly themselves, preferring to use a managing agent instead. It's a decision most of our buy-to-let landlords make and just adds another layer of inconvenience to managing these properties.)

I expected the usual problems I encounter with private letting agents. As a rule, as long as their private tenants are paying the rent, they could be using the place to summon Cthulhu to overthrow humanity for all the agents care. They're not bound by the same rules of social responsibility as we are, and this can often mean that they are unwilling to take action against their tenants for bad behaviour. To do so will usually cost them money in legal fees (as well as lost rent while they find replacement tenants).

To encourage them to do their job (even the most thrown-together of private tenancy agreements will have some clause about bad behaviour), I often contact the owner and say, 'Your managing agent has to deal with the people living in your place, or we will deal with it and hand you the bill.' Money is a great motivator.

This time was different. I told the managing agent (who had a name that wouldn't sound out of place in a P.G. Wodehouse novel and had a fruitily aristo accent redolent of port and tweed) what had been happening, and about the warning letters that had been sent to his tenants. I mentioned the distress it was causing the elderly neighbours, and asked that he do something about it.

'Good Lord, yes, we can't be having that,' he said. 'I'll serve them a Section 21[4] and they'll be gone before you know it.' This was like turning up for a street fight with

4 A Section 21 notice is a notice that private landlords serve on their tenants to notify them that they are ending the tenancy. They don't have to give any reason to end the tenancy. The

knuckledusters, body armour and a shotgun only to find your opponent waving a white flag and brandishing a conciliatory bunch of flowers.

So the problem tenants would be evicted within a few weeks and peace would return to the housing estate. A cracking result for me and a potentially massive headache avoided. Everybody's happy.

They're not, though, are they? Nuisance though they were, half a dozen people had just been made homeless based on a five-minute phone call between two people whom the spectre of homelessness would never visit. Maybe those tenants didn't really believe they could lose their home. Maybe it was just a couple of them causing problems and the rest were powerless to stop them. Maybe they didn't realise how much of a nuisance they were being.

But the workload demands that I can't think about that; I can't think about them frantically searching lettings websites for somewhere else to live, or how they would be packing up whatever possessions they'd managed to keep in their cramped former home. I couldn't stop to think that I was casually making people homeless and that I was readily stepping in time to the steady march of

---

rent could be up to date and they could have been model tenants, but if the landlord wants them out, that's that.

capitalism that allowed people to be treated so badly without consequence.

Another case for me to close off my workload, so there's that, right? Right?

24 July

An appeal hearing. Kara is a sociable sort of person who likes nothing better than to have a load of people round to her flat for a fun evening taking crack cocaine and heroin. She doesn't discriminate, whichever you prefer is fine with her, just as long as she can have some.

It's a common occurrence that drug addicts with tenancies will allow their properties to be used as shooting galleries in return for a share of their visitors' drugs. As you can imagine, the specific quantity of drugs to be shared with the host is never formalised in a written contract, so relations can sometimes become fractious when one party feels the other side is abusing the arrangement by being either too greedy or too parsimonious. Such is the nature of addiction that the host will always feel the guest is not being generous enough and the guest will feel the host is taking the piss.

The trade-off is not always like for like, though. I managed one property where the tenant (Larry) was a drinker and his guests were class A users. They could keep all of their drugs as long as they arrived at his flat with a can or two of booze as a door entry fee.

Larry was one of the most remarkable people I've encountered while doing my job. Barely five feet tall but with shoulders broader than an Olympic swimmer, he looked as if a hobbit had mated with a Rubik's Cube. The years of drinking had beaten him up, making him appear decades older than the thirty-five years his birth certificate would suggest. With stick-thin limbs and skin the colour of a mustard stain, he also sported a perfectly hemispherical belly that looked so taut you imagined it would go 'bdowwwn!' like a timpani drum if you flicked it. It was full of fluids his beleaguered system was unable to process, growing gradually larger over the months until he looked as if he was smuggling a space hopper under his shirt. He would then go missing for a week and reappear looking relatively skeletal, after a hospital stay during which they had drained away the evidence of his addiction.

It was during one such hospital stay that his neighbour in the flat below reported a water leak into their flat. Out-of-hours plumbers attended Larry's flat, located on the top floor of a high-rise block, to find nobody at home. Permission was given to force entry (we are allowed to force our way into a property if there's a fault that could cause harm to others) and once inside, the plumbers found a fully operational hydroponic cannabis factory.

After fixing the leak, the plumbers re-secured the front door, called the police and waited in their van outside the tower block for the officers to arrive. They saw Larry lope into the block and a couple of minutes later, the lights in his flat went on. Shortly after that, he came back out of the block and approached their van.

'You just been in my flat?'

'Yes, mate. There was a leak.'

'You saw what was in there, yeah?'

'We did. We've called the police. Sorry, we have to, it's our job.'

'No worries, I understand. 'Night, lads.'

Larry made his way back into the block of flats. And shortly after, every single scrap of the hydroponic farm – lights, tubing, seed trays, the lot – came sailing out of the window of his flat, twenty-two floors onto the pavement below.

It was a perfect example of how what you know and what you can prove are two different things. Larry told police he'd been away, had lent his keys to somebody, and had no idea the cannabis factory was there. The CPS eventually decided not to press charges. They could prove Larry knew about the cannabis factory on the night in question, but not before then. They could prove he went back into the block, but not back into his flat. Nobody saw who threw the cannabis factory out of the window. Larry said it was somebody else. And the CPS were not satisfied they could prove otherwise.

Now, you may feel you know what happened in Larry's flat. But that doesn't mean you could prove it.

After that, Larry stuck to having his flat used as a shooting gallery, as it was a far lower-risk prospect. From visits I'd done to his home, I knew he had no heating or electricity in the place. In the bitter depths of winter, I'd wonder how he was getting on in his flat, the wind whipping through his windows 300 feet in the air. I assumed that a curious drug addict, carrying a bottle of White Lightning for admission, would find his body before spring arrived.

But every year, despite all medical logic, there he'd be, having survived another season: sloshing his cartoon belly past the emerging daffodils and melted snow back to his flat, with a bag of cans and a couple of heroin addicts in tow. And as far as I know he's still alive. I'm beginning to suspect he may be immortal.

After numerous complaints from neighbours about Kara and her friends, we had eventually had the property closed down and everybody kicked out via a premises closure order. While this solved the immediate problem, it created a new one. Kara was not allowed into her own flat, and she had no postal address to which we could send her paperwork. Given her lifestyle, she was doubtless couch surfing or moving from squat to squat. So if we wanted to take tenancy action against her, we had to wait until the closure order expired and she was allowed back into her home before we could serve the mandatory NOSP[5] on her. We had to allow her to return to the home in which she had caused chaos before we could start the process to get her permanently removed from the home in which she had caused chaos.

The notice was served and, as was her right, she had appealed the decision, the hearing for which appeal is being held today. The appeal itself is heard by three senior

5 The mandatory notice of seeking possession is another new power that was introduced in the 2014 ASB act. Before then, if you served notice on somebody for breaching their tenancy and took them to court, the court had several options. They could say you hadn't proven your case and tell you to sling your hook. They could grant you the eviction you asked for. Or they could suspend possession. Suspended possession is the court saying, 'You have proven your case and I will grant possession, but I'm not going to evict the tenant just yet. If they stick to the following rules – paying their rent arrears back, not being a nuisance, and so on – for the next 2/3/4/etc years, then the possession order will be dropped. But if they don't stick to those rules, you can come back to court and ask for the possession order to be made absolute (i.e. un-suspended).'

With a mandatory possession order, it's different. You can serve a mandatory possession order if a tenant has done one of a specific set of things (committed a serious criminal offence in or near the place in which they live, breached an injunction), one of which is if another court has granted a premises closure order against the property. If you've followed your policy and the law properly, and if the decision to serve the notice isn't successfully appealed, when you get to court the judge has no option other than to grant eviction.

Is that another way a person can be made homeless without a court having the recourse to decide it was the reasonable thing to do? Yes, yes it is. Well spotted.

managers outside of the ASB team, to ensure they come to an independent decision. The law and the procedure are explained to the panel and the tenant. The evidence we have relied upon for our notice is laid out in the meeting. Then we give the reasons why we feel the decision was proportionate (in ASB we have legal remedies to deal with problems and when we use them, we have to prove not only that we are allowed to use the remedy, but also that it's the reasonable thing to do).

After reading through the thirty-odd pages of evidence, Kara is given the chance to give her version of events and to mitigate any proven allegations. Faced with a mountain of police stops, a drugs raid on her address and a dozen statements from neighbours complaining about the nuisance, her defence is that she's done nothing wrong and she won't do it again.

The meeting ends and the panel retires to make their decision. The decision is reached in the time it took you to read that last sentence. The panel decide our team were right to serve the mandatory notice and the case will now be referred to our legal team to apply for eviction.

August

Password: Breakdown101

Medication: Mirtazapine 45mg, Omeprazole 30mg

1 August

Helping a housing officer from another housing association to serve an injunction granted against one of our tenants. Our tenant, Oscar, had been going to the flat of his acquaintance/ex/current partner (depending on who you believed) called Tracy and causing a commotion while he was there. For instance, he'd often shout up at her window like a pissed Romeo, only instead of wishing he were a glove upon Tracy's hand that he might touch her cheek, he'd call her a fucking cow and a slag.

To protect Tracy (and her neighbours), the housing association has applied for an injunction to ban him from coming around any more. I offered to help serve the notice along with our police team for several reasons. I wanted Oscar to know that his landlord knew what he had been doing and took a dim view of it. The presence of police officers would help hammer home how seriously this was being taken. From a risk assessment perspective, any person with a record of violence should be approached with caution, and the added protection would provide any housing officer, repairs officer, or anyone with a reason to go to the address an added level of security. And most of all, putting the fear of God up a domestically abusive arsehole is as fun a way as you can spend an afternoon.

The police are still making their way from the van when we knock on his door, and when he answers, he's a mixture of aggressive and suspicious, demanding to know who we are and not allowing us to finish a sentence when we try to tell him. The other housing officer and I are average height and build, so he employs the standard shithouse behaviour that probably works most of the time. The change in his demeanour when the two attending police officers walk into view is something to behold – like taking a blowtorch to an ice lolly. The dismissive swagger is immediately replaced with obsequiousness and cooperation.

We explain the court order and strongly recommend he adhere to it if he wants to avoid being arrested. He reassures us that he wants nothing to do with Tracy as she is both fucking mental and a bitch whom he wouldn't touch if you paid him, apparently. I'm sure with natural charm like that he won't be single for very long.

6 August

Back in court with Lizzie after she breached her injunction. Yesterday afternoon, she was heard shouting abuse at her uncle and the police were called. When they arrived, she tried to leg it, vaulting over several back-garden fences like Simon Pegg in *Hot Fuzz* before eventually being arrested. This in itself was a breach of the order, for being somewhere she shouldn't have been. The fact she called the arresting officers every shade of fucking bastard wankers while mums walked past with their kids on the way home from school also meant she had breached the part of the order asking her not to use abusive language in public.

She'd spent a night in the police cells without her usual intake of crack (police are very picky about people smoking crack in their cells) and was now in a court custody suite with three Serco[1] officers waiting for a judge to be free to hear our case. I think her mood might best be characterised as 'somewhat impatient'.

She had been served with the injunction the last time she was arrested, but not the legal bundle,[2] so I go into the

1 Serco is the private company employed to transport prisoners from one place to another. It is exceptionally popular with people handing out government contracts for reasons that would evade any person who has had any prolonged dealings with Serco.

2 The legal bundle is the set of papers that constitutes all the evidence we will be relying on in court. We are obliged to serve this as soon as possible (preferably at the same time) when

custody suite, and explain who I am (we hadn't yet met) and what the papers are for. When I tell her we are applying for the order to keep her away from her uncle's house to be made permanent, she calmly informs me that I am a fucking cunt and the second she leaves the court building she is going to fucking kill me.

'I'd rather you didn't, Lizzie, thanks,' I say, and leave the room.

The police officers who had arrested her the day before are in the waiting room, as they will need to give evidence once we are in court. I advise them of what Lizzie has said, advise them that this constitutes a further breach of her order, and ask that they re-arrest her for this new offence. Everyone in the waiting room is then treated to the sound of Lizzie verbally abusing the officers again as they re-arrest her. (They don't arrest her once more for verbally abusing them, reasoning that they could end up in an infinite Escher-like feedback loop of profanity and arrest.)

---

serving an interim injunction. The defendant will want to get legal advice, and that advice will be shaped by the story the legal bundle tells them.

The laws around disclosure are very clear on this point: anything relating to the case has to be given to the other side, even if it's detrimental to your case (if you find out that your defendant reads to blind kids when he isn't donating blood and adopting kittens, tempting though it is to keep that quiet, you're not meant to).

It's another area in which film and TV give you false hope. You can't spring a surprise piece of evidence while the case is in progress, any more than your barrister can badger the witness with increasingly insulting questions until they blurt out, 'IT WAS ME, I DID IT AND I'D DO IT AGAIN!'

When you produce a defendant in court for breach of injunction, you have to be fitted around the existing court lists, since it's an unplanned hearing. This usually results in having to wait around for several hours. This does not sit well with Lizzie in her custody suite, so she decides to threaten the three Serco officers with a chair, spit at them and threaten to kill them. She is eventually calmed down and we are put before a judge to hear the case. As she enters the court, Lizzie asks the judge if the handcuffs can be taken off as they are chafing. Unaware of her previous behaviour, the judge instructs Serco to remove them.

The details of the two breaches – the one that caused her to be arrested initially and the one that happened in the custody suite – are explained to the judge. Lizzie confirms that she wants legal advice, so the hearing is adjourned for a week. Lizzie is asked to wait in the courtroom while the judge goes to draw up the remand order. He is trusting Lizzie to return in a week's time, he explains, and this is the reason she is not being remanded in custody.

The second the judge withdraws to his chambers, Lizzie decides she doesn't want to wait in the courtroom. Or the waiting room. Or, indeed, the entire building. With the handcuffs removed, she is free to walk out, so that's exactly what she does. When the judge returns, the sheepish Serco officers explain what has happened, and his decision to bail

Lizzie is reversed. As soon as police spot her, she is to be arrested and remanded in custody until the next hearing in a week's time.

I ask the five uniformed officers (two police, three Serco) why they were unable to restrain Lizzie and am told they did not feel it was safe to do so. I will always defer to the expertise of people who do jobs that I don't, so I refrain from suggesting that maybe they should get a job they can actually do properly.

Given the earlier promise Lizzie had made to me, I wait in the court for a while before walking a different route home. It also marks out another little patch of the area I cover in which I will have to look over my shoulder in the future. Class A drug addicts deep in withdrawal might not have the best memory for faces, but I do.

From my own experience, and the experience of those I've worked with, it's seldom that ASB officers are physically assaulted, or at least, successfully physically assaulted. Half the trick is moving out of the way before the fists start flying, so all you have to deal with is some threatening gesticulating rather than a smack in the mouth. I suspect this is more down to the experience of those doing the job, and the ability to know when violence is on its way before it actually arrives, than the readiness or otherwise of our clients to assault us.

8 August

A meeting to deal with the family at 7 Bushey House, attended by me, a housing officer and a copper from CID. Safe to assume we won't be discussing somebody hoovering their stairs after 9pm or giving their neighbour dirty looks.

The Greenland family were a tight-knit unit in every sense of the phrase, living as they did with seven family members in a three-bedroom flat. Adult siblings were forced to share a bedroom and the living room had been repurposed as an extra bedroom for the parents. When a family is living in such chronically overcrowded conditions, it's hard not to encroach on each other's lives. Privacy is a luxury that doesn't exist here, and if the eldest daughter farts in one bedroom the youngest son will open a window in the other. Knowing what everyone in your family is doing, every moment of the day, can wear you down. Especially when one of them is a crack dealer.

Christophe had been spotted street-dealing crack by police several months previously. He kept returning to his home every hour or so, presumably to store whatever money he'd made and to restock on drugs. It made sense to have as little of both as possible in your possession, as both police officers and enterprising muggers would be quite keen on taking them off you.

Given the frequency with which Christophe returned to base, officers decided there was no point in a street arrest, but more than enough evidence to suggest that an early-morning visit to his home might produce results.

It did.

Several dozen wraps of heroin and crack were found in the bedroom used by Christophe and his brother Sean, alongside the usual wad of cash and multiple phones. It was impossible to say for certain who they belonged to, so police arrested and charged them both. Police had not seen Sean out on the street dealing drugs, but it was reasonable to suggest he knew the drugs and cash were in the same room he slept in every night.

No other members of the family were charged, with Christophe's parents expressing shock at the fact that their son – who was in and out of their home thirty times a day, and was unemployed yet wore designer clothes – was a drug dealer.[3] Maybe they just thought he kept nipping to the shops to buy a single scratchcard, and he was extremely lucky and kept winning? Maybe they were too scared to tell him to move out, despite the fact that they had not once

___

3 It can often be the case that family members genuinely don't know what people in their own homes are up to. One eviction case we had that was successfully defended involved a bed-bound woman who never used the upstairs of her house, and her drug-dealing grandson, who lived upstairs and whose bedroom looked like Scarface's shed. The court were satisfied that there was no way of her knowing her little darling had more customers than Greggs.

made any indication of this or asked for any help in getting him kicked out? Maybe their rent account was always bang up to date because they were financially diligent and not because they had some kind of undeclared income from a certain family member? Who knows?

It's possible the raid may have created a blockage in Christophe's cashflow, because six weeks later two strangers started hacking at the family front door with an axe. After several blows had bounced off the unexpectedly sturdy uPVC door (double glazing companies are missing a trick in not using this as a feature in their adverts), the two unknown visitors lit a small fire on the doormat and ran away. The fire was quickly put out and the police called.

The next morning, Christophe's parents were waiting for the HPU to open at 9am so they could insist on being accommodated elsewhere. It was not safe to carry on living where they were, they said, as the unknown assailants could come back at any moment and their lives were at risk. The whole family – including Christophe – needed a new home far away from Bushey House.

While I would not wish to presume to know what you're currently thinking, I can probably hazard a guess. You might be thinking that Christophe had brought this to his family's home. You might be wondering why they still wanted him living at home (he was in his mid-twenties and a strapping enough lad to fend for himself). You might be asking why they should be given a new place to live elsewhere because of their son's drug dealing. You may, if you're of an especially suspicious frame of mind, wonder how aware of Christophe's profession his parents were.

This brings us back to the old problem of what you can know and what you can prove. The local authority could not prove that his parents were complicit in his drug dealing, nor that they knew exactly who had Jack Nicholson-ed their door. You may well *think* that kicking Christophe out would solve all their problems, but can you prove it? No.

So police were compelled to agree that yes, a serious attack had taken place on the home and yes, the chances of another attack occurring were quite high so yes, moving the family away would greatly reduce this risk to the whole family (some of whom were minors and were understandably terrified). And because of this, the HPU had been obliged to find the family temporary accommodation far away from Bushey House. But not another three-bed place like the one in which they were currently living: a five-bed house. Because local authorities are not allowed to make a family 'overcrowded', even if the family has made themselves overcrowded by deciding to have kids.

Overcrowding is a massive problem in any area where housing demand is at a premium and poverty is commonplace. People carry on living at home into adult-hood, because the alternatives are trying to find private accommodation that will accept people claiming benefits (remember those signs in windows in the 1950s and 60s that said 'No blacks, No Irish, No dogs'? In the modern era, 'No housing benefit recipients' is a sign private landlords can place in adverts with impunity and there's nothing legally to stop them), a mate's sofa, or a park bench.

People can make themselves overcrowded in the place they have been allocated, and often do. The desire to have kids is a thing that's always eluded me, but apparently it's quite popular. And so a couple in a one-bed flat will start having kids, slowly making their home more and more over-crowded. The right to a family is enshrined in the Human Rights Act, and I would never dream of questioning that, but one of the reasons I don't own a hang-glider (other than a crippling fear of heights) is that I have nowhere to put one. So, y'know.

Local authorities, however, cannot move a family into a property with insufficient space, thus intentionally making them overcrowded. As families grow in size, the number of properties suitable for their needs dwindle. If any social housing had been built in the last few decades, this might not be quite as much of a problem. Apologies if that seems needlessly logical and blatantly obvious.

The reason I am meeting with CID today is that the family has decided that they want to move back home to Bushey House, and police want to assess the risk in allowing them to do so. You might ask why Christophe and his family no longer want to live in a comfortable five-bed house in an area where Christophe can't deal drugs because the local dealers would spot a new face on their patch and kick him around the place like a fucked kite. That is a question you may well ask. You might ask what would compel them to move back into a crowded home targeted by persons unknown who, at this point, had not been convicted. You might ask.

Christophe and Sean had pled not guilty to the drugs charges, nobody had been arrested for the attack on their door, the parents had a valid tenancy at Bushey House, as yet no criminal offence had been proven as having taken place, no breach of tenancy could be proven to have happened, and the parents denied knowing anything about any of it.

So what can we prove and what do we know? What do we want to see happen and what do we know will end up happening? What is the right thing to do and what are we obliged to do? The family move back into their overcrowded home a few days later. We will await the outcome of the criminal case with interest.

12 August

An urgent call from a resident. He's tired of the shenanigans of the people living above him. He tearfully tells me that he cannot continue to live under these kind of conditions. I am asked if I can visit him urgently to look at the state his neighbours have made of his garden. Once given permission to leave the office, I make my way over.

At the door, I'm asked to take my shoes off [4] to walk through his flat (which, in fairness, is so immaculate it makes some of the places on *Grand Designs* look like a squat), just so I can put them back on to go into his garden.

The lawn is so fastidiously mown that for a moment I honestly think it's that Astroturf stuff greengrocers put on their shelves. It's cleaner than the carpet in my house. Whatever havoc has been wrought on this manicured haven, I'm struggling to see it.

The resident points to the trellis on the rear wall of the

4 Whether or not to remove one's shoes on a visit is always a grey area, not least because I'm not always sure my socks haven't got holes in them. Technically I'm not obliged to say yes, and I can terminate the visit there and then if they insist, but life (and your work day) is too short to bother with that. Often people ask for cultural reasons, and people are usually very apologetic when they ask if I mind. A more recent development is being offered little shower caps for your feet.

There have been times when I've refused (if it's a property I've not visited before and the tenant is an intravenous heroin user who owns a dog they don't clear up after, for example), but by and large it's not a big deal.

As soon as I'm asked to take more than that off, that's when I start charging extra.

garden, which is covered in clematis and nasturtium so neat they look as if they're standing to attention awaiting a drill inspection. After staring at them for several moments, I can see a small, lumpy plastic bag nestling between the blooms, incongruous as a moped in a Michelangelo painting. It's clear that it's been thrown over from the balcony of one of the flats upstairs.

Snapping on my disposable rubber gloves, I carefully pull the bag free. Still unable to work out what the bag contains, I unpick the knotted handles and peer inside. The smell of very used cat litter leaps to the back of my throat, causing me to jolt and accidentally tip the entire contents of the bag onto his lawn. So that's how I spend a fair portion of today: picking pieces of cat crap off somebody else's lawn while they mutter threats of reporting me to my manager.

I just hope that the cat that lived upstairs wasn't watching me clear up their shit, because that would have been a level of humiliation too far.

13 August

Return hearing for Lizzie's injunction breach. Against every logical possibility, she's actually here. We're just not entirely sure why. Lizzie hasn't arrived under her own steam – she's once more accompanied by three Serco officers (who are each a foot taller and twenty years younger than the previous set who let her stroll out of court last time). She hasn't been found and arrested as per the judge's order last week, with Serco bringing her from the police station. Neither has she come from jail on another matter; no production order from prison was requested. The Serco officers aren't paid to question how they came to be in charge of a prisoner, so there's no way of finding out from them, either. But here she is.

Rather than stopping to ponder what benevolent god delivered Lizzie to the second floor of the court, we simply thank our lucky stars that she is here, and the hearing goes ahead. But not before Lizzie's barrister (let's call him Dick, because I'm childish) has managed to annoy every person he talks to.

Dick is every cliché you may have in your head of what a smarmy, over-privileged legal professional might be like (almost all the solicitors and barristers I've ever encountered have been, and I hate to disappoint you, normal people managing impossible caseloads and getting paid far less than you might think).

Watching Dick in action for two seconds immediately tells me that he was privately educated, has a higher self-image than Narcissus after a facelift and views everybody around him as inconveniences. He makes the rookie error of annoying the usher (never annoy the usher, they can make your day in court a miserable one) by barking his name at her and telling her he needs time to read through his papers. He then demands paperwork from our barrister that he can't find in his own legal bundle and refuses to meet with Lizzie (I doubt Lizzie was ever taught Latin at prep school so Dick would have little in common with her) to take instructions from her.

This all means we're nearly an hour late going into court. The judge, we can be assured, will have been fully briefed as to why he's been kept waiting, and by whom. As a result, the hearing itself does not go well for Dick: requests for an adjournment are refused, every error in procedure is brought to Dick's attention. The more flustered he gets that life isn't holding the door open and waving him through, as it doubtless has done for the past thirty-odd years, the worse he performs (and presenting a case in court is a performance). By the end, pretty much all our barrister needs to do is look exasperated and gesture at Dick.

The injunction breach is deemed proven and Lizzie is given a few weeks in jail to have a bit of a think about her behaviour, and possibly about getting somebody else to represent her when we're back next month for the full injunction hearing.

16 August

Spent today representing somebody who the organisation wished to dismiss because she failed her police check due to a minor offence committed when she was barely out of her teens, which seemed in her view, my view and the view of the union excessive.

To do my job you have to pass an enhanced DBS (Disclosure and Barring Service) check. This checks the PNC to see if at any time you've come to the police's attention as a wrong 'un – convictions, cautions and so on. It's to ensure that you are of good moral character and not liable to be open to blackmail.

One side-effect is that in your day-to-day life, you have to behave to a higher standard than most people in non-sensitive jobs. Get into an argument with somebody being gobby on public transport, give them a backhander, receive a caution for common assault and bang goes your career. You have to learn to bite your lip and walk away from situations. It's all very 'Coward of the County'.

(Although unlike in the 1979 Kenny Rogers song, I don't have a girlfriend called Becky and nobody calls me 'Yellow'. At least nobody that I'm aware of.)

Given how often the job involves drug dealers and drug addicts, they also want to see you've had no involvement in drugs yourself. Ahem.

There's nothing more tedious than people recounting the times they did drugs, as anybody who's watched Oliver Stone's film about The Doors will tell you, so I want to avoid that. But in the interests of full disclosure it's only right to say that I've had some experience. Cannabis, amphetamines, cocaine, LSD, ketamine, poppers, ecstasy and opium, to be precise.

I've not indulged in a good decade and a half. As a previous cigarette smoker and a currently enthusiastic drinker, I know how much of an addictive personality I have, so I made the decision that me and drugs don't mix.

This was brought home to me many years ago when I almost became a cocaine dealer. My friend worked at my local, a pub that even by my standards[5] was pretty rough. Once, when somebody kicked off at a member of staff, a few of the regulars barred him by dangling him over a motorway bridge and telling him not to return. That level of rough.

As well as the usual pool table, fruit machine and dartboard, the pub had its own coke dealer. A large guy in quietly expensive sports casual wear, Vic moved around the pub like a shark through a coral reef. He never seemed in a hurry to do anything and gave the impression he could beat

---

5 Pubs can be roughly divided into three strata: bars, pubs and boozers. Bars are the kind of place that put a napkin under your drink, smell like air freshener and have snacks served from mason jars. Pubs are the kind of place you'd feel safe taking an older relative for a Sunday lunch, have toilets that work and have a kids' play area with no sharp edges. Boozers have the horse racing on the telly, still don't take debit cards and will serve every regular in the place before deigning to serve you. Of the three, my preference is boozers.

you to a pulp with one hand while constructing a roll-up with the other.

The pub's owners were aware of Vic's occupation and tolerated it. It was the kind of pub where drugs were going to get dealt anyway, so they reasoned they'd rather it was the personable Vic – who never caused a fuss and sat quietly at the end of the bar sipping lime and soda – than whatever local headcase would take his place.

I spent a lot of time in the pub chatting to my mate and the rest of the regulars, and as a result I got to know Vic well. I'd never dabbled with cocaine before I met him, but this changed with alarming rapidity.

The time of my first line to the time I quit – terrified for my safety, my health and my sanity – was no more than a couple of months. It turned out I liked it a *lot*. The occasional line led to going halves on a gram to doing it every night. This culminated in a two-day binge with Vic (on his personal supply rather than the stepped-on coke he sold in the pub), during which I started hallucinating and was convinced I was about to have a heart attack.

While this was happening, Vic told me he planned on moving up a tier as he was tired of the grind of hanging around the pub, so he needed somebody he trusted to work for him. He made me an offer: £500 a week cash in hand plus a few grams for myself if I started selling for him.

Every life has forks in the road, and fortunately I took the road marked 'Fuck that, what am I doing with my life?' I politely declined Vic's offer, but wished him all the best. A month later, he came into the pub with a stitched-up diagonal slash mark from his right eyebrow across the bridge of his nose to the left corner of his mouth. Somebody had jumped him in the toilets of another pub for his coke and his cash. If I'd taken the other fork, that would have been me.

I only mention this to say that we have entirely the wrong attitude towards a person's drug history when it comes to holding down responsible jobs. We prefer people with squeaky clean records and absolutely no lived experience to work with people tangled up in drugs. I'd like to think that when I deal with addicts and dealers in this job, I have at least some small insight into what their lives are like.

I am aware how exceptionally lucky I've been that my drug experiences never developed into trying something there was no coming back from. Or something I couldn't give up as easily. Or something that came to the attention of the police. I'm also aware that being white and vaguely middle class greatly reduced the chances of police wanting a word with me as I stumbled through life with something in my pocket that could carry a prison sentence.

I understand that there need to be checks to ensure the wrong people don't end up in a job in which they could do harm. But it does feel as if there needs to be some middle ground, where people can put their fuck-ups to good use.

19 August

Another possession appeal hearing. Back in January we were told that Raul had been arrested for drug dealing (it was as a result of this that I found, or rather, smelled, Albert the Cat Man). A few months later, Raul pled guilty to eight counts of possession with intent to supply (PWITS[6]) and was given a few years in prison.

A Mandatory NOSP had been served on him in prison,

---

6 The 'intent to supply' part of PWITS isn't always straightforward to prove. It's not just about the quantity of drugs found. If somebody has a big brick of weed but can reasonably argue they intended to smoke all of it, and there's no evidence to suggest they were planning on selling it, you won't get the 'intent to supply' part.

I had a case where somebody managed to convince the court of exactly that. A parcel from overseas had been intercepted by Royal Mail in their suspicious parcel department. A quick check revealed it contained two and a half kilos of cannabis. Police arranged for a controlled delivery – the postie asked for a signature for the parcel and our tenant duly obliged – before kicking the door in and arresting him. At court, he told the judge that he had bought the weed – about eight grand's worth – for himself, using his dole money to do so, apparently. His plan was to invite his mates round and smoke the lot. In the absence of any contrary evidence, they chose to believe him.

Conversely, you can have a relatively small amount of drugs in your house, but if they're all separated out into deal bags next to multiple mobile phones and a list of customers, the 'supply' part is a given. Possession with intent to supply is usually referred to by its acronym, pronounced 'peewits', making it sound like a flock of cute little birds rather than a dangerous and often violent occupation.

and he had decided to appeal the decision. They don't really allow convicted drug dealers to leave prison so they can pop down to their housing office, so a couple of Raul's mates would be arguing his case. Raul's mates are as skilled and as organised a pair of litigants as you would expect from the friends of a drug dealer who was raided twice in the space of six weeks and who had posted social media messages about what a gangster dealer he was.

They tell us the drugs were for Raul's personal use, despite the fact he had pled guilty to possession with intent to supply. They say that Raul just smoked a bit of weed now and then, despite the fact cocaine and spice were found in the flat. Raul had fallen in with a bad crowd, so we should let him move back into his flat (where that bad crowd knew where to find him). They say Raul had never caused problems before, ignoring the thirty pages of warning letters and file notes I had presented from Raul's past, which recorded him racially abusing and threatening members of staff.

Given the circumstances, I'm not sure there's much anybody could have done to convince the panel to overturn the decision to evict him. But by the time they have finished, Raul's mates have not only convinced them it is the right thing to do, they have also convinced them that Raul has really bad taste in friends.

20 August

It's normal to spend all day at work wondering how long it is before you can go home and have a drink, right? Or rather, how long it is before you can get a drink to have on the journey home? Or wonder if anyone would notice if you went to the pub on your lunch break? All normal, right?

23 August

Emergency multi-agency meeting for Sally. Back in January, we were told she might be in some trouble. Known to have serious mental health issues and drug dependency, her erratic behaviour (standing on a street corner punching herself in the face, reporting multiple phantom pregnancies) had been brought to my attention. Referrals to mental health and social services were made at the time but sadly never really went anywhere.

Sally's life was undeniably chaotic, but she showed a skill that many people with similar lifestyles learn: engaging just enough with support services. If somebody's life is swirling around the plughole and they refuse to answer the door to anybody, they run the risk of help being imposed on them (which is always difficult but can, via court orders, be achieved if it's deemed absolutely necessary).

However, if they engage fully with support services,

they may have to actually face up to their problems. If all you've known is heroin and transient friends and shoplifting and occasional assaults and broken windows and alienated family members and health scares, leaving all that behind can be difficult. Regardless of how horrific a life like that might sound, there's a comfort in familiarity, even if what you're familiar with is quotidian misery.

Rehabilitating drug addicts isn't just about the substance they're addicted to. Difficult though withdrawal undoubtedly is, it can be endured and mitigated with therapy and medication. What's a lot harder is to make a break from the lifestyle. If your entire social circle sits in a squatted building smoking crack bought with money they made from shoplifted batteries, you can't sit there sipping herbal tea and politely declining a rock for yourself.

So the trick is to engage with support services, but not too much. Go to your first couple of drug rehab appointments, but no more than that, or you might have to try and give up taking drugs. Work with your social worker just enough to get your housing benefit claim sorted, but not so much they start trying to address your underlying issues. Support services are so overworked and under-resourced they're not going to try too hard to chase people up to offer them help they don't want. It's like doing just enough to stop the plates of your life from falling off their sticks.

And this had been what Sally had managed, until recently. After the referrals were made earlier this year, she had spoken to officers just enough that they were satisfied she wasn't in immediate and serious harm. Then, she had slowly tailed off her engagement to the point at which nobody really knew what was going on in her life. And once more, that life was spiralling out of control.

Another important plate to keep wobbling on its stick is your tenancy. You don't want to get evicted because of your behaviour, but obviously there's no way you're going to stop having your flat used as a shooting gallery/doss house/hide-out. But things had started to slip, and people had started noticing that Sally's life was getting somewhat rowdy once more. Her friends were drawing attention to Sally's flat: pissing in lifts, screaming up at her fourth-floor window to be let in, dragging an abandoned mattress into the lobby area of the block of flats so they could have a kip. People tend to notice stuff like that.

So, a multi-agency meeting to decide how to unpick all of this. Police had visited the property several times recently, and they show us the footage from their body-worn cameras. The bedsit is strewn with drowsy-looking people who seem not to know each other, or that Sally is the actual tenant of the flat. Burnt foil, cigarette lighters, cider cans as ashtrays, bedsheets over the windows. No visible faeces or blood on the walls or floor, though, and there is actually food in the fridge, so I've seen worse. It is clear, though, that Sally has ceded control of her flat to whoever wants to use it. These weren't just friends hanging out to smoke crack. These were acquaintances of friends of complete strangers they'd met waiting for a drop-off.

Police couldn't force them to leave the flat unless it was clear that Sally didn't want them there, but there was no way of knowing that because Sally wasn't at home. They could have searched each of the occupants for drugs (police are allowed to do so if they have reason to suspect somebody has drugs on them, and this was the kind of bedsit that would only ever have drug addicts staying there; you'd need a stiff shot of heroin just to face crossing the threshold) but they had better things to do than spend several hours processing half a dozen prisoners with a couple of rocks (at most) each.

As they left the bedsit, Sally was entering the building. The footage shows her once more being just cooperative enough with the police that they would go away. Yes, she knew there were several visitors in her flat. Yes, she was fine with them being there. No, she couldn't remember all their names. Yes, she would call the police if there was a problem.[7]

---

7 Of course she wouldn't. No self-respecting drug addict would willingly call the police to their own home, not even if a burglar was tapdancing on their throat.

Social services advise the meeting that there was one more person in that bedsit than the police had thought. Because Sally had told them that she was pregnant. Maybe everyone in her bedsit was there to throw a surprise baby shower?

Smoking crack in a bedsit with a steady parade of transient crackheads is not what most obstetricians would recommend for expectant mothers, so clearly this is a cause for concern. Sally had announced she was pregnant a number of times in the past, but had never had a pregnancy carry to the point at which she was visibly expecting. When questioned, she would always say she'd had a late period, or that she had miscarried. Because her GP was just another support person she kept at arm's length, we had no way of knowing whether these were inventions caused by the combination of drugs and mental illness, or were true. But as always, you have to assume it's true, just in case.

In a meeting like this, you look for whether there are any positive aspects in a person's life: support network, good behaviours, and so on. This is the shortest part of the meeting. As she lives with her drug addiction and history of mental illness, Sally has no family she can call on for help. It is believed there may be relatives living in Scotland, but Sally has made vague references to child abuse in her brief engagements with social services. Again, whether this is true or not, we have no way of knowing.

Sally doesn't appear to have any insight into how unmanageable her life is becoming or the danger she is in. She is not addressing her drug addiction with rehab services or working with the mental health team to see what treatment she needs. Her benefits claims have lapsed once more because she hasn't renewed them. As well as being at risk of eviction due to rent arrears, we would soon be obliged to take action against her tenancy for the ASB she and her visitors are causing. Oh, and the lock on her front door isn't working properly.

If Sally isn't able to keep people out of her flat, we could consider a partial premises closure to ban anybody but her from going in there. There is precisely no chance that Sally will stick to this order, but at least it means police can arrest anybody they find in there. Eventually, word will get around locally that Sally's place is no longer a viable hangout. Whatever the drug-addict equivalent of TripAdvisor is, she will start getting one-star reviews. The least we can do is fix her front door to give her a fighting chance.

This means I will have to do a door-to-door canvass of her neighbours to gather statements to justify the court action. And, as always when canvassing, listen to whatever entirely unrelated gripes the residents may have. When I return to the office, I look up the block Sally lives in. It has over seventy flats in it. That was going to be a long old day.

29 August

CLACK. CLACK CLACK CLACK. CLACK CLACK. CLACK CLACK CLACK CLACK CLACK.

This is the soundtrack to my morning because a visitor to the office (our office has hot-desking, which is corporate-speak for 'we don't think enough of you to give you your own desk') appears to be texting every single person on his contacts list. He's so busy doing this, he never got round to switching off the keyboard noises. It's possible that the stress of work is affecting my tolerance towards other human beings but seriously, I have to go and make a coffee to stop myself from screaming at him.

CLACK CLACK

(In my head, this is him typing, 'Help I'm being throttled'.)

September

Password: Workload101

Medication: Mirtazapine 45mg,
Omeprazole 30mg, 45 units of alcohol

2 September

Christophe is found guilty of possession with intent to supply class A drugs; his brother is found not guilty. The judge
decides to make an example of Christophe and send out a
message to other drug dealers that society will not tolerate
such behaviour by giving him community service and a
£200 fine (the equivalent of ten drug transactions, or an
hour's work for Christophe). He's back home the same afternoon and there's absolutely no reason to believe he won't
carry on where he left off.

The guilty verdict does, however, give us the option of
serving a mandatory possession order on the family. The
decision to do so will rest largely on whether the parents
kick Christophe out of the family home or not. The law
allows us to serve the notice at any point up to twelve

months after the conviction, so we have time to see how they react. We have to balance their neighbours' desire not to live next to a convicted drug dealer with the seriousness of making an entire family (including minors) homeless because of the actions of one person.

3 September

Another day, another crack house. This time it belongs to Angela, who came to us several years ago from another town, fleeing violence. Some drug dealers had decided to slash Angela across the face and there was every chance they would try again at some point. She claimed not to know why they had attacked her, but said it definitely wasn't because she had been given a load of drugs to sell and had decided to smoke them all instead, leaving her owing them a substantial sum of money she had no hope of paying back. Definitely not.

A quick check into her criminal past showed that she had several convictions for drug dealing, including one spell in prison in Southeast Asia, as well as the usual litany of petty offences a class A addict manages to accrue. Despite all this, she had to live somewhere, and that somewhere was a small block of flats we managed.

Angela had initially managed to keep her lifestyle to herself, with the neighbours unaware of the colourful past of the new tenant. But the occasional visitor had turned into regular visitors, which turned into regular shouting and arguing from the flat, which turned into people passed-out outside her front door.

I arranged an unannounced welfare visit with the police to check on how Angela was doing. Police won't bother trying to get a warrant for drugs in a property unless there's a suspicion there's drug dealing going on and Angela wasn't currently suspected of that. But a polite knock on the door with an ASB officer present, asking if Angela is home so we can have a quick chat, is a way of taking a look inside a property without needing a warrant.

Angela's door is answered by a scrawny guy in his forties who looks like somebody turned Keith Richards inside out. I tell him I need to speak with Angela and he shuffles back inside without saying another word. Taking this as an invitation to go inside, we walk into the living room. A full house of crack-den bingo.

The first thing you notice is the smell: a heady mixture of unwashed body, burnt tinfoil, stale urine, roll-up cigarettes extinguished in empty beer cans and the acrid odour of crack. Every surface is cluttered with beer cans fashioned into crack pipes, cigarette lighters, dismantled Rizla packets and crumpled toilet paper. Every window has a bedsheet pinned to it to keep the place nice and murky. The whole floor of the lounge is covered in sofa cushions, blankets and duvets, turning the entire room into a pass-out-wherever-you-like flop house. Two guys are playing *Tekken* on a PlayStation 2 and a portable television, none of it valuable enough to be worth pawning for drugs. Two or three more are passed out in the room.

Inside-out Keith Richards shoves Angela awake and resumes his spot on the sofa. I explain to Angela who I am and why we are here – or rather, I tell her that neighbours are worried that they haven't seen her in a while, so we are carrying out a welfare visit. In truth, Angela's neighbours would probably throw a street party if they heard she was leaving, but it is a necessary fiction.

Angela says everything is fine and asks us to leave. There is nothing in plain view that anyone could be arrested for, so we do exactly that. The visit has helped to confirm that the place is being used by local addicts, but we knew that anyway. Not a complete waste of time, but we saw nothing major that could prompt further action.

5 September

An evening at a residents' association meeting. I will never forget the first one of these I attended. I had been an ASB officer for less than a month when an urgent residents' meeting had been called regarding a hostel we managed that had recently opened. The hostel was for people who had just left prison, and since it opened, the amount of drug-related activity in the surrounding streets had sky-rocketed. Car crime, aggressive begging, discarded needles and the like had become rife. The area where the hostel was located was gentrified, so local residents were horrified to leave their seven-figure townhouses for their morning jog only to find somebody had pissed against the antique Tuscan sundial in their front garden.

Somebody from our organisation had to go to the residents' meeting that had hastily been arranged, and none of my other colleagues wanted to. I explained that I had only just started being an ASB officer, I knew nothing about this hostel and I would not be able to answer any questions posed to me. Nevertheless, I ended up going.

My only hope was that nobody would turn up at such short notice – a hope that very quickly evaporated when I arrived at the community centre in which it was being held and over 200 people were already there. By the time the meeting started, it was standing room only. For the next ninety minutes, it was me and a sergeant from the local Safer Neighbourhood police team against a Saturday Waitrose's worth of furious, well-to-do residents.

Meetings like these are not about answers, they're about questions. I would be halfway through addressing one angrily shouted question from the back of the room when somebody down the front would shout something else out, and I'd have to abandon that answer and start another one. Nobody got any worthwhile information out of me or the sergeant, but they got the chance to let everyone else know how cross they were.

It was exhausting – like playing verbal dodgeball. But the worst part of the evening was when Trigger from *Only Fools and Horses* insulted me. Roger Lloyd-Pack, the actor who played Trigger in the sitcom, was one of the local residents present that evening, and he said that both I and the sergeant were incompetent. Being called incompetent by Trigger. That's the kind of thing that stays with you.

Tonight's meeting was a breeze by comparison. I wasn't called an idiot by Father Dougal, and Baldrick didn't call for my resignation, so overall it went well.

9 September

Drinking at home has now been bolstered by drinking at lunchtime. Not every day, nothing excessive, maybe just a pint with lunch, but a drink nonetheless. Always somewhere away from the office, always somewhere away from the estates we manage. It's hardly *Leaving Las Vegas*, but the fact that I feel like I need it now and then is a worry.

10 September

Cases, cases, cases: well over sixty now. Where to begin? Which ones to deal with? Which ones are urgent? Which have resolved themselves?

A torrent: serious drug activity from my neighbour, threats from the family upstairs, property possibly used as a brothel, verbal threats, neighbour shooting up in the stairwell, drug dealing in the car park, smoking on the landing, constant loud parties, threatening behaviour, drug dealer with constant visitors, drug addict neighbour, urinating in the lift, racial harassment, neighbour with noisy kids, drug house next door, neighbour threatened me, bringing loud visitors to the block, noise nuisance from domestic violence, noisy neighbours, smoking weed on his front step, lads smoking weed in the stairwell, property raided, neighbour stole my bike, lads hanging around in the stairs, general noise nuisance, cannabis smell from neighbour, noisy neighbour, noisy neighbour, people climbing up scaffolding, drug den, verbal harassment, abuse from neighbour, drug dealer next door, property raided for drugs, neighbour intimidating me, assaulted by neighbour, crack house, verbally abused, gang fight in stairwell, homophobic abuse, drug users in block, loud parties in garden, drug dealer next door, verbal and physical abuse, cannabis smoker next door, attack with a screwdriver, noisy neighbour, cannabis smell, drug users in block, drug users in block, loud music and smell of skunk, cannabis dealer next door, noisy visitors, drug den, drug den, racial abuse, youths loitering, drug users in block, hate crime, rough sleepers in block, vandalism, drug den, neighbour smoking cannabis, drug users on stairwells, cannabis user, drug dealers in block, loud neighbour, religion-based harassment.

Every case is a small world of woe to untangle. People are complex and demanding and difficult. They all want help and to be reassured. Some of them might be lying, or at the very least exaggerating, and you can only find that out by patiently going through the evidence, or lack of evidence, to look for patterns and absences and inconsistencies.

A case that shouts at you might turn out to be a one-off incident that will never be repeated. A mundane case might suddenly flare up into threats and violence and necessary emergency assistance. Habitual liars suddenly start telling the truth. Reluctant neighbours suddenly decide they want to give a statement. Complicating factors like death and illness and financial setbacks and arrests will knock the trajectory of a case into a spin.

Which one is a big fuss about nothing? Which one will end up in court? Which of them are at home right now, crying because they've had enough? Which one is a public inquiry waiting to happen? Any idea? Because I haven't.

12 September

Back in May, Emma had fled her property after her abusive partner put her in hospital. That incident – when I believe-believed her – felt like a turning point at the time, and news I receive today proves that it was.

Emma is settled in her new place, located many miles away from where she used to live. It's a residential treatment centre to address her class A addiction of several decades. Her old home has been boarded up to stop her partner or any of his friends from using it as a shooting gallery. She has expressed no desire to return, either to her flat or her ex-partner.

She has finally achieved escape velocity and broken free of a relationship that would have killed her, either through violence or drugs, if it had carried on for much longer. Her tenancy in her old home can be ended, and once she has completed her drug treatment, she will be given a new place to live and a chance at a new start in life.

The system, when it works, can be a miraculous and joyous thing to behold. So can people's ability to surprise you by grabbing a second chance with both hands. Emma still has a long way to go, but the direction in which she's headed is one that holds the potential for happiness that would have seemed impossible a year ago.

Once I close a case, I usually don't get to see how the story ends, especially when that person moves away from the geographical area I manage. I'll never know how things will eventually play out for Emma, but I'm going to allow myself the indulgence of optimism.

Good luck, Emma.

14 September

Not a good day. Tim calls our team and says he has serious concerns for the wellbeing of his neighbour, as well as the wellbeing of his own kids. Tim's next door neighbour is Anne, who's in her seventies and lives with her son Alex. And Tim worries that if something isn't done soon, Alex is going to end up killing his mum.

Tim tells me that Anne can be heard pleading with Alex to leave her alone and to get out of the flat. This is usually accompanied by thuds and crashes, and Alex screaming abuse at his mum. Tim has tried to speak to Anne about it when he sees her in the communal stairwells or the nearby shops, but she always manages to deflect, change the subject or tell him she's too busy to talk.

Tim's kids are now scared to leave the flat in case Alex is there. They're old enough to understand the words Alex uses to insult his mother but not old enough to understand he probably won't attack them if he sees them. They dread having to go to bed at night as their bedroom is adjacent to Anne's living room, where most of the arguments take place.

Tim has called the police but by the time they arrive, Alex has scarpered or has convinced his mum to tell the officers that everything is fine. Alex is well known to the police, but unless he's doing something they can arrest him for when they arrive, or Anne confirms she wants to make a report, there's little they can do.

Tim has tried to get the neighbours involved, asking that they call the police themselves, or report the problem to our team. Even if Anne is too scared to say anything, if loads of people make a report to the authorities, surely they will have to do something. The neighbours don't want to, though, because they've all seen what Alex can be like when he kicks off and they don't want that monsoon of anger pointed their way, or at their own kids.

Tim has tried everything he can to help Anne, yet help hasn't seemed to be welcome. But now Anne is sitting in his living room, too scared to go home, and she has finally admitted there's a problem. There's a window of opportunity to speak to Anne, and it could close at any second.

I drop what I'm doing and make my way to the housing estate where Tim and Anne live. Walking through the red-brick 1930s-built blocks of flats, I'm struck by how calm the estate is. The kids are back at school; many of the residents are at work. The occasional noise of a car passing by or a brief snippet of music from an open window is all I can hear. Behind one of these windows, somebody's life is going unimaginably wrong, but down on the pavement calmness reigns.

Tim lets me in to his flat and in the living room is Anne, still wearing her coat, two bags of shopping at her feet. Her eyes are red-rimmed from crying, one of them sporting a fresh bruise. Her bare shins also show a multitude of bruises of varying ages, as if she's played a five-a-side tournament without shinpads. She looks tired and terrified, and on the verge of collapse.

Our team is lucky to have officers with a number of different strengths. Some people are really good at the methodical, process-driven work of drafting legal papers in preparation for court. Some are better at lateral thinking to explore new avenues for resolving cases. And some are exceptionally patient and empathetic, drawing out information from frightened people at a pace that they feel comfortable with. I do not consider myself to represent that last skillset. Maybe it's a male psychology thing but my natural tendency is to focus on solutions and get the ball rolling as soon as possible. But it's immediately apparent that Anne will need handling carefully or she'll withdraw, change her mind and go back home, and the abuse will continue.

On average, you can take a fairly comprehensive statement from a witness in about forty-five minutes. It's unlikely, past that point, that any further information can be gleaned and it's usually the limit of a person's patience. Anne's statement takes just shy of two hours. Every time her train of thought wanders off, I have to let it take its course before gradually getting us back on track. Two cups of tea and a toilet break are required. But we eventually get the story of what life has been like for Anne over the last few years.

Alex is addicted to both heroin and gambling. He came to both comparatively late in life, having previously been married with a decent job. When he was made redundant from that job in his late twenties, the decline started. He would gamble to try to make what little money he had go further. The phrase 'You'll never meet a broke bookmaker' will tell you what a prudent financial decision that was. The strain took its toll on the marriage, which ended soon afterwards.

Alex met the wrong old school friend on the wrong day at a perilously low point in his life, and when that friend offered him heroin, he made the wrong decision. And he had continued making that wrong decision several times a day for the last ten years. He moved back in with his mum. He was her only son. She wasn't going to see him out on the streets. If some deficiency in her parenting had caused his addiction, maybe she could make up for it now by giving him a place of safety.

Alex would disappear for days on end. This could be because he'd been arrested, or a bet had finally come in, or a successful bout of shoplifting had given him the funds to buy a decent quantity of drugs. She knew not to ask where he'd been, or why, because the answer would either be a blatant lie or a painful truth.

When his gambling, stealing or begging couldn't supply him with sufficient funds for heroin, he would look to his mum. When wheedling and begging didn't work, or when he ran out of lies as to why he needed the money, the threats would start. Then the slaps, the punches and the kicks. He would take whatever change she had in her purse – she had long ago learned not to take out any significant amount of money at any one time – and leave.

This information comes out in sudden bursts punctuated by long silences as Anne stares down at her hands. Shame: that is the overriding emotion I get from her. She is ashamed of the kind of person her son has become, but more, much more than that, she is ashamed of herself: for raising a son that could do such things, for allowing him to treat her this way, for not standing up to him. For having to tell a complete stranger all this.

The latest assault was too much. Anne is worried that he will end up really hurting her. I think of the bruises on her face and shins, as well as the crescent of purple semi-circles she showed me on her forearm where he'd grabbed her. The patch of missing hair on her scalp he'd yanked out. I try not to consider what 'really hurting her' would have to look like.

Anne is certain that she cannot report this to the police. She knows that she cannot face going through that, going to court and telling a judge what her only son has done to her, condemning him to even more time in prison.

I explain what we can do to help. I'll refer her to social services so somebody can visit her regularly and make sure she is doing all right. This alone takes a fair amount of sell-ing. (In a previous life I was a salesman, but I grew to loathe the job and the kind of colleague it could attract. While some ex-colleagues from that time are still very close friends of mine, I'll never forget the time somebody at the next desk closed a deal, stood up and shouted 'bish, bosh, lots of dosh' without a hint of irony.)

The experience has helped me in this job, though, by 'selling' people on the idea of getting help, or giving a state-ment, or closing a case. (I never say 'bish, bosh' though.) So I sell Anne on the idea of social services getting involved in her life and that it isn't a cause for embarrassment or shame.

Then I have to sell her on the idea of going to court with us – not to press criminal charges; I know she won't agree to that. But we can get an injunction to keep Alex away from her flat and from the entire block: to give her some peace and some safety, and to make her son realise he can't keep doing this. We have a long conversation about what will happen to him if he can't live with her any more. I tell her about the help that is out there for Alex if he just asks for it. She is just as concerned for his wellbeing as for her own. He is her only son.

Eventually, reluctantly, she agrees. Tim agrees to give us a supporting statement and we will apply for a without-notice injunction tomorrow, meaning her son will have to move out straight away. We will go back to court about a week later to get a full injunction to keep him away. We'll book a taxi for her for tomorrow morning and I will meet her at court. She can tell the judge why we need the injunction, and the court, faced with a woman covered in bruises and a patch of hair yanked out, will almost certainly agree.

Anne has managed to get this far without crying. Maybe it is relief, or realisation that things can't carry on the way they have been. I can't begin to imagine what is going through her mind.

I rush back to the office and send the paperwork to our legal team so we can be ready for court the next day. I call a minicab firm for a car for Anne and explain she might be a bit emotional. I get a statement from police confirming Alex's offences relating to drugs and violence. I go home, via the off-licence. Not a good day.

15 September

I arrive at court with copies of the legal bundle, just in case the court has misplaced what we sent it yesterday or our barrister has forgotten to bring it. There is no way I am letting this case be postponed for another day for something as basic as that.

The courts typically start hearing cases from 10am onwards. Given that a without-notice hearing is slotted in around the judge's existing caseload, it's very rare that you are called in at 10am, unless their first case of the day isn't going ahead. Nevertheless, I had ordered Anne's taxi to get her there in plenty of time. She hasn't arrived by 10am, so I call her number. No answer. With a lurching feeling in my stomach, I call the cab firm to see if she is on her way.

I speak to the minicab controller. He says the driver arrived at the block of flats at the time specified. He rang the intercom buzzer and a man answered. The driver said her car was waiting downstairs. The man explained the car wouldn't be needed now as they had sorted everything out. He then put Anne on to the intercom. She asked the driver to go away.

My heart bounces down to my knees and up against my throat. Without Anne present, the judge could easily refuse to grant the order. Alex had obviously talked – I really hope it had just involved talking – his mum into not going ahead with the injunction. Imagining how he had managed that makes me queasy.

I have to make a call as to whether to go ahead with the hearing or not. Anne might not want to proceed with the injunction. Going ahead against her wishes might actually increase the risk to her from her son. It might be that she wanted us to proceed, but was unable to get away from her son. God knows what threats he might have made to her before she asked that cab driver to go away.

I reason that we can still apply for the without-notice injunction. If Anne refuses to cooperate with proceedings, we still have the option of withdrawing the application at the return hearing. I would rather have an injunction for a week or so (the time between today's without-notice hearing and the return date) than none at all.

When we eventually have the case heard, the judge has reservations. I have been in front of this judge many times before, who has always taken the view that if something could be resolved via the criminal courts, then it should be theirs to deal with. As far as the judge is concerned, Anne's son should be arrested for assault and dealt with that way.

Nevertheless, the without-notice order is granted, with a power of arrest attached. Once served on Alex, if he is spotted in Anne's block he will be arrested on the spot.

I call our police team and ask them to meet me outside the block so we can go together to serve the order on Alex. I also ask for a social worker to be present to do an initial assessment with Anne. We meet a couple of hours later. Every one of us is very keen to meet Alex, serve the court order on him, then escort him out of the building. When we knock, Anne answers the door. I try to gauge whether she is glad to see us or not, but her expression doesn't betray any emotion. An officer accompanies her into the living room along with the social worker, so Anne doesn't have to be there as we kick her son out.

Alex is asleep in his bedroom, which is littered with burnt foil and betting slips. I explain who I am and why I am there, and that he has to gather his things and get out. I do so without making it clear what I think of him, which is as difficult a task as I've managed in this job. He tries to explain he has sorted things out with his mum and this isn't necessary, but I explain the court has made its decision and that, at least until the return date, this isn't up to him or his mum. 'Grab your things and get out.'

After he continues to prevaricate, the police officers intervene, telling him he has five minutes to gather his stuff before he is escorted from the premises. When he shouts for his mum to explain this isn't necessary, he is told this is irrelevant and he should pack it in. Once it becomes clear we won't be swayed, he stuffs a few items into a carrier bag, swearing under his breath, and is accompanied out of the block.

Police confirm they will do some welfare checks over the next few days to make sure he stays away. I have with me a pre-prepared letter for every resident in the block, explaining that Alex is banned from entering, and that they should call the police if they see him. Tim is thanked for his help, and he says he will keep an eye on Anne to see how she is getting on. It's hard to know what Anne thinks of all this. She is an injured, frightened woman, ashamed of how her son has treated her, and ashamed that it has come to the attention of the authorities. Alex has convinced her for so long that she needs him around to look after her – bruises and missing hair notwithstanding – that I think she is scared about what the future might look like.

Even now, professionalism forbids me from voicing an opinion on Alex. But you know the kind of things you say when you step barefoot onto an upturned plug? That.

19 September

I had an unusual problem with a complaint somebody made today. The property they were complaining about didn't exist. The complaint itself was fairly standard: noise from the neighbours above, shouting, doors being slammed late at night. Whenever I get a new complaint like that, I open our housing database to see if the people are our tenants or if the property has been bought and is owned by a leaseholder. It might give me an idea of how we are going to deal with the issue.

While I was speaking with the person making the complaint, I was scrolling back and forth across the property list screens to find the property in question, but it just wasn't there.

Obviously a glitch in the system, but it was tempting to close the case down because the people they were complaining about were clearly imaginary.

20 September

Representing a colleague at a disciplinary meeting. I've been a union rep for several years, after being asked to join by another union member in the organisation. I'd like to think this was because they thought that I was a trusted and respected member of staff, but in truth it was just as likely that I was asked because I am a gobby bastard with no career ambitions, so I don't mind being in the bad books of senior management.

I enjoy this side of work almost as much as my full-time

role, as it gives me the opportunity to use the same set of skills but on the other side of the fence. As an ASB officer, I'm usually trying to prove somebody did something bad and suggesting a suitable course of action as a result. As a union rep, you're usually working with your union member when they have fallen foul of either the workplace sickness policy or the disciplinary process.

I have come to notice the slight look of disappointment and annoyance on the face of a line manager whenever I walk into a disciplinary meeting with a union member, as they know that what should be a straightforward meeting is probably going to be a lot more difficult than they had hoped.

I treat it much the same as I would an ASB case. I will always meet with the union member ahead of the meeting to find out as much information as possible about what has led to the meeting we are about to go into. How many days have you had off sick? When were they? Were you offered any support when you returned to work? Do you have regular one-to-one meetings with your manager, like you're supposed to? Have they ever brought this issue to your attention before? And so on.

In the meeting itself, I'll make sure that company policy is followed scrupulously and that the union member is being given a fair hearing. If the problem is about performance, I'll want to know what chances they have had to improve their work, whether other team members are similarly struggling (and if so, are they being pulled up about it too?) and what evidence there is that standards aren't being met.

It seems that in most organisations, line managers are people who used to do the job of the people they're now managing and were good at it. This in no way prepares you for people management, which requires an entirely different set of skills. Boring skills like record-keeping and form-filling. Stuff that nobody wants to do. But it's stuff that they have to do if they're going to take action against a union member. They frequently haven't. I think they often drop their planned disciplinary action just to avoid reading the 2,000-word reports I regularly send them explaining why their case has no evidential value.

Today is no exception. Two of our horticultural staff – responsible for trimming hedges, mowing grass, trimming trees and the like on our estates – have been accused of verbally abusing a resident. If proven, they will lose their jobs. The resident in question is well known to every department of our organisation, but most of all to the people who collect service charges from our leaseholders. This leaseholder gets her bill every year and every year she quibbles about every penny she has been charged. She will regularly log a raft of complaints about poor cleaning of her block, ASB not being resolved properly, shoddy workmanship on estate improvements and poor behaviour of staff. The undercurrent is always that she will withdraw her complaint if we knock some money off her bill.

So this year, she has alleged that these two members of staff, with over thirty years of service in the organisation between them, were verbally abusive towards her. I was given the report the independent investigator had compiled and went through it at the disciplinary meeting. Some of the 'evidence' and recommendations included:

'1. It is possible the resident thought the officers were being rude to her because one of them has quite a grumpy-looking face.' I asked the investigator if they were genuinely considering sacking somebody for having resting bitch face?

'2. The incident, which included rude gestures, was witnessed by the resident's partner.' On further investigation, the partner in question 'witnessed' it fifteen miles away on the other end of a phone. I asked how it was possible that somebody could make a gesture that was so rude you could hear it?

'3. We recommend that the two officers are banned from entering the estate for any reason, even outside of work hours, and should not be allowed to associate with each other.' I asked the investigator if they had the number of a good human rights lawyer, because if they intended to enforce this kind of restriction on staff members, they were going to need one.

'4. The officers took photographs of the resident to mock her.' This was a new allegation, which the person I was representing had not previously been made aware of. One of the first things I say to somebody I'm representing is, 'Please don't lie to me. It won't help your case and if I find something out in the meeting that they have proof for, it could blow up in your face.'

This officer had assured me that he had never and would never be abusive towards residents, so I took a gamble. I asked whether he would be happy to show the investigator the pictures on his phone. He had no idea this allegation had been made, so he would have had no reason to delete any of the photos he was supposed to have taken.

He agreed and unlocked his phone. I scrolled through his photos to the date on which the incident was meant to have taken place, and sure enough, no photos of the kind alleged were on his phone. The investigator agreed and I handed the horticultural officer his phone back. I just hoped the investigator hadn't noticed the set of photos dated two days before the alleged incident, which showed my colleague had an enthusiasm for a very specific niche of pornography.[1]

---

1 If you're curious, Japanese women dressed as characters from *Star Trek*.

In any event, the allegations were found to be unproven and the officers were allowed to go back to work. If they'd had a more supine or less diligent union officer dealing with their case, or had no union representation at all, I genuinely believe they would have been sacked.

You insure your house, you insure your car, and some people even insure their health. Joining a union is insurance for your job. And most of the benefits you currently enjoy at work would not exist without union members in the past being the same kind of gobby and pedantic as I am. If this sounds like nakedly leftie recruitment sloganeering, that's because it is. Join a union.

26 September

Christophe is back to his old drug-dealing ways, I have been told. People living nearby and members of staff who have visited the block say he has been seen hanging around the main entrance door, doing handovers to people. He's apparently up and down the stairs a dozen times a day going to and from his flat, too.

Evidence of this, along with his previous conviction, would provide an overwhelming argument for having the whole family evicted. I get approval from my manager to have CCTV installed in the communal stairwell to see if it picks up any suspicious activity. Given how blatant his behaviour reportedly is, I'm sure something will show up.

The only other explanation is that his community service is saying hello to twenty to thirty crack addicts every day, which seems unlikely.

October

Password: Sleepless101

Medication: Mirtazapine 45mg,

Omeprazole 30mg, 60 units of alcohol

1 October

Site visit with the CCTV contractor to assess where the cameras can be installed to see whether Christophe is doing some kind of buns-of-steel stair-climbing challenge or has gone back to dealing drugs. As the ASB officer, I will say where the cameras need to cover and the contractor will say where they can practically be installed.

Camera technology has changed beyond recognition from when I first started the job. They used to be bulky units the size of your forearm that sat on pivot mounts as discreet as a teenager's slow-dance erection. Vandalising them was as easy as it was pointless, given how often they managed to break down of their own accord. The footage the cameras produced, on the rare occasions on which they actually worked, was often so poor that the only thing you could say with any certainty was that some form of mono-chrome biped had lurched into view at some point during the one-second jumps between frames. This could be the flytipper or drug dealer you'd been looking for, or it could be an orangutan dressed as Frank Sinatra tapdancing to a selection of hits by Lawnmower Deth.

In order to retrieve the footage, you had to go to the camera's location and retrieve the physical copy of the footage, thus advertising to anyone watching that the cameras were being monitored. Once back in the office, you then had to painstakingly slow-forward through the tape until a grey blob flashed onto the screen.

Before installing cameras, you'd ask residents to let you know when an incident occurred, but often the timescale you were given would be 'The stairs were clean when I came home from work at 6pm and when I left for work at 8am the following morning, there were needles and piss every-where.' Just the fourteen hours to review, then.

Modern CCTV equipment does give me the opportunity to feel a little bit James Bond (especially given that I have alcohol dependency issues, I'm from Merseyside like Daniel Craig and, like Daniel Craig, it's clear I'd rather not be here). New cameras can produce twenty-four frames per second full-colour footage with audio, and are so tiny they can be hidden inside existing light fittings and electrical ducting. I have visited sites where cameras have been installed, having seen some footage they produced, and have still been unable to work out where they are.

The new cameras can be accessed remotely from any location via an app on your phone, meaning if somebody calls up and tells you there's an incident taking place right now, you can see live footage of what's happening in a stairwell several miles away while you're sitting at your desk eating a sandwich, although given the kind of things people tend to report happening, you might not want to be eating while you watch it. The app can pick out activity from the footage, so instead of scrolling through hours of dead footage, you can go directly to the highlighted parts of the activity bar to see what has been picked up (usually somebody coming back from the pub or the postie).

It's not perfect. No matter where you install the cameras, you can guarantee something important will happen just out of shot. You cannot cover every square foot of your housing estate, both because it would be financially prohibitive and because it would be a gross abuse of people's right to privacy. But Christophe doesn't strike me as a criminal mastermind, so I'm confident that if he is misbehaving, the CCTV will capture it.

3 October

Training day. It has been decided that we might benefit from some time management training so we can better plan out our days. I spend the training thinking about my case workload and wondering how my time might be better spent focussing on that than on whatever group exercise our trainer is asking us to do now. I'm aware that I might be missing the point of the training somewhat.

7 October

The officers that take our team's incoming calls are on their training course today, so I'm one of the ASB officers that has been asked to cover the phones while they're away. In a way, this is a throwback to how I first started doing this job.

I graduated from university with a degree in English literature and philosophy. While I found the subjects largely fascinating (apart from semiotics, a topic enjoyed solely by the kind of perverts and lunatics who would rather dissect a hummingbird than watch one in flight), I was aware it would have very little practical application unless there were people out there who would pay for me to come to their homes and tell them how Descartes influenced the role of the narrator in the novel. This meant looking for whichever job would pay the rent, as I wasn't born into the class that thought of work as a career and could afford to keep failing until the right thing came along.

Following the soul-destroying sales jobs, and while working in the warehouse, I saw a job advert to work in the call centre of an RSL answering the phones. The job required you to be able to answer any question asked of you, or if you couldn't, to know who to pass that question on to. The training was extensive to a degree I'm fairly sure would no longer be deemed practical, as we spent nearly a month learning about all the various aspects of social housing, visiting the housing estates we managed, and listening in to calls, before we were let loose on the residents ourselves.

I quickly found that I actually quite liked helping people. I even enjoyed dealing with the obnoxious ones, as it was a challenge to see if you could get somebody who started a phone call by screaming abuse at you to end their call by thanking you.

You got to know your repeat callers and the ones that no amount of soft skills would win around. The most infamous was Mick, a man whose perpetually shitfaced state flew in the face of all medical logic, as he was never just a bit drunk, nor was he ever incoherently arseholed. Whether he called at 9am or 5pm, he would consistently be the level of drunk where you're able to string words together, but you do so to order a kebab. In many ways, he embodied the Aristotelian concept of perfect balance known as the 'Golden Mean' that I'd studied a few years earlier, although Mick would probably think that was a brand of lager.

The call centre had a rule that it would accept incoming calls until 5pm on the dot, at which point the line switched over to an answerphone message, but anyone in the call queue had to have their call dealt with, no matter how long that took – a bit like election night, when you're still allowed to vote if you've joined the queue before 10pm. One of their other rules was that you could issue two warnings to callers who swore at you, and you were allowed to hang up on them if there was a third outburst of pottymouth.

Both of these rules came into play one Friday at 5.01pm when I grudgingly took one of the three outstanding calls and found Mick on the other end of the line. Mick had a number of things he wanted to talk about, it became clear, as my colleagues started putting their coats on and making the universally recognised gesture – eyebrows raised, slight nod, cupped hand shaken near the mouth – of going for a pint.

Pointing at my headset and rolling my eyes in reply, I persevered with Mick. The average call with Mick could take more than half an hour as he pinballed his way from one perceived grievance with his landlord to the next. I knew that I couldn't be criticised for being scrupulously polite and professional towards him, so I became so polite and professional that he got annoyed.

Rather than letting him ramble on about whatever came into his head, I asked if we could focus on why he had called. This frustrated him to the point that he called me a cunt. I begged his pardon and asked him to repeat what he'd just called me, so he called me it again. Two strikes. I warned him that I wasn't there to be sworn at and that I would rather he mediated his language in the future.

'WHO THE FUCK ARE YOU FUCKING TELL-ING TO MEDI—'

click

I was out of the building by 5.15pm.

9 October

Injunction breach hearing. This wasn't one of my cases but, given that injunction breaches have to be heard by a judge within twenty-four hours of the arrest, whichever officer is available from our team will attend the hearing to instruct counsel. We do it so often that we now have the process down to a fine art and can be out of the door and en route to court within twenty minutes of being notified.

I print off three copies of the injunction, the power of arrest document, the certificate of service and the schedule of previous breaches, and I'm ready to go. The bundle of papers for this case is relatively slim, maybe no more than thirty pages. However, one of the things about the legal process that isn't often discussed is what an ecological disaster it is due to the sheer weight of paper involved.

At the other end of the scale, what follows is a perfectly possible size of legal bundle for a full hearing. I've had complaints about a particular property: I've taken statements from witnesses, invited the guilty party in for an interview, statemented them, and sent them a written warning, including a typed version of the statement they gave – that's about forty pages of evidence. The problems have continued or worsened, I've received more complaints, I've asked for supporting information from the police, I've made contact with support services (mental health, social services) to see if the perpetrator is known to anyone – add about another forty pages. We decide to get an injunction out against the person to stop the nuisance, so I write a lead statement and send instructions to our legal team, and they make an application for a court date, and they then notify the person in writing that we're taking them to court – that's another thirty pages. The injunction hearing goes ahead, is granted and served on the perpetrator; assuming there have been no adjournments (which can add as little as a further twenty pages, but as many as a hundred per adjournment, depending on what additional evidence either party decides to adduce), that's another forty pages.

The injunction doesn't solve the problem: we take more statements from witnesses to prove this, as well as an up-to-date police statement; we fill in all the necessary paperwork for a PPCO, have the consultation meeting and make a court application – at least another eighty pages. The PPCO is granted: we use this and the fact that the injunction was breached as grounds to go for mandatory possession against the property, we serve the notice on the perpetrator, they appeal the decision (with supporting documents for their appeal), an appeal hearing is convened, the appeal is unsuccessful, the perpetrator is notified of this decision in writing and we apply to court for possession of the property – that just added another sixty-ish pages.

When we turn up at court for the possession hearing, our legal bundle will need to contain all of the above, as well as an overarching ASB officer statement, telling the whole story from soup to cheeseboard so the judge doesn't have to read the whole thing. I've erred on the side of caution when estimating the number of pages for the above but it's safe to assume your legal bundle will be at least 300 pages long. Oh, and because you can never assume the court received a copy, the defendant brought theirs or your own barrister will have one, you need to print three copies.

Actually, any witnesses you call to the stand will need one in front of them to refer to during their own statement. Best make that four.

Twelve hundred pages of unrecycled paper for a single hearing. The court will not want to keep any of them, which is understandable given the number of cases they hear every day (by way of example, our local court building has about a dozen courts, with each judge in each court hearing anywhere between one large case and a dozen smaller cases per day). Trying to get the court to dispose of your court bundles is like trying to get somebody to look after your pet wolverine while you're on holiday. So you'll be taking them away to dispose of yourself, hopefully via recycling and definitely once they've been shredded, because they contain incredibly sensitive information.

It's monumentally wasteful, especially given that in the majority of cases everyone does remember to bring their own copies, so you've printed out half a tree for no reason. In a modern criminal justice system, a single bundle could be uploaded to a central, secure cloud server and accessed confidentially by the parties involved, and access during the court hearing could be done via tablet computers. But given the fact that we have a criminal justice system that is underfunded to the point of criminal negligence, that may be trying to sprint before we can even crawl. Right now I'd settle for waiting less than six months for a bailiff to execute an eviction warrant.

But anyway, back to our injunction breach. It is a fairly standard case for our team. A rough sleeper has been using the communal parts of our tower blocks to sleep, use as a toilet and inject heroin. She was offered drug treatment and refused, and so she was warned that we would get an injunction against her if we kept finding her blocking the stairwells of our properties. She kept getting found there, so we took her to court.

The injunction was granted a couple of months ago and she has subsequently breached it twice. On each occasion, she admitted the breach and the judge gave her a suspended prison sentence, with the last judge issuing a dire warning that the next time she breached the order she should expect to actually serve the sentences she had been given.

I arrive at court and head straight to the gents' toilet to dry off. Outside, the wind has whipped icy rain horizontally into my face and I'm drenched. I check in with our defendant and she seems in good spirits, holding a cup of vending machine tea and chatting to the custody officers. By her feet is a small rucksack containing her belongings. The police officers confirm she insisted on bringing it with her when she was arrested, as it would be stolen or discarded if she left it behind.

After a short wait, we're called in to court. The rain pelts against the rattling windows of the small room as we wait for the judge to appear. Once the formalities of why we are here, when the injunction was issued and so on are out of the way, the judge – whom I've been in front of many times, and who always shows a kindness and patience towards defendants who may not know the way proceedings work – addresses the defendant, asking if she knows why she's here.

'Yes, miss. I got an injunction and I wasn't meant to be where I was so they arrested me.'

'Now, I don't want you to incriminate yourself. First I have to ask whether you want to deny what they have said you've done. You have a right to, you know. If you do, you have a right to get legal representation and they—'

'No, miss, that's fine. I don't need a lawyer. I did what they said, I was in a block I wasn't meant to go in.'

'I need to make sure you're OK for us to proceed. I see here you've breached the order twice so if you're found guilty today, there's a risk you might go to prison.'

She hooks her rucksack with her foot and pulls it closer to her chair. 'I know that, miss, that's OK.'

The details of her arrest are confirmed by a police officer and the breach is deemed proven, especially because the accused is sitting there repeatedly confirming it happened. All that's left is the sentencing decision.

Judges are given guidelines on sentencing for breach of injunction, with aggravating and mitigating factors banded together into differing categories of importance and seriousness to form a matrix which gives a starting point and sentencing range, depending on where the breach falls (for instance, a first-time breach with no related violence or abuse will fall on one corner of the matrix, with a ninth breach that involved violence, racial abuse and risk of re-offending right at the other) – the idea being that it offers a more consistent approach to sentencing.

The judge reiterates that this is the third breach of the injunction and the defendant has two outstanding suspended sentences on her record. One hand on the strap of her rucksack, the defendant nods along and says she understands. The judge decides that prison is not the answer to the defendant's problems, and that, while the breach has been proven, no further order will be made (i.e. no more prison time added and her suspended sentences will not be activated). She recommends that the defendant abides by the injunction in the future.

The defendant looks crestfallen. Already a frail figure, she falls in on herself, seeming to dissolve into her chair.

'But, I thought I'd be going inside. I brought my bag.' She lifts it so the judge can see, in case that might make a difference.

'No, no. You're free to go.'

The defendant is taken back to the custody room where she'll be formally released and allowed to leave the court building, which sits several miles from where she was arrested.

I walk out into October, my face slowly numbing in the cold, back to the office, to carry on where I left off.

10 October

An update on Candice, whom I've not heard from since January. Her mental health worker tells me she has been taking her medication, has reconsidered her dream of becoming the world's oldest debutant jockey and has managed not to throw anything – not even a dirty look – at her neighbours for months. Hurrah.

11 October

Another day in court because Iain, he of the vicar-bothering and former-colleague-harassing, is, to use a less than legally exact phrase, back on his bullshit. The allegation is that he entered the council building he's banned from, for reasons unknown. What is known is the precise date and time he did this, because the whole thing has been captured on CCTV. Ahead of the trial, I went through the laborious process of obtaining the footage from the people who manage the building. They refused to give it directly to me without a formal request from the police, so I forwarded the request email to our police team, who then emailed the building controller basically saying, 'We'd like what Nick asked for below, please', and had the footage burned onto disc.

Any evidence that doesn't involve a piece of paper or a person saying things is always fraught with danger as you are relying on technology working in a particular environment on a particular day. You only use audio or video evidence when, in cases like this, it's the difference between proving your case or not. I had to rush to get the evidence together so I don't actually watch the footage I'm assured shows Iain entering the lobby area of the building until I'm in a side room with our barrister on the day of the hearing. I switch on the laptop I brought from the office (expecting the court to have functioning air conditioning is wildly optimistic, so there was no way I was going to assume they had a laptop we could use) and scroll the footage to the alleged time of the incident. I have been expecting, and have tried to avoid, IT issues. What I haven't expected is that when I look at the footage, it isn't Iain.

I can't quite make out the face of the man in the footage, but what I can say is that he's about four inches shorter, ten years balder and three stone heavier than how

I remember Iain looking. My barrister asks how sure I am. I tell him that unless he's stepped into a transporter along with Danny DeVito and had his genes spliced in the last eight months, I'm pretty sure it's not him.

When Iain arrives, I'm even more convinced the guy in the footage is somebody else, so we start trying to work out what our approach is going to be. It's possible that if he can't remember exactly what he was doing at that time and on that date, we can sow enough doubt in the judge's mind that it could possibly have been him. I meet Iain in the waiting room and ask if he wants to watch the footage on my laptop to confirm whether it's him or not.

'No, there's no need, I've seen the footage and it is me,' he replies.

Pause. Blink. Side glance at barrister. I knew the camera added ten pounds but I didn't know it squished you and shaved your head. Still, if he says it's him, it must be him.

'Oh. Right. Yes. Of course. So you'll be admitting to the breach, then?'

'Yes, but I had a good reason to be there.'

His 'good reason' for being there forms the central pillar of his defence once we get before the judge. Iain states he was given a letter from his former employer asking that he hand back to the company the photo ID issued when he worked there. We've never been given a copy of this letter, as he's never entered it into his defence and has issued a copy neither to the courts nor to our legal team. He's allowed to rely on this letter because it's fair to say his story has one or two holes in it, amongst them being: one, he claimed the letter was hand-delivered to him by somebody who didn't give him their details, which would never happen; and two, he could only produce a photocopy of the original letter, claiming to have lost the actual letter.

The letter wasn't dated or signed, and had no name of sender at the bottom. It wasn't on headed paper. It was riddled with spelling mistakes. The address of the sender was in several different fonts. The department the letter was supposedly sent from doesn't deal with photo ID issues. The council wouldn't ask for an ID back several years after somebody had been fired. If they did, they would ask him to post it back, not go into a building he's banned from entering.

The barrister puts all these points to Iain, finally suggesting to him that the letter is a complete fabrication, concocted by him as an excuse to visit the building. He strenuously denies this.

The judge is inclined to agree with our barrister and deems the injunction to have been breached. A few more weeks of suspended prison are added to his record, along with a stern warning to stop with his bullshit (this may have been expressed more formally).

14 October

More training, this time on anti-terrorism measures. We are being trained to look out for early signs of radicalisation amongst our residents, as well as potential red-flag behaviours such as leaving empty 100kg bags of fertiliser outside your ninth-story flat that doesn't even have a window box, or somebody muttering into their sleeve while standing near a tourist landmark. Much of it is sensible advice, and it makes sense for people doing a job like ours to be keeping an eye open. Most front-line services will receive similar training, and if it helps stop an atrocity, it will have been worthwhile.

One statistic that comes out of the training echoes what I and other ASB officers are seeing with increasing frequency: racist attacks are rapidly on the rise. The police officer delivering the training states that in the years to come, white nationalist terrorism will completely overshadow that committed by the likes of ISIS, and that anti-terrorism policing will have to radically change its focus to try and keep up. Quite how the media and government are going to demonise a section of society that isn't brown and looks exactly like 82 per cent of the population in order to sell papers or win votes is anybody's guess.

16 October

Meeting with Anna, a drug outreach worker at the nearby hospital. One of her clients, Ray, says he's having problems with some teenagers that hang around on his estate. I've never had any dealings with Ray previously, so I agree to meet with Anna to go over what the situation is ahead of Ray's arrival.

She tells me that Ray is a sort of former heroin user, inasmuch as he sticks to his methadone prescription but occasionally falls off the opiate wagon when the mood takes him. Ray, she says, is being harassed by a bunch of lads in their late teens and early twenties who sit in the stairwell of his block of flats to hang out. They've taken to insulting and threatening Ray when they're hanging around the place, sometimes demanding money from him to buy weed. Ray has a history of mental illness and this situation is not helping with his desire to stick to a mostly-methadone life. We discuss a broad plan of action based on what he tells me and how much he's willing to engage.

When Ray arrives, I briefly think there's been a power cut as he literally blocks out all the light in the room. To call him enormous would do a disservice to the word. He looks like somebody dressed a wardrobe up as the Honey Monster. When he sits in a chair opposite me I expect it to shatter into matchsticks as if in a cartoon. But when he starts speaking, it's clear that somewhere in the middle of this behemoth is somebody whose mental state is like a fractured china teacup. He delivers the subterranean bass of his voice downward to his clenched hands, avoiding eye contact. At first glance, he looks as if he could pull your average crack user inside out like somebody shelling pistachio nuts, but speaking with him, it's clear how easy a target he could be for somebody able to spot his weaknesses.

When I ask him to talk about what's been happening, he answers in monosyllables that I frequently have to ask him to repeat, because his struggle to express himself causes him to mutter and cut himself off mid-word.

'How long has it been happening, Ray?'

'It's. Dunno. Umm. Months. Maybe Ju . . . months.'

'Can you describe what the main lad who gives you abuse looks like?'

Shrug. 'Small. He's, like.' Shrug, pause. 'Little guy.'

We talk in general terms about how he can report harassment if he wants to, what we'll do with that information, and what we can and can't reasonably do to help him. At this stage there's no point in trying to pin him down to specifics as the strain of even admitting it's happening seems almost too much for him to bear.

He thanks me and Anna, ducking under the door frame

on his way out. Anna says she will keep an eye out for him which, I refrain from pointing out, won't be too difficult.

18 October

I'm pulled aside for a quiet word. Apparently, it's become evident that I am less than a rollicking bundle of joy in the office. Tell-tale signs have become gradually more noticeable. These have included drinking more coffee than an AA meeting, ending phone calls to other departments by putting down the receiver and muttering 'Oh, fuck *off*, why can't you?' to myself, and on one occasion loudly calling my computer monitor a stupid prick.

I'm asked if there's anything that can be done to help. I've no idea where to begin, so I just say no and go back to my desk.

19 October

Following the joint meeting back in August, I visit Sally's block of flats, along with a colleague, to see if anyone else has been affected by her flat hosting more drug addicts than backstage at Glastonbury for the last few months.

Starting at the top floor and working our way downwards, we end up speaking to almost fifteen of the block's seventy households, which is a remarkably high percentage. Normally during a door-knock on a block of flats on a weekday during work hours, you're lucky to find one in ten of the properties occupied, and often the people who are in have no idea what you're talking about.

Not so with Sally's neighbours, who all have varying tales of woe about living in the same building as her. It looks as if we should have enough impact statements from her neighbours to go for the partial premises closure that the meeting agreed was the next step. As we're finishing up, I notice Sally walking towards a group of three late-teen lads sitting on a low wall next to her block of flats. A brief exchange takes place, with her money going into the pocket of one of the lads and whatever she just bought going into her mouth, lodged between her gum and cheek so it can quickly be swallowed if a waiting copper leaps out of a bush during the thirty-yard walk from the dealers to the main entrance door to the flats. She goes inside and into her flat. Shortly afterwards, a crack addict straight out of central casting arrives.

Another entirely useless skill the job has taught me is being able to work out what an addict's drug of choice is from a distance. A combination of gait, complexion and general appearance can usually steer you towards which is their main poison (it's rare that people in the grip of addiction show loyalty to one drug over all the others; whatever oblivion is on offer will usually be gladly accepted). It's like being the guy at the fairground who used to guess people's weight, only I'm able to guess what's going to eventually kill somebody.

Two things alert me to the possibility that the woman standing outside Sally's block might be a fellow crack addict. The hawk-like, hurried body language, graveyard of missing teeth and the clothes hanging off a skeletal frame are one set of clues. The fact she bellows, 'SALLY! SALLY! OPEN THE FUCKING DOOR!' at the top of her voice is another. She is soon buzzed inside and I watch as she makes her way into Sally's flat.

There's no evidence like direct evidence, so alongside the numerous neighbour statements, I write a statement of what I've witnessed myself.

20 October

Our office has a cat, called Bob. Not officially, of course, but the cat lovers of the office (me being one of them) noticed a few months ago that there was a big bruiser of a tabby cat that hung around the car park outside where we worked. He had battle-scarred ears like clipped train tickets and knackers the size of walnuts, and was clearly used to fending for himself out on the streets.

Before long he had his own food bowl, box of biscuits and supply of wet food that would be employed whenever he came around. Bob didn't take long to realise he'd found a building full of easy marks, and these visits became an almost daily occurrence. None of us liked the thought of him rooting through bins to keep himself fed, so we gladly kept him in Felix in exchange for the few seconds of begrudging head scratches he'd allow us while he ate.

To begin with, Bob felt he had to song-and-dance a little to get our attention for food, plaintively meowing to show us how hungry he was. Not any more. Now, he just plonks himself down immediately outside the main door, not budging when people need to get past him, knowing that food will soon be on its way.

Today, I walked past a corner shop a few hundred yards from the office. Outside was Bob, tucking into a bowl of cat food. I asked the shopkeeper whether Bob was hers. 'No,' she said. 'But he's a stray and this must be the only food he gets, the poor thing.' Bob looked up from his food, stared right through me, and carried on wolfing down the tuna and prawn.

A team full of ASB officers who like to think they know a con story when they see one, fooled by a cat. (Of course we keep on feeding him.)

27 October

Listening exercise. Household noise nuisance is often, more than drug dealing, violent confrontations or prolonged harassment, the hardest kind of case to resolve. Broadly speaking, household noise nuisance is a way to describe everyday living done at an unreasonable volume: slamming doors, dropping objects onto laminate floors, scraping furniture, shouting and so on. Unless the noise is loud, blaring music, it's unlikely to be affecting anyone other than the person living below. By the nature of this kind of noise, it's unlikely to happen for a prolonged enough period to get an officer out to independently witness it. Contrary to popular belief, recording audio of the alleged noise is of little use. Without knowing what context the noise was made in, it's just as possible the person complaining got their mate to go into the next room and rattle the door to get their neighbour into trouble (and the job has taught me that this level of pettiness is not only possible but also fairly common).

It's very difficult to establish that the noise is even happening. When you have one person saying the neighbour upstairs is being noisy, and the person upstairs says they're not, that doesn't leave an awful lot of evidential leads to follow. People will often claim they have 'independent' witnesses to the noise, who turn out to be relatives or close friends. This is independent evidence in the same way that asking your spouse if they think you're looking fat is independent evidence of how much you weigh.

Complainants will often say the person allegedly making the noise is doing so deliberately to annoy them, and over a period of time it can lead to people living in a constant state of alertness. They will sit in silence, TV turned down to a whisper, waiting for the next bump or scrape from the neighbour, seizing on the slightest noise as evidence of their unreasonable lifestyle. Often, the case then morphs into a harassment investigation, as the supposedly noisy person alleges the person below is making complaints just to harass them.

I had one case many years ago where the 'noisy' tenant said she was at the end of her tether. She'd paid for expensive carpets throughout her flat, wore headphones to watch TV and never wore shoes indoors, but the guy downstairs kept banging on his ceiling, hurling abuse upwards at her.

She told me this during a visit I paid her in her flat one afternoon. 'See for yourself,' she said. 'Walk to the kitchen and back and see what happens.' I was halfway back from the kitchen, having stepped lightly along the way, when thumping could be heard from below and a voice muffled by the despairing woman's inch-thick carpet shouted, 'Fucking noisy bitch.' The case was closed and the man making the complaints was politely told to wind his neck in.

But today, I'm in a flat, about to close a door. This is what over a decade of experience has trained me to do. A colleague's entrenched noise case has led us to try a listening exercise. Soundproofing regulations and technology are so bafflingly irregular, we can't always be sure that what sounds noisy below isn't just somebody acting normally above. Buildings that passed soundproofing standards fifty years ago are unlikely to meet today's standards, and alterations to buildings can adversely affect it.

So you have an ASB officer downstairs with the aggrieved party, and one upstairs with the alleged noise-maker. In the upstairs flat you do normal things – walk across the floor in shoes, drop a small object onto the floor, close a door – and the colleague listens downstairs to see if it seems unduly loud. You then repeat the actions, but do them all deliberately noisily. Then you swap flats and do it all over again, so there's no room for subjective error. It's precisely as enjoyable as I've just made it sound.

Having completed the actions in the 'noisy' flat above, it was my turn downstairs with the complainant – always the less fun half of the process, as they're always poised, waiting for the slightest decibel. I told our aggrieved tenant that I assumed she didn't live her life standing in her hallway with the TV off, so this might not be the most reasonable of tests. She demurred, turning on a radio to the same volume as a mouse pissing on blotting paper, and we waited for my colleague to complete the actions, first normally, then loudly.

Time passed. The sound of traffic continued outside. Somewhere in the distance, a sparrow coughed politely under its wing. Nothing. I phoned my colleague and asked when they were going to start door closing and so on.

'I already have. Twice.'

I waited for her to come downstairs before leaving. I didn't especially want to be there when our complainant, who had been hounded by an incessant din from upstairs for months, was told she was making it all up.

28 October

Since the cameras were installed into Bushey House, there have been no further complaints from the residents to suggest Christophe's business is still up and running. Occasional police patrols to the area haven't stopped anyone and caretaking staff are not reporting the usual litter associated with drug dealers working in the stairwell. The cameras cover the bottom stairwell and main entrance door to the block. I haven't proactively monitored the footage since the cameras went in. It's a busy block with lots of families with children, so there will be people coming and going all the time.

My concern is that Christophe, or one of his associates, saw the contractors installing the equipment and has been scared off. The people doing the installation don't wear uniforms announcing why they're there, and if anyone asks what they're doing they know to say it's just scheduled electrical maintenance. Even so, if Christophe et al. know they're being watched, that might explain why everything has gone quiet. I pick a day at random and sit down to scroll through the footage to see if it offers any clues.

What it shows me is that Christophe is not only still a drug dealer, he is also still an exceptionally stupid one. As with every set of cameras we install, we have to put up signs warning people that they are entering an area in which they may be filmed. The signs themselves are about two feet high by one foot wide and dayglo yellow. For this installation, we placed four signs in total, two outside the entrance door, one on the stairwell and one on the wall inside the block immediately next to the entrance door.

It's this last one which is clearly visible on one of the two cameras we fitted. Starting from 6am, I watch a procession of people walk past it on their way out to work or to school. A postie comes and goes. There's the caretaker cleaning the stairs, whistling to himself.

10am: hang on, there's Christophe, jogging down the stairs barefoot, wearing a Manchester United dressing gown. He opens the entrance door and gestures to somebody out of shot. He lets them into the block – their scrawny, soiled hoodie covering their face; scabbed hands – and he counts out a dozen items too small to discern into their palms. They leave the block and Christophe walks back upstairs. At one point, his face is perfectly framed by the camera hidden in the electrical ducting.

11.15pm: Christophe is back again, dressing gown flapping as he jogs down the stairs. He lets his friend back in and they tip two hoodie pockets full of loose change into Christophe's hands. Heroin addicts don't tend to buy their fix from a street dealer using a £50 note. Christophe restocks his runner, who goes back out to make him more money. This process is repeated several times more throughout the day.

I check the footage for a few more days either side of the one I picked, and sure enough the story is pretty much the same. He seems to have three or four runners working for him. There's one occasion when he gets them all into the lobby next to the entrance door to give them all a pep talk. 'You can't fuck about doing this, yeah? This is a proper job. You don't wanna do it, fuck you, I'll get somebody who will.' He's clearly missed his vocation as a line manager.

Christophe's arrest and conviction were as a result of him dealing on street corners himself. By graduating one step up the ladder to having people out there selling for him, he probably feels he's insured himself against further arrest. If they get picked up by police, he'll just drop them like a sack of wet washing and find somebody else to deal for him, and if they drop him in it, he'll pay somebody to break their hands so they can't shoot up for weeks.

All of this is, if drug-dealing is how you make your living, the smart thing to do and part of your standard career progression. It's a well-thought-out plan that has every chance of working. But not if you do it all while you're being filmed and you're standing right next to a two-foot-high dayglo yellow sign telling you that you're on camera. I choose a selection of illustrative clips and forward them to our police team to see if it piques their interest.

31 October

I was late for work today because I spent half an hour sitting on the edge of my bed having a bit of a cry. By the time I get to work this is changed to 'overslept' – the irony being that I haven't had a full night's sleep in months.

November

Password: Lotterywin101

Medication: Mirtazapine 45mg,

Omeprazole 30mg, 75 units of alcohol

1 November

Our management has decided that our team needs to publicise the good work it does a bit more, and should do so in a forward-looking, twenty-first-century type of way, so they have generated a Twitter account for us all to use.

Everyone on our team views Facebook as impenetrably futuristic, so the idea of using Twitter will take some getting used to. We even have a quick training session on how to log into the account, how to send a tweet, and the perils of liking a tweet sent by an account with a name like MAGA4EVERSOROSNEVA4277265.

The trainer asks if anybody has any experience using Twitter. I've been on the site for nearly a decade and have a few followers. I think about my recent tweets, which have compared the prime minister to a water bed full of evil porridge, suggested a pop singer looks like an orc's dad, and generally used language fruitier than a pint of Beaujolais Nouveau served in a hollowed-out melon.

'Nope,' I say. 'Never heard of it.'

4 November

An update meeting with social services. A few months ago I received a noise nuisance report. The complainant said his neighbours were always shouting and screaming at each other, and he could hear items being thrown around the place and doors being slammed. This was often accompanied by a brace of large dogs, who lived in the two-bedroom flat on the fourth floor, barking loudly.

In addition to this, he could hear the adult woman of the household shouting abuse at the young girl who lived there. He said the woman was the girl's stepmother. She would frequently call the girl a 'fucking idiot', say she was 'fucking useless' and chide her for getting things wrong. The girl in question was ten.

As well as gathering evidence on the noise nuisance, I contacted social services, given that the situation brought up more red flags than a Communist birthday party. We had worked together to speak to the family first about the noise and then about what we could do to help them with the flat, which was in a dilapidated state.

Perfectly sane people who can function in everyday life and appear otherwise rational can live in the most squalid conditions imaginable, with hoarding being the most commonly known iteration of this. One hoarder, Niall, who lived on my estate years ago, was completely undetectable to the outside world. Every day he left his home dressed in a suit and worked in an office doing a responsible job, and every day he came home to a flat in which he could barely move. His bedroom was stuffed floor to ceiling with unpacked bedroom furniture still in its wrapping, along with multipacks of kitchen roll and various cleaning products. He also had stacks of newspapers and magazines, often with dozens of copies of the same edition. Every other room was similarly full, meaning his kitchen was unusable, and only the sink and toilet were accessible in the bathroom, the bath being used to store dozens of unwrapped bath towels and packs of shower gel. He lived on takeaway food, the wrappers of which were waist-high in his living room. He slept on one half of his sofa, the other half buried under a mountain of God knows what. The hallways were also crammed with stuff, and you could only walk between rooms by shuffling sideways between precarious stacks of garbage.

The way we deal with hoarders has changed significantly over the years. The solution used to be threats via the court or tenancy action, and attempts to forcibly dump the accumulated rubbish into skips, which is both legally and practically unenforceable. A box full of out-of-date bottles of ketchup might seem like junk to you, but it's still a possession to the person who hoarded it, and you can't just go into a person's home and throw out their stuff. If some git from the council entered your house by force and threw out your collection of Penguin first edition paperbacks or novelty fridge magnets, you would want to sue them into next year. Hard as it is to believe, the hoarder may view that ketchup with a similar level of attachment and may feel equally as motivated to sue you.

The reason that clearing out a flat is practically unenforceable is that it does nothing to address the underlying issues of which hoarding is an outward manifestation. Modern thinking believes that hoarding is a form of OCD and should be treated in the same manner. Niall's wife had left him some time ago and he found it difficult to clear the flat of her belongings. This led to him struggling to clear out his own rubbish. He then bought stuff to address the clutter. Then more stuff. Then buying multiple boxes of the same stuff became normal. Before he knew it, his home had gone beyond the point at which he felt he could deal with it.

Our approach to dealing with Niall was to start slowly: clear enough stuff so he could access the bath (he'd been using his work shower exclusively for months). Then maybe we would focus on the perishable stuff in the rooms, cleaning down a designated section of one room. This could eventually progress to keeping a whole room clear. It took months, but he eventually got his flat back to normal and, to my knowledge, he kept it that way afterwards.

Our noisy family had a home that had got away from them, but they didn't hoard. Instead, the place was so ingrained with filth it was impossible to see what colour the kitchen floor was meant to be or whether the carpet had a pattern or not. On top of this, the whole place was infested with fleas from their two large dogs, whose faeces sat in dried piles in the corners of the rooms. The school had noticed the young girl's unkempt state and flea bites, and had also voiced their concerns to social services.

As with Niall, we had to use baby steps to deal with the issue. Social services would refer the parents to counselling to deal with how they dealt with anger. Environmental services would treat the entire home for the fleas. At some point I would have to tell them that the dogs would have to go, but I knew that would spook them into withdrawing cooperation. They agreed with social services that they would clean one room per week. If the kitchen was clean enough to inspect, I would look into whether I could get some new units fitted to replace the current kitchen cupboards, which were millimetres thick in grease and all missing their doors. It seemed to be going well. The complaints of noise nuisance dwindled, and both the daughter's school and social services said they were engaging with them. Then they disappeared.

Their absence was noticed almost immediately. The neighbour said that, while they were glad of the peace and quiet, they were a bit puzzled that the family seemed to have upped and left. The school reported the daughter as absent and were unable to contact dad or stepmum to find out why. They didn't answer the door to social services. After a few days, a police welfare visit showed that they had indeed left, and left in a hurry: half-finished meals on the kitchen table, drawers pulled out with clothing missing. A set of plugged-in hair clippers in the hallway sat on a nest of the dad's shaved-off hair.

An alert was put out. The dad was from a small town in Northern Ireland, so notice was sent to authorities up there to look out for them. The NHS was notified to inform police if or when the family tried to register with a dentist or GP. The stepmother was originally from Spain, so I asked whether passport control could be put on notice. I was told there was an insufficient level of risk to justify this. I asked what more risk they needed to see before they would change their minds. I never received an answer.

Today's meeting is a follow-up to see if the family have popped up anywhere. It has been a couple of months since they disappeared. In the interim, we have received a letter from the dad, containing the front door keys, saying he wants to end the tenancy. He has given no reason for leaving and no forwarding address.

Social services say the family hasn't turned up anywhere. Right now, there is nothing more they can do. So, as an ASB officer, with the combined lack of resources and time and influence and power that the job entails, all I can do is close it down as an active investigation (no more noise nuisance, right?) and try to forget all about them.

The number of cases I've had to forget about because there was nothing more I could do to help has mounted up over the years. They sit like boxes in Niall's living room, unaddressed and mouldering, bursting at the edges: slowly but surely closing in on me. By now, there are too many to deal with properly. I wouldn't know where to begin.

5 November

I receive a phone call from one of the lockups/offices used by our caretaking staff. A temp has been told, not unreasonably, that she has been fired after being found reading a newspaper in a café when she was meant to be out on our estates being a caretaker. She had not taken this news well, and started screaming at the team leader, hurling at him whatever words came to mind to reinforce quite how unhappy she was with this new arrangement. The team leader had managed to barricade himself in his office and thought the best people to speak to about this would be us, 'because this is definitely anti-social behaviour'.

I ask whether he has called the police yet, and when he says he hasn't, I suggest that might be the ideal thing to do. There's often an assumption that, being somebody who deals with anti-social behaviour, you have special magic powers that can resolve any unpleasant situation. I'm the wrong side of forty-five, five foot eight and have a gammy leg, so I'm not sure what he thought I was going to be able to do, other than recommend that the next job advert should say 'People who make a habit of totally losing their shit need not apply.'

6 November

A phone call from Colin, who has found something else to be unhappy about. He tells me that he had a terrible night yesterday, and the noise he had to put up with was completely unacceptable. He's had to put up with noise for years and nothing ever gets done. He had to turn up his television to drown out the din and no doubt there will be complaints now from his neighbours about that.

I rack my brain to go through the extensive number of different households Colin has complained about over the years, discounting the ones that have moved out, and manage to narrow it down to roughly five.

'Can you tell me who it was that was causing the noise?' I ask.

Colin tells me that the noise was coming from everywhere. No matter which room in his home he went into, he could hear it. It was all around him. This is a new one on me, as I've never had somebody allege that a troublesome neighbour was floating around the building like an antisocial poltergeist.

I ask how late into the night it went on, wondering whether we could send out our evening patrol officers to try and hear it for themselves. Colin tells me it finished at about 11pm, so that's not really an option.

'What kind of noise was it?' I ask him. I wonder whether he could make out a particular voice so I could start to work out who to contact and have them reply that, no, they have no idea what I'm talking about. This is what normally happens when Colin complains about a neighbour.

Fireworks. Colin has called me to say he could hear fireworks. On bonfire night.

'Colin, you do know it was Guy Fawkes last night, don't you? You have to expect to hear fireworks on November 5th.'

Colin is less than happy with this. He says he's heard about the community trigger and warns that he's going to activate it. He says it's applicable because he's had to complain about the same thing on three separate occasions and nothing has been done to stop it. Exasperated but curious, I ask him when the other two times were that he had complained about firework noise.

'Bonfire night last year, and the year before that,' he replies.

7 November

Having filed for Raul's possession appeal hearing back in August, I'm given notification of the court date, which is February of next year. Assuming the court hearing goes off without a hitch, we will then have to wait for an available bailiffs' date to carry out the order.

Bailiffs are probably best known in this country for repossessing people's electrical equipment in greasy, exploitative daytime television shows whose mission statement is to suggest poor people shouldn't be allowed to have nice things. There's an assumption that bailiffs have to look like an angry side of beef in a cheap suit, but all of the bailiffs I've ever dealt with have been grey-looking blokes who you'd guess were probably called Keith.

When we evict somebody, the bailiffs aren't present to

physically remove anybody (the police would be called if that was necessary), to empty all the person's belongings out of the property (we'd dispose of any remaining items once the eviction had been carried out and the property secured) or to board up the door to stop them getting back in (we'd book a locksmith to do that). They're there to 'enforce' the court order, which is a nebulous way of saying they're there to make sure it's been done properly.

As you can probably imagine, days with evictions in them are seldom days on which I skip to work with a song in my heart. If we've got that far, something has gone seriously wrong in somebody's life and the coward in you silently prays that the people you're evicting will have already moved out before the bailiffs arrive.

On the plus side, eviction days can make you feel better about the slightly untidy house you left behind because nothing says 'bollocks to doing any housework' like knowing you're going to be kicked out of somewhere in a few weeks' time. People can leave behind a mess that is almost beyond comprehension.

The worst home I ever saw belonged to Gavin, a permanently annoyed father of four who had harassed an entire housing estate to the point of his being evicted. Gavin was almost incapable of keeping his counsel, a trait best illustrated by the last time he got arrested before he was kicked out of his house. A local copper was chatting to parents and their kids one afternoon as the school was closing for the day, doing your basic community policing work. Gavin steamed over like a man possessed, bellowing, 'Are you badmouthing my fucking kids? You're always fucking doing this.'

The officer advised him he was doing no such thing and asked that he temper his language, especially as there were kids (or 'fucking kids', as Gavin would have put it) present.

'Don't fucking tell me to stop shouting,' Gavin shouted. 'I'm just sticking up for my fucking kids.'

The officer took Gavin to one side and spoke to him in the calm, measured tone that police usually use when they're a millimetre away from getting the handcuffs out. If you're ever spoken to by a copper in this tone, I'd really recommend you stop doing whatever it is you've just been doing. He told Gavin that he needed to calm down. Nobody was talking about his family. If Gavin carried on swearing like that, he would be compelled to arrest him for a public order offence and surely neither of them wanted to waste the rest of their day with that? Having seemingly placated Gavin, the officer walked back towards the group he'd been chatting with.

Gavin shouted after him, 'Well, I was just fucking saying, wasn't I?' And was promptly arrested.

A few weeks later, the bailiff date for Gavin's eviction arrived. The police agreed to come along just in case Gavin decided to voice his opinion on proceedings, but were not needed as Gavin had departed the day before. When we got inside, it took a few minutes to fully take in how he had lived his life. Downstairs was a mess, but no more than that. But the entire upstairs of his house – three bedrooms, a bathroom and a hallway – were literally (and I mean *literally*) knee deep in what can only be described as 'stuff'. Toys, clothes, bedding, newspapers, bits of furniture and God knows what else. It was as if a filth fairy had sprinkled two tons of landfill around the place. This wasn't hoarding, this was untidiness taken to an Olympic standard. In the end, it took seven full-sized skips to clear the house, and three months of work before it was in a condition suitable for other human beings to live there.

Hopefully, Raul's home won't be in the same state, but it's likely to be April of next year before we find out. In total, it will have been seventeen months between him doing the thing he will get evicted for and him being evicted. This is because we have to follow court schedules and abide by the law, even if our residents don't. In a way, we have been very lucky with Raul's case because his drug dealing didn't impinge too much on his neighbour's day-to-day life and he's been in prison for much of those seventeen months.

When we have somebody being an absolute nightmare in their home and continuing to be one while we wait for the slow grind of the court process, it can be hard to justify to their neighbours why it takes as long as it does.

9 November

Since February, Lynne has managed to be fully assessed by knowledgeable practitioners who have come to the clinical conclusion that there is sod-all wrong with her. However, she has taken down the posters from her window so her neighbours no longer have to read her theories on why Eamonn Holmes is actually the 267th Pope and why porridge doesn't exist. And she has managed not to shove anybody down any stairs at all for months. So a decision has been made to let sleeping dogs lie and take no further action against her, a decision that caused the sad demise of my stapler when I found out. I replace it with one of the eight staplers Simon managed to amass in his short time with us.

11 November

People say that drinkers 'self-medicate' with alcohol. If this is the case, the medicine I'm drinking almost every night is almost homeopathic in its inability to treat the symptoms.

13 November

An unspoken truth about this job is that for a statistically significant number of cases, the best thing you can do is nothing at all. People report their neighbours in a flurry of indignation and self-righteousness, demanding answers and demanding justice. It's easy to get caught up in this and start putting wheels into motion that, once moving, are difficult to stop.

Given the precarious nature of social housing in this country, 'being reported to the council' is a serious business for many people. There is a phrase – 'intentionally homeless' – that hangs over the head of anybody with a council or social housing tenancy. To be intentionally homeless means that, either by act or omission on your part, you have made yourself homeless. This may be because you just handed the keys in and cleared off, but in the overwhelming number of cases it's because you breached your tenancy in some way. You may have failed to pay your rent or been kicked out because of your behaviour. The reason being 'intentionally homeless' is such a big deal is that if that's how your last tenancy ended, the council are under no obligation to rehouse you. They are obliged to house any child under the age of eighteen, but not the parents if they're over eighteen. And yes, that risks the kids being placed into care.

So people tend to react badly to 'being reported to the council'. It's like having a schoolmate report you to the headmaster, if the headmaster could punish you by making you sleep in a shop doorway instead of detention. What could have been a minor feud that would have been forgotten in weeks becomes a major issue for both sides, and not one easily forgotten. I will always make people aware of the risk of this happening before asking if they definitely want me to proceed with an investigation. But too often, Tenant A would rather be right than happy, and will decide that yes, he does want me to start canvassing neighbours and dragging the woman next door into our office because she told Tenant A to piss off for the first time in the ten years they've lived next door to each other.

Having an unmanageable workload sometimes has its positives, and this is one of them. It can sometimes be weeks before you manage to speak to the complainant, by which time calmer heads will have prevailed, and the complainant will have decided that it was just a one-off. If you had been on the ball from day one, taken a main witness statement and pressed the case forward, you might, with the full consent of the person making the complaint, have irreparably damaged the relationship between neighbours.

Even when there has been serious, proven ASB, standing back and waiting to see what happens can sometimes work out for the best. This has proven to be the case with Mr Rashid and his tempestuous offspring. Back in June, I had decided that we had to proceed with possession of the property because there were no signs of the situation improving. It wasn't something I was looking forward to, both because it would result in making a family homeless and, to be honest, because the amount of paperwork involved would be more of a ballache than galloping on a bony horse over rough terrain. So it kept getting put to one side. But today I was given confirmation of a breakthrough.

After more rows with each other, Mr Rashid threw his kid out of the family home, saying he was sick of the problems he was causing, both in the family home and in the block as a whole. This is seldom anything but a temporary measure, but by some minor miracle, it has all worked out for the best. The child has settled in a sheltered accommodation scheme designed for youths looking to live independently. Once he turns eighteen, he will be given accommodation of his own. Since living in the scheme, he's stuck to curfews and has not brought any of his previous problems with him.

Meanwhile, Mr Rashid has managed to secure a mutual exchange out of the area. A mutual exchange is when two tenants of the council or social housing essentially swap tenancies and move into each other's homes. As long as the properties are the right size for each set of tenants and they don't owe any rent, the swap can go ahead. In Mr Rashid's case, and for this I need to make a small offering to whoever the god of housing is, his new home is with another social landlord. So even if the kid moves back in and the problems start up again, they will be Not My Job.

Small mercies.

15 November

During a conversation in the office, somebody brings up the name of a former manager of our team and reminds me of one of the stupidest questions I've ever been asked while doing this job.

Managing ASB officers can't be easy. We tend to be stubborn, contrary and pedantic. You sort of have to be to do the job properly. We often leave the office at a moment's notice as the job demands, and we're often out on visits scheduled for an hour that end up taking four. Our stress levels are through the roof, so you have to be a bit more accommodating to less-than-polite behaviour when somebody needs to vent.

But most of all, you need to actually know how to do the job. It's not a case of entering (x) amount of officers and (y) amount of work, producing (z) output. A line manager will sign off on decisions that have serious legal ramifications, so you need to know that the correct decision-making process was reached and can be legally defended if challenged.

Basically, you need to be anybody but Zak. Zak was the kind of person with whom you'd count your fingers after having shaken his hand. He could walk through a revolving door without moving it. He had a surface, bland, politician charm that he used to his full advantage to climb up the promotion ladder. One of his tricks was that he knew the first name of every person in the organisation, the job they did and one personal fact about them, like whether they were expecting a baby or liked windsurfing. People would be disarmed by this, I was dismayed to discover, rather than realising he viewed people as data in an Excel spreadsheet.

Zak somehow became manager of our team, despite never having investigated ASB, and our first meeting as a team with him got off to an imperfect start when his first words were, 'Right, well, ASB. It's not rocket science, is it?'

After mapping out his vision for our team (never trust anybody who uses the word 'vision' in a workplace context unless it has the words 'I work for' before it, and 'Express' after it), he gave us the team objective for the year.

'OK, what I'm hearing from people across the organisation is that drug dealing is a problem on our estates. So, I want us to rid our estates of drug dealing. How are we going to achieve that, guys?'

There was an embarrassed pause. Feet were shuffled. Despairing gazes were avoided. Eventually, I made a suggestion.

'Zak, I reckon what we need to do is have a country-wide drug education programme that talks in an honest way about drugs and their effects. This would lead to a slow decriminalisation of all drugs to be sold via government-monitored outlets. Alongside this we have to work on access to education for teenagers and have better employment opportunities. I reckon if we can do all that we can rid our estates of drug dealing, no problem. Three months, tops.'

We never really got on after that, Zak and I. He left the organisation soon afterwards to be a resources manager for another housing association, possibly because buildings don't tend to do sarcasm.

The reason Zak came up today is because our staff conference for next year has been announced and it was at a previous conference many years ago when we first met him as a team. The venue in which the next conference is going to be held is also used for live music. I was there a few months ago seeing a band from my teenage days, and got recklessly drunk and jumped around like an idiot who had temporarily forgotten he wasn't fifteen any more. I toy with the idea of doing the same at the staff conference while they're handing out awards for 'Most Improved KPIs of the Year' but I doubt they'll have arranged a mosh pit.

17 November

The perils of having both your personal Twitter account and your work Twitter account on your phone. I almost told the world that it was the considered opinion of the entire organisation that I work for that a certain well-known comedian is a complete bellend.

I mean, he *is* a complete bellend, but I doubt that would have been seen as a mitigating factor.

19 November

Just before lunchtime, I receive some news I'd long suspected was coming but still didn't want to hear when it arrived. I switch off my computer, go home and don't come back for a couple of days.

23 November

First aid training. I'm having trouble concentrating because the guy delivering the training looks and sounds disconcertingly like the football pundit and former Manchester United striker Denis Law. What's making it worse is that nobody else in our team has the slightest interest in football; I can't even nudge them to point it out, so the thought is just bumping around the inside of my skull like a bee in September.

Another distraction is that he finishes every section of the training with the phrase 'And that's all you can do, really', which is probably meant to reassure us that we're not expected to be trained paramedics by the end of the course, but sounds increasingly like a lament on the futility of human struggle in the face of an uncaring universe.

('So you raise the arm, put pressure on the wound and wait for the ambulance. And that's all you can do, really.' 'Keep them warm, try to reassure them, and wait for the ambulance. And that's all you can do, really.' 'Run it under cold water for twenty minutes. And that's all you can do, really. That's all any of us can do. We struggle not because we think we can cheat death, we struggle because it proves we are alive. As Camus famously said, within the depths of us there lies an invincible summer, which—'

'Will this be on the test?')

Most of the people we're likely to encounter in need of first aid will be class A drug users on the stairwells of our blocks, possibly following an overdose. Somebody asks whether the mouth-to-mouth part of CPR is absolutely necessary, given the fact we're unlikely to be carrying protective mouth shields around with us, and given the likelihood that the patient is likely to have a heady cocktail of illnesses commensurate with rough sleeping, needle sharing and ill health.

'You can just do the chest compressions, but all you'll be doing is moving blood around their body that's got less and less oxygen in it. That'll probably last them about five minutes before the brain starts dying.'

'So if you were in our place, would you give them unprotected mouth-to-mouth?'

'Oh, God no.'

One unfortunate side-effect of doing first aid training (I've had to do several top-up courses over the years) is that you spend the next few days on your commute to work looking round to see if anyone is looking a bit peaky so you can try your moves out on them. Once, I thought I had a whole train carriage full of potential test subjects for my training but then I realised it was a Monday morning and everybody just looks like that.

25 November

I'm not given to believe in the paranormal or in superstition (except when it comes to watching football, when I'm convinced that some action or omission on my part will somehow affect the performance of a highly trained athlete several hundred miles away, as well as bending the laws of physics to deflect a ball away from its trajectory). That said, my years as an ASB officer have made me feel there may be something in the theory of psychogeography, specifically the part that says certain areas retain a memory of people who have lived there and cause the same issues to be repeated.

There is no rational reason why a certain street or block of flats should consistently experience the same issues due to the people living there, but time and again it happens on the estates we manage. This isn't down to external factors like proximity to a transport hub or the underlying poverty index of the region. It's not down to the makeup of the buildings, either, as many of them are of an identikit 1950s/1960s construction that eschewed individuality for cost-cutting. Neither is it down to a selective lettings policy. Such is the demand for housing that the days of socially engineering areas or tower blocks to be solely for young families, the elderly and so on are over. As soon as a property becomes available, it's offered to the people at the top of the waiting list, who may have been on that list for many years.

Nevertheless, I and the officers I work with will tell you that certain geographical areas, certain streets and even certain individual blocks will be plagued by the same issues. One colleague seems to deal almost exclusively with people struggling with class A drug addiction, another colleague has as many cannabis farms sprouting up in the properties they manage as the rest of us put together. One has become an expert in dealing with people struggling with loneliness by making repeated and unfounded reports of ASB to our team.

On my patch, there's a block with no more than fifteen flats, and I would estimate that at least ten of the households have a tenant who suffers from serious mental illness of some kind or another. It has a slightly higher than average turnover of tenants, so in the decade I have managed it, I've seen a number of people come and go. In that single block, there is the woman with severe agoraphobia whom I've never seen leave the confines of her flat, the guy who is so sensitive to outside noise that if somebody farts in the next street he will call up to complain about it, the woman who's drinking herself to death because she never got over losing her daughter, the paranoid schizophrenic who blots out the voices in his head by singing Kylie songs loudly – and badly – at all hours of the day and night, the woman who's convinced she's going to become a millionaire because she's invented a new type of deodorant and has bought five thousand plastic tubs to start production at some point in the future, an elderly woman struggling to maintain her tenancy with progressive dementia, two bipolar tenants and a smattering of people on antidepressants.

Meanwhile, another block I manage which is less than a five-minute walk away is over twenty storeys high and has 130 homes, and in the last decade I have probably dealt with half a dozen cases relating to people living there. And even then, the cases I have dealt with have generally been low-level noise nuisance stuff.

Both blocks were built at roughly the same time, from the same materials, and are in the same neighbourhood. Both have a mix of one- and two-bed flats, so the makeup of people living there is, sociologically speaking, broadly the same. The estate they're on isn't in Nevada, so I can't even put it down to one of them having been built on an ancient Native American burial ground. There is no way to explain the disparity between the two.

Such is the clumping of issues across estates – mental health problems (most prevalent on my patch for no explicable reason), addiction issues, elderly and vulnerable complainants, gangs – that you often find yourself called upon to help another officer out because on their patch, the problem occurs so infrequently.

I do wonder whether this happens across the country, and if people in other local authorities and housing associations have their own borderline personality disorder street or seasonal affective disorder maisonettes.

27 November

In court with a cannabis factory. Cannabis cultivation is a big problem on our estates. As I've mentioned, aside from the issue of legality, cannabis factories are often so poorly constructed that they pose a safety risk to other residents, so when we find them, we take the strongest action possible against the tenant involved.

Cannabis factories have often troubled me as something that I can't professionally condone but I can personally completely understand. Imagine you're in your early twenties. A difficult childhood and maybe some learning difficulties meant you left school without any qualifications. Now let's say you did some daft stuff as a teenager that brought you to the attention of the police. You're in a flat you can't afford to furnish and can barely afford to heat. What few jobs there are out there are not going to be given to somebody with no work experience, no qualifications and a criminal record.

You see other people your age whose fate rolled a six instead of a one. They have some nice clobber, can afford to go to the pub of a weekend and maybe even drive a car. Not unreasonably, you feel that this is the kind of thing you'd like in your life, but that seems unlikely to happen unless you win on a lottery ticket you can't even afford to buy.

One day, a friend of a friend takes you to one side and offers you a large roll of tenners, tax free and no need to tell the dole about it. In return, all you'll have to do is sleep on the sofa in your flat for a few months and tend to some plants every day that will be growing in your bedroom. You won't be able to have friends round while they're there, but it's not like you've had much of a social life anyway, given how skint you are. Once the plants are gone, they may even throw in a small bag of the crop as a thank-you.

Anyone saying that, dealt the same hand in life and offered the same arrangement, they would definitely turn it down, is not being entirely honest with themselves. Given the same set of circumstances, I'm struggling to think why I would say no. So I completely understand why we see such a proliferation of cannabis factories.

From the grower's point of view, this arrangement is a no-brainer. The return on investment is high, even factoring in the losses caused by police raids. The person whose flat they've used is almost always vulnerable in some way, otherwise they might have turned them down, so it's not as if they're going to grass on them to the police.

Even so, growers have found increasingly inventive methods of cultivating crops in ways that can't be linked back to them. Seedlings need intensive care in a carefully controlled environment. On one of our estates, we noticed there was a car that seemed to have been abandoned. It was still taxed and insured, and it looked roadworthy, so there was no reason to tow it away, but it had not moved for months and none of our residents said it belonged to them. We sent a sniffer dog to the estate and it indicated when it got to the boot of the car. Police forced the boot open and there, lined entirely in black bin liners to blot out any stray light, was a small hydroponic cannabis farm with dozens of little seedlings, all of it powered off the car battery.

The cannabis farm for today's court hearing is a different matter, though. Police raided the flat and found that every room in the property had been converted to grow dozens and dozens of plants. Wiring looped from the ceiling, dripping with condensation, and silver ducting pumped air throughout the property. There was barely room to walk between the plants, let alone sleep, eat or live there.

The property is in the name of Kirsteen, who is in her mid-twenties, currently studying law at college and whose family lives a couple of miles away. Police visited the family home and Kirsteen, who had her own bedroom and was clearly living there, was promptly arrested. As we often do in these cases, I gave Kirsteen two options: she could surrender her tenancy immediately without further action against her, or she could defend the possession action in court and run the risk of not only being made homeless (or as homeless as somebody with their own room a bus ride away can be), but also having to pay our court costs.

Full of a confidence that was entirely unfounded – we had more photos and police evidence of the massive haul of cannabis in Kirsteen's flat than we knew what to do with – she refused to surrender her tenancy, so we served her notice and said we'd see her in court, hence today's hearing. I'd been in front of the judge who was due to hear our case and knew that, as long as you had all your evidence to hand and could show proper procedure had been followed, he tended to be a brisk and reasonable type.

Kirsteen had consulted with the duty solicitor in the minutes before the hearing, not having sought legal advice or entered a defence beforehand. We briefly set out our case: the property was not being lived in and was used for illegal/immoral purposes, electricity had illegally been abstracted (i.e. the meter had been bypassed), and un-authorised alterations had been made to the property that rendered it dangerous.

Kirsteen's solicitor then sets out her case. He claims that she has temporarily moved back in with her parents due to a recent bout of depression. She had previously lent a set of keys to a cousin and she believes this cousin must have made a copy for persons unknown who had then set up the whole farm in her flat without her knowledge. The duty solicitor continues, 'Given these facts, sir, I would look for an adjournment so my client can have a psychiatric assessment and following this we—'

'No,' the judge replies.

'—can assess w— I'm sorry, sir?' The duty solicitor seems thrown by the interruption.

'No,' the judge reiterates. 'What possible story are you going to come back with in a month's time that will convince me not to evict this young lady? No, absolutely not. I'm not wasting everybody's time like that.'

He grants outright possession of the property back to us and agrees that, as we've proven our case, Kirsteen should pay the legal fees. At least she'll have something to talk about on Monday at her law course.

December

Password: Finished101

Medication: Mirtazapine 45mg,
Omeprazole 30mg, 90 units of alcohol

2 December

I'm getting hints of sandalwood and vanilla, which are quickly followed by a strong punch of spruce pine needles and an almost disinfectant tang. These are superseded by elements of peach before finally resolving in a heady fug of jasmine and lavender.

I turn to the caretaker, who is looking at me with an expression of bewilderment. 'And how long have they been here?' I ask.

'Bit by bit over the last week or so, but there's been loads put up over the weekend. When I got here this morning to do my weekly clean I could barely breathe.'

We both look back down the corridor we've just walked along, located on the second floor of a block of flats. The walls and ceiling are painted in the usual corporation colours designed not to fade or discolour and to make cleaning easier, rather than according to any aesthetic considerations, and are somewhere in the middle of a Venn diagram of white, green and yellow. The floor tiles follow the same sickly colour scheme, alternating between a sort of vomit-y grey and a slightly different sort of vomit-y grey.

Decorating the corridor, like baubles on a pestilential Christmas tree, are little points of bright colour: orange, pink and green. Some round, some lozenge-shaped, others triangular, dangling from the light fittings that run down the centre of the corridor. Somebody has slowly but surely filled the corridor with enough air fresheners to mask the smell of a dead sperm whale washed up on a beach. Spending more than thirty seconds in that corridor feels like grinding a department store perfume counter into powder and snorting lines of it.

I ask if the caretaker has seen anybody putting them up during her rounds but she's seen nothing. Similarly, no residents have mentioned having seen anything. We don't have cameras in the block to give any clues, either. Who would do such a thing?

I walk halfway back along the corridor and knock on a flat door. After a pause, a tall, wiry man with a halo of ginger hair answers the door.

'Oh, it's you, Nick. How can I help?'

'Mr Angstrom. You wouldn't know anything about all these air fresheners, would you?'

4 December

All employees have had to attend a workshop on 'staff culture' and today is my turn. I share comedian Alexei Sayle's view on the use of the word 'workshop' in this context ('anybody who uses the word "workshop" who's not connected with light engineering is a twat') but am nonetheless obliged to attend.

One of the exercises they get us to do is write down the names of companies we respect and one reason why we respect them. I'm guessing they want us to think of nationally known organisations so I resist writing 'my corner shop' and 'because they sell me booze'.

We then have to list the qualities we would want our residents to write about us. Again, I anticipate they're looking for buzzwords like 'openness' and 'reliability' so I refrain from suggesting 'hasn't flipped a table over and started smearing his dung on the walls despite some pretty strong provocation'.

We're encouraged to think of our residents as 'customers', and while I understand the sentiment – historically there has been a tendency to view social housing tenants as being lucky to have the accommodation they have, and a feeling they should be grateful for whatever level of service they get from housing providers – it falls far from the truth. If you're on a low income and have managed to navigate the whole process – form-filling, waiting, bidding for available properties – to the point at which you have a tenancy, you're stuck with whoever manages your property. It's not like buying a pint of milk or a pair of socks; like switching energy providers or cancelling your broadband. You can't decide to go and be a social housing tenant with somebody else, or at least not easily.

I do think we have to make sure we treat our residents as well as we can, not because they're customers, but precisely because they're not. They're totally reliant on us for housing so we have to make sure we do it properly.

6 December

Colin has another complaint. This time it's kids harassing him and trying to extort him by causing noise nuisance until he gives them money to go away. Further questioning reveals that the kids in question were going door to door singing Christmas carols. I advise him that we will make a note of his complaint.

9 December

Investigating a harassment complaint made by Mr Hewitt. This will be roughly the ninth complaint of this nature that

I have investigated for Mr Hewitt in the last ten years. No investigation has ever led to any concrete evidence of actual harassment having taken place and usually ends with a disgruntled Mr Hewitt telling me there's no point in keeping in touch with him if I don't intend to take his complaints seriously.

In my more charitable moments, I feel sorry for Mr Hewitt. He seems to live a solitary life, based on my previous dealings with him. His flat is very sparsely furnished, without any of the usual items you'd expect to see in a middle-aged person's home that mark out a life having been lived. There are no pictures on the walls – neither photos of family and friends, nor paintings or pictures that might have caught his eye. There are no ornaments on his shelves: no tacky gifts from a child on holiday, no certificates of past accomplishments, no collection of thimbles or spoons or crystal figurines or any other kind of hobby. Neither are there any books, or records or DVDs to hint at what entertains Mr Hewitt during his long days sitting at home. He has a small television in his living room, which is usually on when I visit, but I get the impression it's there to break the silence rather than as something he actively enjoys watching. The silence would also not be broken by friends visiting, as Mr Hewitt has none that he's ever mentioned, nor by pets, as this is another thing missing from his life.

He dresses neutrally for a man of his age and background and has an accent free of any local inflection. He looks exactly the age he is, and is neither in poor health nor notably sprightly for somebody in their late fifties. I have asked if he wants me to look into any social activities offered by the local council that might get him out of his home once in a while. People reporting harassment, whether that harassment is real or imagined, can often become shut-ins, feeling trapped inside their home because Out There is where the bad things happen. This can exacerbate the stress the situation is causing them and create a cycle of sensitivity to the slightest noise or sideways glance from a neighbour. Getting them out of a routine, having something worth leaving their homes for, or an interest to occupy their minds, can often be just as valuable as any investigation or court action.

Mr Hewitt has always declined, though. Everything from cookery classes to car maintenance to DJ turntable skills has been turned down. He's not interested in that kind of thing, whatever thing it is you have to offer.

Over the years he's complained about pretty much every person that lives near him, and the general thrust is always, 'They are doing (x) and the reason they are doing (x) is to harass me.' A peculiarity Mr Hewitt shares with a lot of complainants is that he feels his neighbours' behaviour is directed at him and intended for his detriment. Often people will say that the toddlers upstairs are being allowed to run around all day to annoy them, or that their parents flush the toilet at 3am just to wind them up.

It's often hard to convince people otherwise, even when you tell them that other people have heard the same things they have, and it neither bothers them nor do they think it's done on purpose to annoy them. Nobody wants to be the bad guy in their own life story, and I think that admitting they were wrong, or being overly sensitive or petty, would cast them in that role in their own minds.

The behaviour 'directed' at the complainant is almost always routine activity, which makes these cases even harder to resolve. The activity isn't the kind of thing you can ask people to refrain from doing without being unreasonable yourself. You can't ask a parent to stop their young child from playing, or ask people not to go to the toilet at certain times, or not to leave for work at 6am. And asking them if they're doing any of these things deliberately to annoy their neighbour is invariably met with a puzzled frown.

This doesn't stop people from making such allegations and has certainly never held Mr Hewitt back. Over the years, the behaviour he's complained about that he feels has been done as an oblique method of harassment has included having grandkids around to visit, watering hanging baskets, coughing, being on the phone all the time and cooking spicy food.

With some trepidation, I ask Mr Hewitt what the issue is this time. He tells me that the neighbour in the flat opposite him has started playing drums. Not for any prolonged period of time (say, the amount of time it would take for an officer to come out and witness it), but in short bursts of a minute or so. Since it started happening, Phil Collins next door has smiled at Mr Hewitt when he sees him in the street, thus proving he knows how much it has been irritating him.

I ask whether he thinks anybody else in the vicinity might have also heard Sixty Second Dave Grohl and might be willing to give a corroborating statement, knowing what the answer will be. Sure enough, Mr Hewitt says that the neighbours wouldn't back up his story because they don't like him so they would rather put up with the drumming than help him out. This is his standard response when I investigate his claims and is a convenient way of explaining the lack of additional complainants.

I offer to go and speak to Ringo straight away, reasoning that he wouldn't be expecting my visit so wouldn't have time to dismantle his kit. If I'm allowed in and I see it in the flat, I can issue a warning there and then. Mr Hewitt reluctantly agrees.

I knock on the door opposite and Keith Moon lets me in. He's a round-faced man in his late thirties who in the space of a short conversation tells me all about his current physical and mental health problems, offers to make me a cup of tea, compliments the coat I'm wearing and asks whether I think it will snow soon. He readily agrees to let me have a look in every room, including the bathroom and kitchen, to see if he has a drumkit set up and ready to play. His flat is ramshackle but clean, with bric-a-brac scattered all over the place in a way that suggests it's been there for a while. There's barely enough spare room on the floor to stand up a single bongo, let alone a drumkit. I thank him for his time and leave.

I go back to Mr Hewitt's flat and tell him how my meeting with John Bonham went. He immediately suggests that his neighbour must have seen me coming when I first arrived, knew what I was here for and hastily dismantled the kit while I was talking to Mr Hewitt. I feel this will be another case destined to go nowhere. I ask Mr Hewitt to get in touch if he has any further evidence and leave him to whatever it is he does all day long, my heart hurting slightly at the quiet, bland tragedy of it all.

11 December

Police confirm they have paid an early-morning visit to Christophe's home. All the family members were present when the police arrived and were asked to stay in their respective rooms while the search was conducted. Several wraps of crack and heroin were found under Christophe's bed, along with nearly a thousand pounds in cash and two cheap burner mobile phones. More damning were the electronic scales found on the kitchen counter alongside packs of red-and-white and blue-and-white carrier bags.

Christophe is arrested for PWITS. No other family members are arrested as there is insufficient evidence to suggest they were active participants in the drug trade operating from the property. There is, however, sufficient evidence on the face of things to suggest that the family knew what Christophe was getting up to.

The evidence will be collated – evidence of Christophe's previous conviction, the complaints from the neighbour regarding Christophe's coming and going, footage from the cameras and the evidence found during the police raid – and I will be recommending that we evict the whole family. This will include the kids that live in the family home and had nothing to do with this. I know that this will be used to paint our team as being heartless and nasty. I also know that adults risked making young family members homeless by allowing drugs to be sold from the address. I'm willing to take responsibility for the choices our team makes. I just wonder if Christophe and his parents are willing to do the same.

12 December

Our work IT department has had another bright idea, this time with a new way of ensuring staff don't get spam emails. In the old, Luddite days you would get an email from somebody purporting to be the Argentinian foreign minister asking you to reset your Netflix password in exchange for 1,000 bitcoin. You would shrug, delete it and carry on with your day.

Under the new system, you get an email telling you that you were sent a spam email but it was intercepted. The email has a link via which you can safely check the spam email before agreeing to have it deleted. If you don't do this, you will keep getting reminder emails telling you there's a spam email awaiting your inspection. Once you do delete said message, you get another email from IT telling you that the spam email has been deleted. I can only assume that a descendant of Franz Kafka is now running things over at IT. The future with teleportation and lasers I was promised as a kid seems further away than ever.

13 December

Weapons sweep. Weapons are an integral part of the drugs trade on our estates. Going to work selling drugs with nothing more than a winning smile and a sharp tongue will soon see you targeted for whatever you have in your pockets.

Guns are thankfully rare on our estates, at least up until now, but knives are a common weapon of choice for people selling drugs. Street dealers have kept up to date with changing legislation and are fully aware that they can go to jail for up to four years for carrying a 'bladed article', as a knife is known in legal terms. I always think they've missed a trick by not calling a gun a 'bulleted article'.

Rather than having a knife in a pocket while they sit and wait for customers and risk getting arrested with it in their possession, dealers will often stash weapons somewhere nearby where they can be quickly retrieved when trouble brews – 'trouble' in this line of work being dealers from a rival gang, or any group of lads looking to make a quick bit of cash by robbing them. So knives will often be hidden in hedges, in bin chambers or behind the wheel of a nearby car.

The weapons in question can vary from a kitchen knife stolen from home to actual full-length samurai swords. The purpose of having a knife is as much to scare somebody off as it is to wound, so if you have one that looks as if you could use it to peel a hippo with, so much the better. This has led to the rise in popularity of so-called 'zombie' knives over other knives that could reasonably be said to have a practical use.

The aforementioned kitchen knife can peel spuds and the samurai sword can hang decoratively on the wall of the kind of bloke who trains with nunchucks bare-chested in his back garden and reckons he knows the real reason Bruce Lee died. Zombie knives serve no other purpose than to inflict serious and often fatal wounds. Not only designed to injure, they are also designed to look as terrifying as possible, as if the xenomorph from *Alien* had sex with a cutlery drawer.

The sale and manufacture of zombie knives is banned in England and Wales, but of course drug dealers treat this law with the same respect with which they treat most other laws. So if we have an issue with drug dealing on a particular estate, we will do periodic weapon sweeps there alongside police, who will take away any knives found in case they may have been used in previous crimes. Sweeps are carried out by simply looking in likely areas, but our team has recently upped its game by purchasing a metal detector, making the whole operation feel like a really bleak episode of *The Detectorists*.

Today's sweep unearthed a single, rusted butter knife half-covered in soil. Police make an onsite decision not to take it into evidence and it's disposed of in a nearby recycling bin.

15 December

People's capacity to do really stupid things is boundless. Walking through an estate I manage, I hear the sound of sawing wood. Turning a corner, I encounter the following scene: in the back garden of a ground-floor flat, there is a tree. Although currently free of leaves, in summer it must block out quite a bit of light for the flats on either side of it. Propped up against the tree is a ladder, and on the very top rung of the ladder is a man wearing a vest, pyjama bottoms and flip-flops. He is holding a hacksaw, which he is using to cut down the lowest branch of the tree, which is thicker than his thigh and spreads out to the back of his garden, over his back fence, the pavement beyond and the road beyond that. On the other side of his fence, standing on the pavement directly below the branch, are two teenagers, who I presume are his sons.

I manage to get his attention by waving my ID badge at him, jumping up and down and shouting to ask, somewhat unprofessionally, what the fuck it is he thinks he's doing. He looks at me as if I've asked the stupidest question in the world and says that the tree dumps leaves into his garden every autumn and blocks the daylight out, so he's pruning it. After confirming that the man is not a qualified tree surgeon, I ask if he knows whether the tree will still be stable once he's lopped off such a large branch. He can't be sure. Above his flat are three more storeys of flats, all directly in the firing line should the tree, which I'd estimate is about forty feet tall, decide to fall over.

My curiosity gets the better of me and I ask what he thought would happen when he cut through the branch, which must weigh the same as a small car. He indicates his two spindly offspring outside, saying they were going to catch it. The possibility of it crashing through his back garden fence, killing one or both of his sons and possibly causing a road accident hadn't occurred to him.

While I'm waiting for our horticulture team to call me back, I ask him what he had planned to do with all the wood he would suddenly find himself in possession of. He tells me he was going to cut it into smaller bits and place it in the recycling bin. This seems a waste, as he could have made coffins for his kids with it.

19 December

I quit. Today is my last day working as an ASB officer for my current employers. It may well be the last day I ever do this job.

This time last month, I got an email confirming that Carla had died. She never left the hospital ward she had been living in all year. She never got better. She never went back home to pick her life up again and try to make things better with her neighbours. She never went to the shops for a pint of milk, or sat in the nearby park watching the kids play on the climbing frames, or lay in her own bed listening to the rain, or had a coffee with friends, or any of the things she might once have expected to do as part of just another day.

The fog of rage and confusion and hate and sadness that had settled over her never lifted. She just got more and more ill and confused and tired, and then, when her body couldn't take it any more, when her mind had betrayed her for the final time, she died.

Her home is no longer her home. What few possessions she had will be collected by whatever family still had any contact with her. The cot she kept, ready for the return of her child, will be taken away. Maybe some other baby will get to use it, curling pink little fists around its bars and jig-gling at the knees when a parent comes in of a morning to pick them up and smell that oddly-pleasing odour of a full nappy. Or maybe the cot will just get thrown onto the tip. Or burned. I've no idea.

Contractors will come in and clean the place up. Make any little repairs that are needed. Maybe decorate it. What-ever tiny traces Carla left on her home will be gone, like Albert before her. A new family on the waiting list, full of hope and anticipation, will view the empty home and imagine where they would put their sofa, their TV, their bed and say yes, they would like to live here, and then they will move in and Carla may as well have never been here.

And I can't do this any more. Not if I want to stay sane. I handed my notice in last month and when asked what I planned to do next, the only thing I could tell colleagues was, 'Not this. I don't know, but not this.'

I'm scared of what kind of a person the job is turning me into. I'm cynical by nature, but years of exposure to just how awful human beings can be to one another is starting to affect every aspect of my life, and I'm beginning to find optimism an entirely alien concept.

This isn't a job you can do, or at least do well, if you've stopped caring about the people you're trying to help. If there isn't at least some spark of empathy there, the daily grind becomes too much. And I can feel it coming. I can feel myself thinking, whenever a really serious, urgent case comes up, about how much hard work it's going to make for me, rather than thinking about what I can do to help somebody who really needs it.

Only time will tell to what degree the job has prompted the need for medication and alcoholic self-medication, or how much of the insomnia and mild panic is due to work, but I feel that if I leave it much longer, it will become beyond my control. Letting it drag me down is unfair on everyone: my colleagues, my family, my friends, my wife and, I suppose, me.

Despite all this, I feel like a fraud. A failure. I'm letting people down, both in my team and in the community I was paid to help. I'm under no illusions that I would ever win employee of the year, month, week or even Tuesday afternoon, but I do know there were aspects of the job I was good at, like preparing legal paperwork for court, putting together statements, planning case strategies. Me not being there doesn't mean it won't get done; it just means it won't get done by *me*, and I'm still enough of an arrogant control freak to think that I might have somehow made it go better. But by quitting I feel I've admitted defeat or, at the very least, that maybe my heart wasn't in it all along.

But now this won't be a battle I'll encounter every day in quite the same way. I'll always care that people with mental health and/or drug issues are being let down, but it won't be my job to put out that particular house fire with a colander full of water any more. Today is about doing all the mundane things that need doing when you leave a company.

My email has a permanent out-of-office message, the ultimate in Not My Job. My desk is cleared. I hand in my work phone, ID badge and fireman drop keys, like a suspended detective in a cop show handing in his gun and badge.

There's a card signed by everyone, and thoughtful presents, and people say nice things and we promise to keep in touch and it's like the last day of somebody you work with that you've seen a hundred times. I don't kid myself that I'll be irreplaceable but I hope that in some small way, I made a difference and me being here actually mattered.

Late in the afternoon, a guy called Sam from another department comes to our office for a meeting. We've known each other to say hello to ever since I started here. Sam notices the card and the gifts and expresses surprise that I'm leaving, and I explain that I'd not wanted to make a big thing about it.

'Well, all the best, you'll really be missed,' Sam says, shaking my hand in goodbye. 'Take care, Neil.'

Epilogue

The news about Carla was the ultimate catalyst for my resignation, but that resignation had been in the offing for a long time. I'd seen the job get harder year on year because I'd seen that living on the edges of society is getting harder year on year. It's like a slowly-inflating balloon: the workload keeps expanding and the balloon stretches to accommodate it; you see it expand past the point it's meant to go, but it somehow still manages to keep together, and keep expanding. The skin holding it all together is now as thin as a coat of paint. It's not meant to take this much, but somehow it is, and now you're wincing and flinching and waiting for the moment when it stops working. Because like a balloon blown past the point of safety, when a hole appears it's not going to slowly unravel. The whole thing is going to burst.

The other problem was that I was far from alone in having had enough. In every department of all the different services I worked alongside – police, social services, housing, the NHS – I was seeing people waiting to bail out in the next round of redundancies, taking early retirement or just walking away from the whole thing. Once they're gone, they take all that experience with them and it's not coming back. And as good as the people coming up to replace them are, experience can't be replaced overnight. The new people will doubtless be dedicated and hardworking, and will grow to know their jobs inside-out, but I wonder how long they will want to stick around. There comes a point when a job becomes too hard for too long and for too little money, after which nobody will want to do it.

There are so many things that society is getting wrong that all affect how well somebody like me can do the job I do – or rather, did. Many people with more letters after their name than me, who went to better schools than me (and know things like 'you should have said "I" rather than "me" at the start of that sentence'), have discussed the housing crisis, but it boils down to something very simple: there are more people who need social housing than there are homes to put them in. The disparity is alarming and it is only going to get worse if we carry on the way we have been.

The 'right to buy' scheme simply didn't work. It took social housing out of the loop, and local authorities were not given access to the funds needed to replace the stock. Successive governments then went on to build fewer and fewer social housing properties. About half the properties we manage – sorry, 'managed' – were bought under RTB, and I would estimate that about two-thirds are now rented out privately. The idea that it helped low-income people own their own homes is proving false. It has simply provided the opportunity for people to become private landlords. If we don't start prioritising the building of new social housing on an unprecedented scale, and start doing so now, what is currently a scandalous failure to help people in need will become a widescale tragedy.

Also missing from society are the dozens of little knots that held the safety net together but have been austerity-ed out of existence: libraries, Sure Start schemes, youth centres, and hundreds of other services that couldn't turn a profit and didn't look good on a whizzy PowerPoint presentation, but helped to stop people falling through the net, and helped to keep this country as a cohesive society rather than a collection of terrified individuals wondering when their world is going to collapse and who they can blame when it does.

Take knife crime as an example. If those in power were serious about stopping the rise in knife crime, they'd stop the paths that lead to people being involved in knife crime in the first place. And that means better schools, better social care, better youth opportunities, better community policing provision: all the things that you can do away with to balance a yearly spend spreadsheet, so you look like you're being efficient. The effects of knife crime cost more in the long term – financially and societally – than any short-term cuts could ever save. As a society, we are demanding action now and results now, and anything that takes time and produces intangible results is seen as a waste of time and money. We are no longer planting trees under whose shade we will never sit.

But our two greatest failures, the two areas where we get so much wrong on such a massive scale, are drugs and mental health. I genuinely believe that a country with a mature approach to drugs and a comprehensive approach to mental health provision would have seen my workload reduce by about eighty per cent.

The current punitive approach to drugs isn't working, has never worked and never will. I understand why some governments want it to continue, because privately run prisons need prisoners to turn a profit, but maintaining the profits of a handful of security firms should not dictate social policy.

I understand people's twitchiness towards legalising all drugs, but all I can say, based on my professional experience, is that some people want to take drugs, and their legality has never and will never be an issue for them – in much the same way that I've never wanted to smoke crack, and the fact it's illegal has always been a footnote in that decision.

Our current model sees criminal gangs making vast amounts of money, enforced with brutality and slave labour (large-scale cannabis factories in the UK are frequently staffed by trafficked people who are deported if they are raided, with the people running the factories walking away free). Their class-A-addicted customers are using adulterated drugs that cause multiple health issues which have to be picked up by a health service already on its knees. To get drug money, addicts turn to crime such as shoplifting, burglary and robbery. You will have been affected by these crimes, either by shops increasing prices to pay for shoplifting losses, your insurance premiums rising alongside burglary rates, or as a direct victim.

You will also be paying for the police to deal with drug addicts committing crimes, processing them through the criminal justice system and then for any jail time they end up getting.

So right now, the only people making money from drugs are criminals and security firms. The people for whom it's costing money are literally everybody else in society.

Years of interacting with class A drug users has shown me that they really don't want to be out hustling to make enough money for their next score of diluted heroin. They want to sit at home, take drugs and when those drugs wear off, take some more. You may view this as a wasted life, and you may well be right, but here's the thing: they are going to do this anyway, whether we decide to criminalise them or not.

If, after a lengthy period of honest, mature drug education across the country via schools, further education,
government advertising and so on, class A drugs were made
legally available on prescription to adults via pharmacies, the
vast majority of users would pick up their prescriptions, go
home, take their drugs and leave everyone else alone. They
couldn't be arsed to break into your car if they didn't have to.

There would still be outliers, of course, and I'm not saying that class A users with prescriptions would become
model citizens overnight. I'd also say that in order to renew
their prescriptions, they should have to attend a counselling session every now and then, even if they have no
intention of quitting.

But if that happened, what few police officers we still
have would be freed up from investigating petty theft, bur-
glaries and all the rest that are caused by class A users to
investigate other crimes. They could be out catching real
criminals, just like the right-wing press want them to. The
prison population would also drastically reduce, which
might allow for less overcrowding and more rehabilitation
work to be done with prisoners.

There have been enough examples of legalised cannabis
working in other countries to see that it could work here,
too. Again, carefully monitored outlets selling to adults
only, with a brand-new tax revenue stream going back into

the nation's coffers, would reduce the workload on the criminal justice system even further.

You might be reading this, gin and tonic in hand, in absolute disgust at the debauched bacchanal I'm suggesting. I can only tell you what over a decade of working with drug addicts, and the victims of drug addicts, has suggested to me. Would I want somebody I love to start smoking crack? No, of course not. But do I think it being illegal would make any difference to whether they did it or not? Also no. And if they did make that decision, would I rather they were taking medically graded and monitored drugs and didn't have to resort to crime or prostitution to pay for their habit? 100 per cent yes.

What we also need to admit is that we are failing the mentally ill in this country at every possible level. Provision is almost non-existent. People are waiting months for diagnosis, the assumption being that if they don't kill themselves in the meantime, they can get help when they reach the top of the waiting list. They then receive treatment which is patchy at best and woeful at worst. I've dealt with countless residents who are clearly unwell and their only interaction with their mental health carer is a ten-minute visit every couple of months. ASB teams often act as the early-warning system for people who are experiencing a mental health crises, or have stopped taking their medication, or whose medication has stopped working. It's only when their erratic behaviour rubs up against those they live alongside that anybody realises there's a problem.

At this point I could quote various studies or rattle off figures that show how many beds are available in mental health wards, or how many psychiatric nurses have been cut, or what percentage of people in the country will suffer mental illness at some point in their lives, but I won't. They're always open to interpretation and I can imagine people's eyes glazing over as they read them, and it doesn't speak to the heart of the problem. But if you're really hungry for some graphs and some statistics, a quick Google search using terms like "NHS cuts since 2010" or "mental health beds shortage" should provide some interesting, if depressing, reading. I'll simply say this: anyone who has had any experience of mental health in this country, whether as a patient or a practitioner or a relative, will tell you that we are failing a large part of society.

People have to reach crisis point before they can access help. This isn't due to a lack of care from those working in mental health provision. I cannot begin to imagine doing the job they do, week after week, with some of the most vulnerable people imaginable, on a shoestring budget. The problem is that they only have capacity to deal with the houses that are on fire; they don't have the time or the resources to fit smoke alarms in the houses that aren't.

We have to treat this as what it is: a major health crisis. I am exhausted by hearing campaigns saying that we need to be able to talk about mental health issues. Because then what? Great, we're all talking about how ill we are, so what do we do now? Where do we go for help? To our oversubscribed GP who may or may not write a prescription, who can offer cognitive behavioural therapy as long as you're prepared to wait, or talking therapy if you're prepared to wait a *really* long time? Maybe pop down to A&E and sit through the worst waiting times in recent years, after which you will almost certainly be told to go and see your GP?

The whole 'let's talk about mental health' trend of recent years has some major underlying flaws. Sometimes it's not OK to talk. In a perfect society it always would be, but look around you and tell me if that's what we're living in. If you are part of some traditional communities, if you have a zero-hours job with an exploitative boss, if you're in an abusive relationship or if you want to get medical insurance, being open about your mental illness can make your life considerably worse in the short term. It's dangerous and irresponsible to tell everyone, 'Hey, it's OK to talk.' Sadly, sometimes, it isn't.

It is also a sticking plaster to cover a gaping wound. 'It's OK to talk about mental health' is the equivalent of 'raising awareness' – it gives the impression of actually doing something to help without putting in any effort or resources. If you're a paranoid schizophrenic suffering auditory hallucinations which are causing you to neglect your self-care, talking about it does nothing without some help to follow it up. (Also, one of the common symptoms of people with serious mental illness is that they don't believe they're ill, so they're not going to start chatting about an illness they're convinced they don't have.)

The campaign should no longer be 'Let's talk about mental illness'. It should be 'We've talked about mental illness, lots of people have it, now what are we going to do to help?' Any answer that doesn't involve additional resources is just so much chin music and can be safely ignored. People who tell you there's no use in simply throwing money at a problem are actually saying they don't think there's a problem.

I've been a drug user. I've been seriously mentally ill (two nervous breakdowns in younger life) and am currently mentally ill (hello, Mirtazapine), so I admit I have a dog in both of these fights. But so does anybody else who wants to live in a country that works for everybody else. If we get this right, there are few finer things we can say we have achieved as a society. Continue to get it so badly wrong and we won't have a society worthy of the name for much longer.

Despite all of this, I still believe the overwhelming majority of people are fundamentally good. I've spent more hours than I care to recall dealing with the worst excesses of human behaviour, but this never made me lose hope that given the right opportunities and treated with respect, your average person is inclined towards benevolence and decency.

My job largely existed not because of how terrible humanity is, but because humanity has some pretty terrible coping mechanisms for stress, ignorance, despair and frustration. These can often involve thoughtlessness, lashing out or reckless disregard for other people's feelings, which can look a lot like vindictiveness or malice, but are often just the howl of the powerless.

Time and again, I witnessed people willing to fight for the wellbeing of their families or communities, willing to place themselves in the firing line by giving evidence. Reporting unacceptable things they had seen because it was the right thing to do rather than closing their front doors and pretending it was somebody else's problem. Countless little acts of kindness, whether that was looking out for a vulnerable neighbour, volunteering to do after-school work to give kids something to do of an evening, or simply thanking a caretaker for doing what is often a thankless job.

I saw acts of breathtaking empathy and forgiveness, too. People who had endured months of nuisance from their neighbours would end up being a key part of their support network once they realised the annoying behaviour was simply a symptom of an unmet need for help. In my experience, victims don't want perpetrators of ASB thrown to the wolves for what they've done, and would rather see somebody turn their life around than see them made an example of or brutalised.

I'm not naïve enough to think that there aren't those who spurn every opportunity to do the right thing, or prey on others out of laziness, pettiness or malice. They do exist, and they do need dealing with, and that can often mean legal action, tenancy action and whatever other enforcement tool is available and proportionate. But too often, this approach is conflated and distorted into easy answers for perceived wrongs in the world: longer sentences; clamping down on the weakest for their weaknesses; seeking people to blame, bogeymen to be scared of, a target to point the finger at; a quick fix for a generation of neglect; believing that looking tough trumps being thoughtful every time.

But this isn't a society I recognise. Based on all of my experience as an ASB officer, I sincerely believe that people – not as individuals performing acts of unusual kindness or conspicuous bravery, but people en masse as a society – are as generous, patient and capable of love as we allow them to be.

So let's try that.

Acknowledgements

Being my first book, it's been a steep learning curve. A big part of that was realising how many people it takes to get one made. I'm just the name that appears below the title. So my thanks go to my agent Max Edwards for his unstinting support, my editor Zennor Compton for making this a far better book than I could possibly have managed alone, and to Rachael Beale for her innumerable editorial nips, tucks & suggestions. Thanks must also go to the entire team at PRH/Cornerstone/Century for their tireless work, input and advice – Susan Sandon, Lucy Middleton, Sam Rees-Williams, Becca Wright, Katie Sheldrake, Klara Zak Georgia Williams, Konrad Kirkham, Claire Simmonds, Sasha Cox, Laura Garrod, Mat Watterson, Rachel Campbell, Kasim Mohammed, Joanna Taylor, Amelia Evans, Annamika Singh, and Jason Smith for his brilliant cover art. Apologies to anyone I may have forgotten – you have my permission to hunt me down and hit me with a copy of this book.

Thanks to all my former colleagues, many of whom are still working in ASB, doing an often-thankless job in difficult circumstances, for all the times they helped me stay relatively sane.

I'm lucky to have some of the finest people on the planet as friends, and their patience and kindness can never be overestimated. To my mum and dad, brother and sister, nephews and nieces – I wouldn't be here today without you. You're the best.

But most of all, thank you to my wife. God only knows why you put up with me, but I'm glad that you do.